Business Rules Management and Service Oriented Architecture

Business Rules Management and Service Oriented Architecture

A Pattern Language

Ian Graham

John Wiley & Sons, Ltd

Other Wiley Editorial Offices

John Wiley & Sons Inc., 111 River Street, Hoboken, NJ 07030, USA

Jossey-Bass, 989 Market Street, San Francisco, CA 94103-1741, USA

Wiley-VCH Verlag GmbH, Boschstr. 12, D-69469 Weinheim, Germany

John Wiley & Sons Australia Ltd, 42 McDougall Street, Milton, Queensland 4064, Australia

John Wiley & Sons (Asia) Pte Ltd, 2 Clementi Loop #02-01, Jin Xing Distripark, Singapore 129809

John Wiley & Sons Canada Ltd, 6045 Freemont Blvd, Mississauga, ONT, L5R 4J3, Canada

Wiley also publishes its books in a variety of electronic formats. Some content that appears
in print may not be available in electronic books.

British Library Cataloguing in Publication Data

A catalogue record for this book is available from the British Library

ISBN-13: 978-0-470-02721-9 (PB)
ISBN-10: 0-470-02721-5 (PB)

Typeset in 10.5/13 Palatino by Laserwords Private Limited, Chennai, India
Printed and bound in Great Britain by Bell & Bain, Glasgow
This book is printed on acid-free paper responsibly manufactured from sustainable forestry
in which at least two trees are planted for each one used for paper production.

Contents

Trademark Notice

ART™ is a trademark of Inference Corp.; Biztalk™, COM™, COM+™, DCOM™, SOAP™, Internet Explorer™, Microsoft Windows™, Access™, PowerPoint™, MSMQ™, MTS™, Excel™, Intellisense™, OLE™, Visual Basic™, Visual Studio™ and Microsoft Office™ are trademarks of Microsoft Inc.; Catalysis™ is a European trademark of TriReme International Ltd. and a US service mark of Computer Associates Inc.; CORBA®, IIOP® and OMG™ are registered trademarks of the Object Management Group™, ORB™, Object Request Broker™, OMG Interface Definition Language™, IDL™, CORBAservices™, CORBAfacilities™, Unified Modeling Language™, UML™, XMI™, MOF™ and the UML Cube logo are trademarks of the OMG.; Haley Authority and Haley Rules are trademarks of Haley Systems Inc.IBM™, AS/400™, OS/400™, CICS™, Component Broker™, DB2™, ENVY™, IMS, Visual Age™ and Websphere™ are trademarks of International Business Machines Inc.; Iceberg™, Tuxedo™ and Weblogic™, are trademarks of BEA Systems; Java™. EJB™, Enterprise Java Beans™, Java Beans™ are trademarks of Sun Microsystems Inc.; JRules is a trademark of ILOG SA;Kappa™, KEE™ are trademarks of Intellicorp Inc; Netscape™, Netscape Navigator™ are trademarks of Netscape Inc.; Nexpert Object™ and Blaze Advisor are trademarks of a Fair Isaac Inc.; NeXT™, NeXtStep™ and OpenSTEP™ are trademarks of NeXT Corp.; Objectory™, Rational Unified Process, RUP, Rose and Requisite Pro™ are trademarks of Rational Inc.; Oracle®, CASE*METHOD™, Express™, are trademarks of Oracle Inc.; Orbix™ is a trademark of Iona Technologies Plc ProcessWise™ and REVEAL™ are trademarks of ICL Ltd.; Select™ is a trademark of Princeton Softech; Simula™ is a trademark of Simula AS; Syntropy ™is a trademark of Syntropy Ltd.; Telescript™ is a trademark of General Magic Inc.; Together™ and TogetherJ™ are trademarks of Together Inc.; Other trademarks are the property of their respective owners.

Foreword

In *Business Rules Management and Service Oriented Architecture*, Ian Graham provides a solid architectural introduction to business rules for IT professionals and architects taking the next steps into SOA, components, and other state-of-the-art software engineering techniques. He speaks of concerns I find just about every IT architect has these days, offering a wide-ranging set of solutions. It's a compelling story.

Let me share with you briefly some of the things Ian gets right in this book.

- Separating concerns of business from those of the infrastructure (the 'plumbing') is fundamental to building better architecture. He deftly explains how both business rules and SOA can help you make that happen.

- SOA and business rules management systems (BRMS) are parallel and complimentary technologies. They're both about the quest for agility – creating new levers to manage (and encourage!) endless, fast-paced change. Is there anything much more urgent than that these days?

- It's all about re-use – but the right *kind* of re-use. A BRMS allows reuse of rules across services. Why does that matter to you? You want your services to be easily reconfigured. When the business changes, you want to be able to change the rules without ever digging into the code. Ian claims (and I certainly agree) that this alone can speed development and ease maintenance even more than the adoption of SOA on its own.

- There are some areas where I'm afraid we need a bit of attitude adjustment. (Those are my words, not Ian's – he's much more diplomatic about it.) Creating a business model is *not* a waste of time. More and more descriptive use cases are *not* going to solve all your problems!

I could go on and on about that last one, but Ian more than does the topic justice, so I'll just invite you to jump right into the book.

- The notion of business rules is on an inevitable collision course with the notion of *patterns*. As one who studied this area a great deal in the formative years of business rules (*The Business Rule Book*, 2nd edition was published in 1997), I applaud Ian for breaking new ground in this important area.

There are many other things I could mention about what Ian gets right in this book. For example, what about legacy systems? Ian points out how adopting a BRMS will assist in the transition to SOA because service-based and legacy applications can be coupled using the BRMS as the common decision engine. What about semantics and pragmatic management of business intellectual property (IP)? Business rules provide a pragmatic, proven answer on that one.

The main thing I want to mention, however, is that Ian says he finds little to disagree with in the *Business Rules Manifesto* (Business Rules Group, 2003). That's an important statement – one that as an IT architect you should find comforting – because it reflects a growing consensus in the industry as to just what business rules are about. I mentioned the 'formative' period of business rules above – well, that period is just about over. By any reasonable measure, business rules are mainstream now. Do have a quick look at the *Manifesto* – it's conveniently included right here in the book for you. Incidentally, the *Manifesto* has been translated into about a dozen languages as of this writing. It's impact is truly global.

It's exciting to see new ideas become reality. That's especially so when the ideas make the professional's job easier, and the resulting systems better for business. Fortunately, Ian's work is highly approachable. If you want to know how to go about building a world-class rule-based, service-oriented architecture, read on!

Ronald G. Ross
Executive Editor, www.BRCommunity.com
Principle, Business Rule Solutions, LLC

Preface

There has been a great deal of interest in business rules management systems (BRMS) for several years now and the technology has matured considerably. At last it seems that the time is ripe and a plethora of commercial applications are beginning to be fielded, driven by the escalating difficulty of maintaining essential computer systems, the onus of greater regulatory compliance, the increasing complexity and volatility of business processes and many other factors. The existing literature is surprisingly sparse and most of it approaches business rules management from the standpoints of database practice and project management or concentrates on perfecting rule syntax. All these approaches are valuable but the origins of the subject are more diverse. It is now time, therefore, for a concise but comprehensive look at the subject that gets away from both database-centred tunnel vision and from the exaggerated (and thus discredited) claims of the erstwhile expert systems community.

The other factor that has moulded the approach I have taken here is the massive explosion of interest in service oriented architecture (SOA), one of the most significant potential steps forward in computing for a decade. Here there is much confusion. Some commentators seem to identify service oriented architecture with web services, whilst others claim that the main idea is to build an 'orchestration' layer that will glue any new services together with APIs to the goulash of legacy systems. Both these claims are wrong and the second one is downright dangerous. With many of my clients now adopting SOA (and some implementing business rules too) I have become more convinced than ever that the key to success with both technologies is to pay serious attention to modelling not only systems issues but the business environment as well. With the help of my colleague Derek Andrews, I have tried to explain this in Chapter 2.

As the manuscript developed, and looking constantly at the interactions between these strands, I found that a constant theme emerged, almost organically, from my researches, practice and discussions: service oriented architecture without business rules management is not going to crack the nut. Similarly, BRMS without SOA is unlikely to address all the pressing needs of business that so desperately need addressing by IT practice. So the propaganda message here is simple: SOA and BRMS; do both, or don't bother with either. *And* do them on the basis of first class requirements engineering and modelling practices too.

Even companies that decide not to invest in a full-blown BRMS product can benefit from externalizing their rules; writing them down in a clear and consistent style leads to immediate benefits. One of my clients, for example, is developing its own customized variant of Ross's RuleSpeak. This will enable their business analysts, users and developers to communicate more effectively and has already led to the discovery of errors and inconsistencies in existing documentation.

What the Book Covers

The aim of this book is to bring together the following key ideas in modern enterprise system development best practice.

- The need to separate business logic cleanly from the software 'plumbing'.
- The need for service-oriented architecture.
- How the former depends on component-based development (CBD).
- Database-centred approaches to business rules.
- Knowledge-based approaches to business rules.
- Best software engineering practice for designing robust, flexible systems and aligning IT with business more closely than has hitherto been the case.
- Using patterns to design and develop service oriented business rules management systems.

The text starts with a business case for adopting BRMSs and surveys the wide range of possible application areas for this technology. Then we present a tutorial on and discussion of service oriented architecture, its role, concepts, and supporting technologies. In this chapter we meet the central role of modelling in the design of successful computer systems, which a major theme of the book. The ideas of greater business alignment and of intelligent software agents are used to pull together the two strands of BRMS and SOA. Chapter 3 is an historical digression looking at the sources of the main ideas of BRMS, but it also discusses trends and emerging standards.

Chapter 4 is a technical tutorial on business rules management systems.

Chapter 5 applies the ideas of the previous chapters to existing and notional BRMS products.

Chapter 6 looks at knowledge elicitation and requirements engineering techniques insofar as they are specific to BRMS.

Finally, we gather together all the book's techniques and guidelines into a pattern language that is intended to be a 'how to' guide to running an actual BRMS/SOA project. Using the language, if done as intended, should generate specific solutions to a range of concrete development problems. The two appendices support the material in this chapter.

I believe that pattern languages are far more powerful and flexible than mere checklists. However, as with a checklist, no pattern language is ever complete and finished, and the reader will undoubtedly want to refer to the work of other authors as well as mine. Notably, I have drawn on the modelling patterns of Peter Coad when discussing SOA, Barbara von Halle's work on method and as yet unpublished SOA patterns under development by Derek Andrews, Hubert Matthews and (to a smaller extent) myself. On rule writing style, I have tried to capture the essence of the works on Ronald G. Ross and Tony Morgan but, as always, there is no substitute for reading the originals. The bibliographical notes to each chapter provide pointers to references of this kind. There are also some references to my own earlier works, notably those on requirements engineering, but I have tried to make such material self-contained within this text.

Intended Readership and Scope

The book is intended to be accessible to readers who do not have deep knowledge of theoretical computer science, but at the same time it attempts to treat the important issues accurately and in depth. It provides a tutorial on the technology and advice on how best to exploit business rules management in practice.

The primary audience is IT professionals (architects, analysts, developers, strategists, managers) and some of their interested customers. It may be of use to undergraduate and postgraduate students studying information technology or software engineering. It will therefore be of interest to teachers of Computer Science and Business IT. I have assumed that the reader has at least a nodding acquaintance with the basic UML notations for use cases, class diagrams and state models.

The book is designed to be read sequentially, although readers with differing interests may safely omit some sections. For example, readers with a less technical focus may skip the material on web services. The impatient reader, who already knows what backward chaining is, may even jump straight into

Chapter 7, which contains the RulePatterns pattern language. This chapter is intended as a stand-alone reference. Here too, the introductory sections (7.1 and 7.2) may be of no interest to people who already possess a sound knowledge of the idea of pattern languages.

While the scope of this book is broad and intended to cover the gamut of topics pertinent to a move to service oriented architecture and business rules management, it does not attempt to duplicate unnecessarily the work of other authors. Notably, there is scant consideration given to such issues as analytics, business rule maturity models, tying business rules to other deliverables, integration of the business rules approach with proprietary methods such as RUP or non-proprietary methods such as that of Halle (2002). These, I feel, are either already adequately dealt with in other texts or deserve a treatment separate from the one given here.

Acknowledgements

Although it contains much original material, this book is largely a survey of other people's work and could not have been written without that work. I would like to acknowledge the contribution of these other authors. Also, many of the ideas contained were honed in discussions with my colleagues at Trireme and participants in various conferences and seminars. In particular, at EuroPLoP 2006, Ademar Aguiar, Jon Bennett, Frank Buschmann, Alexander Fülleborn, Marina Hasse, Michaelis Hadjisimou, Kevlin Henney, Lise Hvatum, Maria Kavanagh, Alan Kelly, Klaus Marquardt and Martin Schmettow all made very helpful comments on some of the patterns presented in Chapter 7. Conversations with members of staff at some of my clients, whom I may not identify here, also provided invaluable insights and helped me keep my feet on the ground; thanks to you too, you know who you are.

Special thanks are due to Derek Andrews for his contribution to Chapter 2 and to him, Clive Menhinick and Hubert Matthews for many interesting and sometimes formative discussions. The remarks of several anonymous referees were very helpful too. Of the reviewers whose names I do know, I especially want to thank Barbara von Halle, Tony Simons, Ron Ross and Paul Vincent for their comments and kind suggestions for improvements. I have tried to incorporate them as best I could.

I am grateful to the Business Rules Group for permission to reproduce their seminal *Business Rules Manifesto* as Appendix A.

The team at Wiley were a joy to work with on this project. I don't know the names of all the production and other back-room workers there but I can express my profound thanks to all of them and to my editors, Drew Kennerley and Sally Tickner.

Even with all this help, the responsibility for any mistakes or omissions is entirely mine. If you can get past any of these that remain, then I do hope you find the book entertaining as well as merely informative. I would be most interested to read any comments you may have.

Ian Graham
Balham, August MMVI
(ian@trireme.com)

Aligning IT with Business

I have not kept the square, but that to come
Shall all be done by the rule.
William Shakespeare (Antony and Cleopatra)

Businesses continue to strive for shorter time to market and to lower the cost of developing and maintaining computer applications to support their operations. Business rules management technologies can play an important role in this.

Well, if you believe that, you'll believe anything. You are already thinking 'Another silver bullet!' But stay with me for at least another few paragraphs, whilst I try to convince you that it may actually be worthwhile to read further.

When I started writing this book, this chapter had the provisional title of 'Why Business Rules?' or some such. As I started laying out the reasons, it became clear that I was ducking the main issues facing the world of IT (information technology) by thus restricting my focus. So I asked myself 'Why are we doing all this?'

According to Standish (1995; 2004), around 66% of large US projects fail, either through cancellation, overrunning their budgets or delivering software that is never put into production. Outright project failures account for 15% of all projects, a vast improvement over the 31% failure rate reported in the first survey in 1994, but still a scandal. On top of this, projects that are over time, over budget or lacking critical features and requirements total 51% of all projects in the 2004 survey. It is not incredible to extrapolate these – frankly scandalous – figures to other parts of the world. What is harder to believe is that our industry, and the people in it, can tolerate such a situation. Clearly we should be doing something differently. The Standish surveys also looked into the reasons why people involved in the sample projects thought such projects fail. The reasons given – in descending order of importance – were:

- lack of user involvement;
- no clear statement of requirements;
- no project ownership;
- no clear vision and objectives; and
- lack of planning.

The first four of these relate strongly to the need for better requirements engineering and point to the developer-centric culture of many IT development organizations, a culture highlighted by Alan Cooper (1999) and others, and familiar to those of us who have worked in or with corporate IT over a long period. Too often, developers expect users to learn *their* language – often nowadays in the form of UML diagrams. In today's fast-moving competitive environment this will not work. Project teams must develop languages that can be understood by users and developers alike: languages based on simple conceptual models of the domain written in easily understood terms. Business process modelling approaches of the sort pioneered by Graham (2001) and business rules management systems both have a rôle to play in this critical challenge for IT in the 21st century.

Furthermore, the level of abstraction at which we work is far too low. IT departments are often culturally and technically miles away from the concerns and thought processes of the customers they serve. The problem is, thus, far broader than the need for business rules management; the real problem we have to solve is how to align IT practice with business need.

To believe that adopting a business rules management system on its own will solve this problem is nothing short of naïve. Business rules management is only a part of the solution. To align IT with business we must also consider innovative approaches to requirements engineering and service oriented architecture. Whilst its focus remains on business rules, this book is about all these issues.

Briefly – because the next chapter will be devoted to a detailed discussion – service oriented architecture (SOA) is an architectural concept in software design that emphasizes the use of combined services to support business requirements directly. In SOA, resources are made available to service consumers in the network as independent artifacts that are accessed in a standardized way. SOA is precisely about raising the level of abstraction so that business processes can be discussed in a language understood by business people as well as IT folk. Business rules are about aligning IT with the business too. It is to them we now turn.

In this chapter, after a short look at the history of the idea and technology of business rules management systems (BRMS), we examine the features and responsibilities of a BRMS, and then the benefits of and business drivers for adoption of the technology. We list typical applications and indicators of the need for a BRMS.

In subsequent chapters we will relate business rules to the concept of service oriented architecture, look at different approaches to and philosophies of business rules management, cover the key technical features of a BRMS (including *inter alia* knowledge representation and inference techniques) and discuss requirements engineering, appropriate development methods and processes. Next we try to distil this knowledge into a prototype pattern language.

1.1 Historical Background

The first talk of business rules management emerged from discussions in the database community as long ago as the late 1980s, notably in a journal called *The Database Newsletter* – although the term was used as early as 1984 in an article in *Datamation*.

However, there is an older tradition in the artificial intelligence (AI) community going back, arguably, to EMYCIN, the first so-called expert system shell. MYCIN (Shortliffe, 1976) was an expert system that could diagnose infectious diseases of the blood – with some success too. MYCIN was not, in any sense, a business rules management system; its rules were pretty much hard coded and concerned a fairly esoteric domain: medicine. EMYCIN (Melle *et al.*, 1981) was 'empty' MYCIN: MYCIN with the rules taken out and two significant mechanisms. First, rules on any suitable domain (including business domains) could be typed in and run under the control of the same logic used by MYCIN. Secondly, an EMYCIN application could be asked to explain its conclusions when asked 'How?' or 'Why?' I will explain how all this works in a later chapter. For now, notice only that EMYCIN separated business rules from both data and the control logic that enabled conclusions to be reached, and this is a key principle of modern business rules management systems. Furthermore, the rules were entirely declarative (unconnected statements rather than the interdependent lines of a computer program); another key principle of the business rules approach.

The first implementations of business rules in databases were more limited in several ways, the first being that rules were usually implemented as stored procedures written in procedural and proprietary extensions of declarative SQL. Other rules, notably those for referential integrity, were implemented in the database system itself, but nothing more complex was to succumb to this approach. The next step forward took some time. Active databases incorporated triggers: if/then rules that caused updates dependent on the values entered into the database. But even triggers did not offer the flexibility of EMYCIN's general if/then rules.

As an example of the gulf between the two traditions, I recall attending the British launch of Sapiens (still a major player in the BRMS marketplace today) in around 1989. I have a fairly low tolerance for sales pitches, but I was aroused from my slumbers when told that the product (basically a database and 4GL) was object-oriented and rule-based. As the technical presentation wore on, it became clear that the 'objects' were merely relational tables; by the end nothing much had been said about rules.

'Can you give me an example of a rule?' I asked.

'Of course. All employees must be over 16.'

'No, I mean a proper rule with an "if" and a "then".'

The speaker paused for a second. 'OK, then. If you are to be an employee then your age must be greater than or equal to 16.'

I decided to hold my peace, and went away rather unimpressed.

The point here is not just that salesmen can sometimes be rather uneconomical with buzzwords, but that there is a misunderstanding about what constitutes a rule (and, indeed, an object in this particular case). I regarded the example given as a range constraint on an attribute, rather than a rule. What is evinced is a lack of common terminology among the two camps.

Consider the following (very slightly edited) dialogue between MYCIN and a human physician.

```
>Is the patient's illness with ORGANISM-1 a hospital
 acquired infection?
>WHY?
[i.e. Why is it important to determine whether or not
  the infection with ORGANISM-1 was acquired while the
  patient was hospitalized?]
>This will aid in determining the category of ORGANISM-1.
 It has already been established that
     [1.1]the gram stain of ORGANISM-1 is gramneg, and
     [1.2]the morphology of ORGANISM-1 is rod, and
     [1.3]the aerobicity of ORGANISM-1 is facultative
 Therefore, if
     [1.4]the infection with ORGANISM-1 was not acquired
     while the patient was hospitalized
 then
     There is strongly suggestive evidence (.8) that
       the category of ORGANISM-1 is enterobacteriaceae
     ALSO:
     There is weakly suggestive evidence (.1) that
       the identity of ORGANISM-1 is pseudomonas-aeruginosa
```

Even ignoring the specialized terminology, it should be clear that the implied rule is far more complex than a constraint saying that staff entered in the database must be over 16. We will see many examples of similarly complex rules in more familiar domains as we proceed. Furthermore, we will encounter more complex constraints that involve more than one attribute, object or database table.

The first step towards a reconciliation between these two camps came with Ron Ross's (1994) *Business Rule Book*, to be followed by his several subsequent publications that show that he is aware of both traditions, though mainly rooted, originally, in the database world. Ross founded Business Rule Solutions in 1997 to focus on applied business aligned models (strategy, process, vocabulary, rules, etc.) that would be completely independent of any IT tradition.

In 1995, a group of IT practitioners produced the GUIDE *Business Rules Project Report*, which also clarified the territory, though remaining database centred. The manifesto of the (now better informed) database-centred approach was finally published by Chris Date (2000). In the same year, the Business Rules Group published the first version of the *Business Rules Manifesto*, which established the ground rules for what constitutes a BRMS and the principles of the business rules approach. By 2002, Barbara von Halle, another database guru, had published the first comprehensive method for applying the approach and Tony Morgan became the first AI expert to publish a book on the subject.

In the interim, products evolved. Some of them were extensions of database or repository products, others evolved from expert systems shells. We will look at some of them later.

As I write, it seems to me that there is now enough maturity in both theory and practice for commercial organizations to apply the business rules approach, along with mature object-oriented modelling techniques, better requirements engineering and the philosophy of service oriented architecture, to the critical problem of aligning IT with business goals and practices.

1.2   What are Business Rules?

Most early definitions (e.g. Appleton, 1984) conflate business rules with database constraints. Ross (1987) is more general, defining a business rule as a rule or policy that governs the behaviour of the enterprise and distinguishes it from others. Elsewhere (1994), he defines a rule as a 'discrete operational business policy or practice', and insists that a rule is a declarative statement expressed in 'non-technical' terms. Of course some business domains are replete with technical jargon, so perhaps 'non-IT' is what is intended. The declarative point is key. Declarative is the opposite of procedural. In a procedural rule language the order of execution of the rules matters; in a declarative language the outcome is the same whatever execution order is selected. Date (2000) makes the same point, insisting that rules convey 'what not how'.

Halle (2002) sees rules as conditions that 'govern a business event so that it occurs in a way that is acceptable to the business'. Date (2000) makes it clear that these 'business events' are to be viewed as events that result in an update to a database; the rules are there to ensure that rogue updates are not allowed. Date too insists on the declarative nature of rules; he sees rules as predicates (statements that are true or false) concerning the database domains.

The GUIDE project (Hay and Healy, 1997) saw a rule as defining or constraining some aspect of a business and 'intended to assert business structure, or to control or influence the behaviour of the business'. Such a rule 'cannot be broken down' without the loss of important information; i.e. rules are **atomic**. But GUIDE too deliberately restricted its scope to row 3 of the Zachman framework (Zachman, 1987); i.e. to 'specific constraints on the creation, updating and removal of persistent data in an information system'. However, there is a major acknowledgement of the rôle of inference. GUIDE said that facts could be derived by mathematical calculation, deductive inference and even induction (i.e. data mining). It went so far as to say that each of these three derivation methods is 'itself a kind of business rule'.

The Business Rules Group, taking on the mantle of GUIDE, has given various revisions of the definition such as: 'a directive that is intended to influence or guide business behaviour ... in response to risks, threats or opportunities'. More importantly, the Business Rules Group has published the Business Rules Manifesto (reproduced as Appendix A). The manifesto provides principles, rather than a definition, insisting that rules are atomic, declarative, logically well-formed, separated from processes, procedures and technology and, critically, written in business terms.

In what is probably one of the best and most sensible and practical books yet on business rules management, Morgan (2002) defines a business rule as 'a compact statement about an aspect of a business [that] *can be expressed in terms that can be directly related to the business, using simple, unambiguous language that's accessible to all interested parties*: business owner, business analyst, technical architect, and so on' (emphasis added). One focus in this book will be on the ease of expression of rules and the suitability of available products for business owners, business analysts, as well as on their technical features.

It is difficult to fault any of the above definitions, except if one were to criticize them in terms of scope and emphasis. I can find little or nothing to disagree with in the Business Rules Manifesto (BRM). To me, Morgan's definition seems to capture the essence of the notion best. However, there is one issue unaddressed so far.

All these definitions emphasize one business. Open business on the web, closer customer relationships, and collaborative ventures all indicate a need to share business rules. Some rules could be about more than one business. Some rules could be imposed by one business on another (e.g. taxation rules). Some rules might be better shared with customers – perhaps in the form of explanations (a BRM principle). Taking this into account and picking up some points from all the definitions, here is my definition for the purposes of this book, based most chiefly on Morgan's.

> **A business rule is a compact, atomic, well-formed, declarative statement about an aspect of a business that can be expressed in terms that can be directly related to the business and its collaborators, using simple unambiguous language that is accessible to all interested parties: business owner, business analyst, technical architect, customer, and so on. This simple language may include domain-specific jargon.**

The term 'well-formed' comes from logic and needs explanation. The rules must be executable on a machine if they are to be of much use in a business rules management system. This implies that they must be convertible into statements in some formal logic: statements that are **well-formed** with respect to that logic.

One corollary of the declarative principle is that business rules do *not* describe business processes; they do, however, constrain what processes are permissible.

Business rules are statements expressed in a language, preferably a subset of a natural language such as English. I see two clear kinds of statements that must be distinguished: assertions and rules. **Assertions** or **facts** have the form: 'A is X' or 'P is true'. These are equivalent forms; e.g. I can convert the former into '"A is X" is true'. Simplifying slightly, until later in this book, **rules** have the equivalent forms: 'If A then X'; 'X if A'; 'When A then X'; and so on. Here X can be a fact or an action.

We can see from Table 1.1 that rule statements can be classified. Date, Ross and Halle all offer useful classification schemes, but I do not want to be so specific here.

Table 1-1 Examples of statements and their types

Eeyore is a donkey.	Assertion
Computers come in blue boxes.	Assertion
NetMargin = 2,000.	Assertion
Bill Gates is wealthy.	Assertion
If the computer's box is not blue then paint it blue.	Action rule
To paint something: acquire funds, visit shop, buy paint, paint article.	Procedure
Wealthy people are always tall and handsome (if Z is wealthy then Z is tall and handsome).	Rule
NetMargin = Revenue − Costs.	Procedure or Rule
Employees must be over 16.	Range constraint or Rule
A borrower may borrow up to 6 books.	Cardinality constraint or Rule
A borrowed book must be owned by the library that the member belongs to.	General constraint or Rule
If any employee has a salary greater than the MD then set the MD's salary to the maximum of all employee's salaries.	Trigger rule

Statements are always statements *about* something. Ross refers to these somethings as **terms**. Other authors refer to the **vocabulary** of the domain or even the **domain ontology**.

Strictly, ontology is the philosophical science concerned with what exists: the science of Being. Here, though, it is used to mean the model of the domain that we work with, including the things we can discuss, their properties and how they relate to each other. I will take the view in this book that the domain ontology is precisely an object model, usually expressed by a UML type diagram; but more on that later. Some readers might like to think of the ontology as the database schema – at least for the time being. The ontology tells us what we are allowed to discuss when we write rules. Without a sound ontology the rules are meaningless, and any attempt at writing them in natural language is certainly doomed. This means that we must modify our definition slightly. We can do so by adding just one sentence.

> **Business rules are always interpreted against a defined domain ontology.**

Having defined what business rules are, there is still much more to say about them, such as how they may be linked together to derive new facts (inference), how they are best written (rule structure) or how they are to be discovered (knowledge elicitation). We will return to these topics (and more) in subsequent chapters. For now, let us take a look at how rules may be managed.

1.3   What is Business Rules Management?

Business rules management is the practical art of implementing systems based on the business rules approach. This can be done in many ways, but the most economical is to use a business rules management system. In addition, there will be some process adopted for managing and organizing projects and conducting tasks such as rule authoring, rule maintenance, and so on. We will return to such issues later.

Let us start with business rules management systems.

BRMSs have the following features and responsibilities:

- Storing and maintaining a **repository** of business rules that represent the policies and procedures of an enterprise.
- Keeping these rules (the business logic) separate from the 'plumbing' needed to implement modern distributed computer systems.

- Integrating with enterprise applications, so that the rules can be used for all business decision making, using ordinary business data.

- Forming rules into independent but chainable **rulesets** and performing **inference**s within and over such rulesets.

- Allowing business analysts and even users to create, understand and maintain the rules and policies of the business with the minimum of learning required.

- Automating and facilitating business processes.

- Creating intelligent applications that interact with users through natural, understandable and logical dialogues.

The idea that the rules are stored in a repository is a critical one. If we are to manage rules there seems no alternative to storing them in some sort of central database. Furthermore, storing the rules in a layer separate from both applications and from the various databases that may exist in a real organization gives obvious maintenance advantages. We might even argue that centralizing the rules makes them more readily reusable. However, there is an opposing force: that of the need for reuse of the objects in our domain model. If the rules (and indeed rulesets) are not encapsulated within the objects that they constrain, then those objects are incomplete and, if reused, may function incorrectly.

Date (2000) also argues that, ideally, rules should be part of the database but then, rather reluctantly, concedes that storing the rules in a separate layer gives the advantage of DBMS-independence. Contrariwise, Bruce (1992) points out that treating rules separately 'avoids the debate over which object (or objects) should encapsulate the rules'. This is indeed a hard problem sometimes, and I will return to the issue in subsequent chapters. All design problems concern the resolution of contradictory forces such as the ones referred to: reuse *versus* independence. In Chapter 7, I present some patterns aimed at resolving these forces. For now, assume that rules live in a repository and are managed thereby.

The business drivers for the adoption of BRMSs are as follows:

- Current software development practice inhibits the rapid delivery of new solutions and even modest changes to existing systems can take too long.

- Accelerating competitive pressure means that policy and the rules governing automated processes have to be amenable to rapid change. This can be driven by new product development, the need to offer customization and the need to apply business process improvements rapidly to multiple customer groups.

- Personalizing services, content and interaction styles, based on process types and customer characteristics, can add considerable value to an organization's business processes, however complex. Natural dialogues and clearly expressed rules clarify the purpose of and dependencies among rules and policies.

- In regulated industries, such as pharmaceuticals or finance, the rules for governance and regulation will change outside the control of the organization. Separating them from the application code and making them easy to change is essential, especially when the environment is multi-currency, multi-national and multi-cultural.

- Even in unregulated industries, companies subject to the Sarbanes-Oxley Act are required to make their business processes (and thus the rules that they follow) visible. If such rules are scattered through multiple applications, duplicated (consistently or otherwise) in different places and embedded in procedural code, this becomes a costly and nigh impossible exercise.

- Business rules and processes can be shared by many applications across the whole enterprise using multiple channels such as voice, web, and batch applications, thereby encouraging consistent practices.

Using BRMSs should decrease development costs and dramatically shorten development and maintenance cycles.

Typical applications of BRMS technology include these:

- Automating procedures for such things as
  - ☞ claims processing
  - ☞ customer service management
  - ☞ credit approval and limit management
  - ☞ problem resolution
  - ☞ sales

- Advice giving and decision support in such fields as
  - ☞ benefits eligibility
  - ☞ sales promotions and cross selling
  - ☞ credit collection strategy
  - ☞ marketing strategy

- Compliance with
  - ☞ external and legal regulations
  - ☞ company policy

- Planning and scheduling of
  - ☞ advertising
  - ☞ timetables and meetings
  - ☞ budgets
  - ☞ product design and assembly

- Diagnosis and detection of
  - ☞ medical conditions
  - ☞ underwriting referrals

- ☞ fraud (e.g. telephone or credit card fraud)
- ☞ faults in machinery
- ☞ invalid and valid data
- Classification of
  - ☞ customers
  - ☞ products and services
  - ☞ risks
- Matching and recommending
  - ☞ suitable products to clients
  - ☞ strategies to investors.

Business rules arise from the objects that one encounters in a business and their interrelationships. These 'business objects' may be found in documentation, procedure manuals, automation systems, business records, or even in the tacit know-how of staff. It is these objects that are modelled by our domain ontology objects.

Morgan (2002) identifies the following indicators of the need for a business rules management system:

- Policies defined by external agencies.
  - ☞ Government, professional associations, standards bodies, codes of practice, etc.
- Variations amongst organizational units.
  - ☞ Geography, business function, hierarchy, etc.
- Objects that take on multiple states
  - ☞ Order status, customer query stage, etc.
- Specializations of business objects
  - ☞ Customer types, business events, products, etc.
- Automation systems
  - ☞ Business logic embedded and hidden within existing computer systems
- Defined ranges and boundaries of policy
  - ☞ Age ranges, eligibility criteria, safety checks, etc.
- Conditions linked to time
  - ☞ Business hours, start dates, holidays, etc.
- The quality manual
  - ☞ Who does what, authorization levels, mandatory records, etc.
- Significant discriminators
  - ☞ Branch points in processes, recurring behaviour patterns, etc.
- Information constraints
  - ☞ Permitted ranges of values, objects and decisions that must be combined or exclude each other.

- Definitions, derivations or calculations
  - ☞ Transient specialization of business objects, proprietary algorithms, definitions of relationships.
- Activities related to particular circumstances or events
  - ☞ Year-end, triggering events, conditional procedures, etc.

If any of these concerns are familiar, then your organization may well be a candidate for a BRMS.

1.4   Why use a Business Rules Management System?

As I have pointed out, according to Standish (1995; 2004) around 66% of large US projects fail. Clearly we should be doing *something* differently.

Another key statistic relevant to the failure of IT in the modern world is the cost of maintenance. It is widely estimated that well over 90% of IT costs are attributable to maintenance of existing systems rather than to their development. This is one of the reasons that object-oriented and component based development is so attractive: when the implementation of a data structure or function changes, these changes do not propagate to other objects. Thus maintenance is localized to the changed component(s) or service(s). However, this benefit does not extend to changes to the business rules if they are scattered around the application or tightly bound to interface definitions. If the interface changes – as well as the implementation – the changes *will* propagate and maintenance will be very costly.

To overcome this we need to separate the definition of policy from implementation and code detail. BRMSs facilitate this. Ideally, the rules are subdivided into modules that are encapsulated in individual objects, including so-called 'blackboard' objects, which are visible to all objects that have registered an interest in them. Such blackboards encapsulate global or organizational *policy*, while rulesets that pertain to specific classes (such as clients or products) can be stored (at least conceptually) within those objects for better reuse.

The separated rulesets need to be maintained and kept under version control. This implies that a good BRMS will store rulesets centrally in a repository. As we shall see later, the apparent contradiction between the need for encapsulation and centralization can be resolved using patterns, notably the POLICY BLACKBOARD and ENCAPSULATE A REFERENCE patterns (cf. Chapter 7).

We think that a good BRMS should allow applications to be deployed in a service oriented architecture (SOA). The rule engine should therefore present itself as a service to applications and applications should be deployable themselves as services (e.g. as web services).

Returning to the linguistic gulf that too often separates developers from their customers, we need ways of writing the rules that are understandable to users. Ideally, this would be pure natural language, but unfortunately it is impossible (in principle, I believe) for computers to understand unstructured human discourse. Our speech is too larded with cultural referents and ellipsis. There are four possible solutions to this problem:

1. Make business people learn computer-understandable languages like Java or UML. The language can be textual or graphical but it must be computer executable.

2. Invent a computer language that *looks like* natural language.

3. Provide user-friendly interfaces that generate rules in a way that is natural to business people.

4. Restrict usage to the subset of natural language needed to discuss a particular domain.

In our opinion, the first strategy is both arrogant and doomed. But it is currently the norm. The last three strategies all require the construction of a vocabulary or domain ontology: a model of the things and concepts under discussion and the connexions among them. It turns out that this is much the same idea as that of an object model in UML. However, there are more or less user-friendly flavours of UML, ranging from approaches that use UML like a language describing a Java program to really quite language-independent styles. For now, suffice it to say that most people's conceptual model of their subject area does *not* fit comfortably into the object model of any programming language. UML can be used to describe the former, but it may also be used to describe more natural conceptual models based on, say, semantic networks (see Chapter 4, Section 4.2.1 for an explanation).

Thus, modern corporations will need to adopt development styles that fit their development culture. This will substantially affect the type of BRMS product that they choose.

1.5 The Benefits

The benefits of adopting a business rules management system may be summarized as follows:

- Faster development.
- Faster maintenance, which is particularly relevant in service oriented architectures, where the maintenance of a rules component is addressed outside of the wider IT maintenance context.
- Clearer auditability.
- More reusable business logic.

- Greater consistency across the enterprise.
- Better alignment and understanding between business and IT.

However, business rules management systems alone will not suffice. They need to be implemented side by side with business-oriented requirements engineering, best practice in object and component modelling and, I believe, service oriented architecture. It is to the latter topic that we turn in the next chapter.

And there are a few pitfalls. There can be technical problems in debugging a system with thousands of rules. Large, badly segmented rulesets become increasingly difficult to manage. This is because rules are sometimes invented in restricted contexts which do not consider all the background assumptions explicitly. As more rules are added to handle particular or exceptional cases, this can affect the global consistency of the ruleset and the ability to select which rules should fire. These problems are best addressed by paying attention to sound requirements engineering practices, solid architectural patterns, the dangers of potential 'entropy' in rulesets and conflict resolution strategies (such as most-recent, least-recent, refractoriness; cf. Jackson, 1986).

1.6 Summary

Software engineering practice has not delivered on its promises and needs to change.

The problem we need to solve is broader than just business rules management; the real problem is how to align IT practice with business need.

There are two traditions underpinning the business rules approach: database theory and AI.

A business rule is a compact, atomic, well-formed, declarative statement about an aspect of a business that can be expressed in terms that can be directly related to the business and its collaborators, using simple unambiguous language that is accessible to all interested parties: business owner, business analyst, technical architect, customer, and so on. This simple language may include domain-specific jargon. Business rules are always interpreted against a defined domain ontology.

Business rules management systems separate the rules from data and control logic and maintain them in a repository. Rules are grouped into rulesets, and inference over and within rulesets is both possible and transparent.

BRMSs have applications across all industries and many types of business problem.

Businesses strive for shorter time to market and lower development and maintenance costs. Business rules management technologies can play an important rôle in this. Using BRMSs together with better requirements engineering and business modelling within the context of SOA should decrease development costs and dramatically shorten development and maintenance cycles.

1.7   Bibliographical Notes

The seminal works on the business rules approach are probably those by Ross (1987; 1994; 2005), Date (2000), Halle (2002), and Morgan (2002).

I have assumed in this chapter that the reader is familiar with certain well-known developments in IT. If any terms are in fact unfamiliar, Graham (2001) contains a discussion of database terminology and introduces the Zachman framework. It also contains useful background on object modelling and my approach to requirements engineering.

Service Oriented Architecture and Software Components

with Derek Andrews

It is to be all made of sighs and tears; –
It is to be all made of faith and service; –
William Shakespeare (*As You Like It*)

In this chapter we digress slightly, in order to locate the business rules approach, within the context of service oriented architecture (SOA), the modern, more flexible approach to structuring decentralized IT systems. We will see that many of the ideas and techniques of SOA carry over directly to the business rules approach, and the adoption of SOA and BRMS together will let businesses deploy or integrate new applications far more easily. One of the key points of this chapter is that SOA, like business rules, is about raising the abstraction levels of interfaces: interfaces that must support the business, not the system.

The examination of any engineering discipline must start by looking at its history, in the hope of determining trends and learning from the mistakes of the past. Programming computers used to be easy, although producing high quality software was never so and remains a key challenge. Over five decades, programming has evolved into a much more complex activity, and the goal of producing good software is as elusive as ever.

In the 1950s, it was a simple matter to persuade an electronic brain (as they were then dubbed) to add up some numbers and print them out or, provided that you knew the mathematics, compute the cosine of an angle. The invention of high level languages such as FORTRAN, ALGOL and COBOL made such tasks even simpler. However, there was a double price to pay. Firstly, you had to choose the right language for the job; COBOL doesn't know much about trigonometry. Secondly, the poor programmer has to know that the COS function is in the language's library. Then came databases, removing the need to worry about much of the complexity of data storage and management – provided that you knew the language and, indeed, the theoretical basis of the database. At the same time we saw the advent of fourth generation languages (4GLs) that made programming easier still. But, here too, there was a price; such languages were predicated on relatively fixed data structures. Just as we wouldn't choose COBOL to calculate sines, we would not choose a spreadsheet to write a computer game.

By the mid 1990s, it was clear that the future of computing was synonymous with the idea of distributed computing. Life suddenly got much harder. Now the programmer not only programs, but does so within an environment that requires the use of a bewildering array of pre-written components supplied within an architectural framework such as .NET or J2EE. During this evolution, the dream of the 4GL largely evaporated, outside of the world of database management anyway. 4GL programming was largely superseded by programming in object-oriented 3GLs such as C++, C# or Java.

The move to component architectures raised the stakes in terms of software design too. The complexity itself means that good modelling of the logical structure of systems becomes critical. The banner of component-based design (CBD) is raised in the battlefield of computing. Szyperski's (1998) ground-breaking book told us how to program with components. Sims (1994), D'Souza and Wills (1999), and later Cheesman and Daniels (2000), began to show us how to design for component frameworks. Much of this work seemed to say that CBD was a major advance over object-oriented methods and superseded the latter, but there were dissenting voices (including my own) that took the view that earlier work had merely deviated from pure object-oriented principles and that CBD was merely OO 'done right' and, in fact, the current commercial frameworks were encouraging a very non-OO approach to design by separating coherent business objects into process layers, data layers, etc. Typical of such dissenters were Pawson and Matthews (2002).

Add to all this the emergence of new technologies such as grid computing, peer-to-peer computing, web services and agent-based systems, and we have a recipe for a goulash of staggering complexity.

The only way to integrate these views and maintain good design disciplines seems to be to regard components and, indeed, all objects as suppliers or consumers of services. Indeed, systems based on a service oriented architecture (SOA) could be said to be the natural next step in software development. If we look back again at the history of software development, we see at the start that programs were written to solve a particular scientific problem; next programs were written to help with business: programs were written to read, process and put data out in a batch environment. Online systems followed; these were for clerks to work with, usually driving a legacy system adapted from batch to handle work in real time. The introduction of the world wide web led to online systems for customers who could then use a system directly, rather than using it indirectly through a clerk. The natural consequence is the online system for anybody (customers, people, partners, other businesses), not necessarily with any human computer interface of the old type.

Business rules management technology dovetails neatly – and essentially – into the SOA approach. The change in philosophy needed to produce systems that support the business is leading to new business opportunities, a different way of developing systems and doing business. However, if our main goal is to align IT better with business, then SOA alone is not enough. We need to separate the business rules from the code to achieve this. In other words, SOA without BRMS is like a runaway train with no wheels; it will soon grind to an ignominious halt.

We now look at the philosophy of SOA and outline the business drivers for and the benefits and pitfalls of adopting it.

2.1   Service Oriented Architecture and Business Rules

Service oriented architecture is an architectural concept in software design that emphasizes the use of combined services to support business requirements. In SOA, resources are made available to service consumers in the network as independent artifacts that are accessed in a standardized way. Many definitions of SOA identify it with the use of web services using standards such as SOAP (originally Simple Object Access Protocol) and WSDL (Web Services Description Language – pronounced *wuhzdle*). However, it is possible to implement SOA using any service-based technology. Though built on similar principles, SOA is **not** coextensive with web services, the latter being a collection of technologies and standards, such as SOAP and XML. The notion of SOA is quite independent of any specific technology.

Critical to this notion of services is their loosely coupled character; service interfaces are independent of their implementations. Application developers or system integrators can build applications by composing one or more services without having to know the services' underlying implementations. For example, a service can be implemented either in a .NET or J2EE environment, and the application consuming the service can even run on a different platform or be written in a different language.

Consider, for example, someone enquiring about the parts needed to construct a floggle and their costs. The service might respond with something like 'You need six widgets @ 6p and one 6 mm toggle @ £1.20. The total cost is £1.56. All items are currently in stock.'

The service meets the need of this type of customer well, but it should be clear that there are at least three underlying services, concerned with bills of materials, pricing and stock. It is almost certainly more flexible to implement these services as separate components and aggregate them into higher level services like the one described.

We can note three further features of SOA:

- SOA services have self-describing interfaces in platform-independent documents. In the case of web services, these documents are presented in XML, and WSDL is the standard used to describe the services.

- SOA services communicate with messages using a formally defined language. Consumers and providers of services typically exist in heterogeneous environments, and consumers communicate with the least possible knowledge about their provider. Messages between services can be viewed as if they were business documents. In the case of web services, communication is via XML schemata (also called XSD).

- Ideally, SOA services are maintained in a registry that acts as a directory listing. Applications can then look up the services needed in the registry and invoke them as required. In the case of web services, Universal Description, Definition, and Integration (UDDI) is the standard used for service registry definition.

Each SOA service may have a quality of service (QoS) associated with it. Typical QoS elements include security requirements, such as authentication and authorization, reliable messaging, and policies regarding who can invoke services. However, more business-oriented service level agreements can also be important. Consider a financial pricing service that gives current stock prices based on current trading in the market. There are two components that implement the same service interface. One is from Reuters – a well-established and reputable vendor – and the other is supplied by Honest John's Prices Inc. Do you care which implementation you take? Of course you do, if reliability is an issue. But SOA is implementation independent, so you shouldn't have to care. The solution is to include a QoS factor in the service interface that measures the 'reputation' of the supplier[1]. Of course, when the services are provided in house the quality may be inferred, and these considerations do not apply.

Service oriented architecture structures software systems in the following style:

- Distributed enterprise application servers provide a collection of services (or transactions).

- By various incentives (which may include quarterly bonuses), developers are encouraged to build systems using this collection of services to supply most of the functions of new applications; roughly speaking we assemble new applications by plugging together existing services.

---

[1]We are indebted to John Daniels for this example.

- These units of transaction can be relocated, load-balanced, replaced, security-applied, etc.

One of the ideas behind component based development is to scale up the object oriented philosophy of encapsulation, interfaces and polymorphism to the component level – a component is just a big object, designed and developed with the same care and attention given to identifying classes, their responsibilities and their collaborations. This approach can be further extended to a service oriented system by dividing the system into a set of components, each of which supplies a set of business services. Done intelligently, this leads to the system being built from a set of loosely connected components, many of which are ripe for reuse, or even better – sharing.

Because of the nature of components, we can try and factor other decisions into their design as well as just responsibilities and collaborations. If we try for a layered architecture (always a good idea) at the lowest level we can identify components that supply business utility services. These components supply utility services that are useful across a family of businesses. For example an address book, a catalogue, or a component that deals with interest rates. This type of component encapsulates few or no business rules, and can be categorized as being 'function-like'. By function-like we mean that they behave as a look-up table might, indexed by a key, or as a mathematical function – a particular input will (nearly) always supply the same answer. A key such as zip code and building number should yield a unique address. A book catalogue should, for a given ISBN, produce the details of the relevant book, and such details do (or should) not change. For interest rate calculations, given a period, interest rate and principle amount; the result should not change (a real interest rate calculator component would not be that simple, but the principle remains the same). These components are, by their nature, very stable and should be reusable within a particular business area. This type of component extends the old idea of a FORTRAN code library, but brings it up-to-date.

At the next level up are components that encapsulate business objects: parties, places or things. These components would, for example, manage customers (or even better people or companies, one of whose rôles is customer), locations for a parcel delivery company, or book copies. These components are still relatively stable in the sense that once written, they tend to have only minor modifications made to them later: usually the need to add additional information or roles. They are re-usable, or shareable, within a particular company. The interface to them is basically Create-Read-Update-Delete, suitably renamed – for a library member the services would be join and resign, lots of query operations to do with being a member of a library and operations to change details, such as a library member's address or their name if this is requested when they get married. It may look as if such components might only encapsulate a single type; but even in a simple example, the component managing members in a library system may have as many as 10 different types in it, and a component containing customer details would be very much larger. Business rules are usually found in these components – hence reusability is likely to be restricted to a particular business area.

At the top level we can define components that manage business processes; these contain objects that record events such as a book loan or a reservation for a title. Business objects will play particular rôles in a business process event, and thus appear in the record of that event. For example, in a library a person plays the rôle of a borrower in a book loan and a reserver in a reservation and as a library member in the library. The rôles link to, and represent, business objects. Business rules about the processes can be held in the corresponding process component. The component managing loans would know about the length of a loan, and the maximum number of books that can be borrowed at one time. A process component is less reusable than the other two types as it contains business rules that govern the process. These components are less stable; they tend to change quite frequently as the organization thinks of better and different ways of conducting its business. Even these can be made easier to write and maintain if they can be split into two parts, a generic description of a particular business process together with a part that tailors the description to a particular business process by providing the business rules the restrict the general approach. This latter part should be written and developed as a plug-in. Returning to the library example, the loan component is about lending books to library members, but with care can be refactored to be used in any organization that does loans (books become lendables and library members borrowers). The business rules about the business process can be turned into plug-ins and can be changed as needed.

Looking at any business process, one part is about the order in which we do things, and the other is about under which conditions we do things: you can only reserve a horror movie if you are over 18, you cannot buy life-insurance if you are over 100, you cannot have a loan if you are an un-discharged bankrupt. These later business rules can be encapsulated in a separate part of the component. To introduce generality into the first part we can allow more general order in which we do things and impose business rule to restrict this. Consider the business process of making a sale; our business rules may demand a prescribed order for the activities that make up a sale as shown in Figure 2.1 (a). This ordering could be weakened to that illustrated in Figure 2.1 (b).

The latter allows the activities that make up the business process to be done in any order, or even in parallel. Consider a Christmas club, where we pay for goods before we finally obtain them, and a 'try-before-you-buy', where they are delivered before being ordered. Business rules are used to enforce the previous order for new or unreliable customers; reliable and well-known customers could benefit from more liberal régimes.

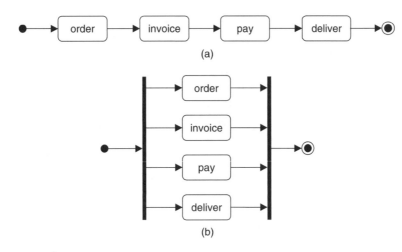

Figure 2-1 Sales processes.

With the breakdown into three types of component[2], it is now possible to examine the build, buy or wrap decision. COTS (Commercial Off-the-Shelf) components are more likely to be utility or business object components, since these components include few or no business rules, and are thus likely to be more general. New application areas managing business processes in an organization are more likely to be built in house rather than bought off the shelf, as these are likely to include rules which are peculiar to the organization. Legacy systems tend not to have layers corresponding to the three component types, but have process, objects, rules and utility services mixed together. Wrapping legacy systems in a component is wrapping legacy business processes and rules – a sure way of perpetuating old-fashioned ways of doing business. Wrapping the legacy at the utilities or business object level, if these types of services can be teased out, is a better idea. Wrapping at the business object component level is necessary; wrapping legacy at the business process layer is difficult and is also wrong; it is most likely that this is the part that will change the most. Old stovepipe systems encapsulate their own business rules, and these rules may conflict with other stovepipes, so trying to combine them is likely to lead to problems – an insurance company may wish to offer a package of mortgage, term insurance convertible to life insurance and medical insurance, and an endowment to pay off the mortgage, and might find that the legacy rules are such that only one person in a million is eligible; this package may need some weakening of the individual rules for each financial package.

---

[2]This discussion refers implicitly to Peter Coad's (1999) 'colour' patterns, where he distinguishes the recurring object types: PartyPlaceThing (green), Rôle (yellow) and MomentInterval (pink). We prefer to call the latter type Episode. Coad's insights are core to one of the patterns in Chapter 7: BUILD A TYPE MODEL (4).

In the long run, if the company is made up from a lot of different companies that have merged, then there may be many versions of the same core component (e.g. customers of the different companies). A strategy needs to be developed to merge all of these into a group of components, each covering a core type. The first thing to do is to get the business rules out of the legacy systems so it is only data that are being merged – not data plus business rules.

Having said all this, it must be admitted that it is just as easy to construct a weak or dysfunctional SOA as it is to mess up any other kind of computer system. Also, quality is much more of a problem; any errors will be visible globally. If your services are no good, your reputation will suffer and your services will lie unused. Worse still, badly dysfunctional services may attract litigation. Another danger is basing a SOA on proprietary product line architecture and thus preventing unforeseen variation.

The route to SOA involves supporting business goals by supplying services to the users of the system so that business can be conducted more easily; it involves the infrastructure to support those services, both from the application and its platform. To do this, it is necessary to understand the business. This cannot be done by just looking at the system users and their use cases; the net must be cast wider. To supply a set of services it is necessary to understand the business and find the real users of the system, and these are not usually the people sitting in front of a keyboard and screen. The real users of the system want to achieve a goal, and a computer system is just a tool to help to achieve that goal. SOA is about designing and developing systems that supply services fit for the purpose of helping users attain their goals.

Decentralized computing provides greatly increased flexibility for both business and IT, but it also creates a danger: business decisions may be inconsistent across applications. BRMS provide a way of managing the decision logic centrally and independently, even where the rules apply locally to different 'zones' within an organization. The key is the use of a repository to store the rules and a rule engine to apply them correctly in the context of a particular application or service. Thus a BRMS can act as a mediator between service oriented applications and the legacy; it smooths the interactions between applications and acts as the decision management component for applications that are implemented as a set of services. These services interact with a decision management service which incorporates a rule engine; this, in turn, has access to the repository. As the intent of each service is distinct, so too is the service's use of rules. Two services might use a common rule, but both may have unique rules or processes related to that rule. Using a BRMS allows reuse of rules across services. This, in turn, can speed development and ease maintenance even more than the adoption of SOA on its own, precisely because the services are easier to configure; when the business changes the rules can be changed without need to recast the services or architecture at the code level.

Service oriented architectures and business rules management systems are an essential component of modern agile businesses. They vastly reduce the problems associated with the evolution of complex and volatile business strategies and policies. SOA and BRMS are parallel and complimentary technologies.

A good BRMS should allow applications to be deployed in a service oriented architecture. The rule engine should therefore present itself as a service to applications and applications should be deployable themselves as services (e.g. as web services).

There are well known and understood technologies to support SOA. The use of these encourages, but does not guarantee, systems that supply services. SOA is not just about using the right tools and infrastructure, there is much more to it than that.

2.1.1 Business Drivers, Benefits and Pitfalls

The drivers for SOA are manifold. Perhaps the most striking is the history of failure of large IT projects referred to in Chapter 1, where we saw that maybe two-thirds of everything we do in IT goes awry. We need better project management. Here the news is good because the Standish surveys report steady improvement over the decade from 1994 to 2005. We need better requirements engineering too, but there is little convincing evidence of dramatic improvement here. In addition, evolving or poorly understood requirements point to the need to involve the business more closely in service definition and delivery. SOA is one way of moving closer to this goal. Evolving technology and platforms can also hit maintenance costs. Defining platform independent services through SOA should mitigate this tendency by providing a baseline of more stable definitions.

At the time of writing, the main focus of SOA adoption is 'behind the firewall'. Therefore, many of these considerations do not apply, but as the number of resources available on the web grows like Topsy, it becomes increasingly difficult to know if the service that you need is out there or not. SOA, as we have described it, makes it possible to search for available services and components much more readily. Finally, SOA is necessary for business-to-business transactions (B2B) on the web. In the short-to-medium term, of course, B2B links will be set up with great care and through negotiation by people – not by machines trawling cyberspace and matching parameters.

SOA proffers several significant benefits to its adopters. The ability to plug in new services without disrupting existing software, modularity based on business concepts rather than technical models, the ability to share and connect services across organizational units, companies and geographical areas. Most importantly, it can bring us closer to supporting business goals, especially when combined with a business rules approach, as we shall see. Adopting SOA, like business rules, encourages the separation of the concerns of business *versus* those of the infrastructure. With a well-designed SOA you can add value to your own business by doing things better and using other people's services, and add value to other peoples' business by adding your services, thus sharing your savings with them.

Defining components as services also offers the possibility of contracting development out to third parties with better control over the results. If we add web services to this picture, the benefits of web delivery being well known by now, we can envisage immediate gains.

2.2 Service Implementation using Components

Component Based Development (CBD) is a sister technology to SOA; they are orthogonal, but sympathetic concepts; it is possible to have one without the other, but they best go hand-in-hand to produce component based systems that provide business services. For all practical purposes, service oriented architecture depends on component based development.

Component based design is aimed, like object-orientation, at improving productivity by offering a better chance of reuse through better modularity. If it is done well, we can build large, complex systems from relatively small components. If combined with an agile development process and if there has been sufficient investment in components, this can lead to a faster development cycle.

A software component is an object that is defined by an interface and a specification. An **object** is something with a name (identity) and responsibilities of three kinds: responsibilities for remembering values (attributes); responsibilities for carrying out actions (operations/methods); and responsibilities for enforcing rules concerning its attributes and operations (often referred to as constraints). An **interface** is a list of the services that an object offers. A **type** is such a list plus the rules that the object must obey (its **specification**). Contrast this with the notion of a class. A **class** is an interface with an implementation. A class has instances; a component has implementations. So what's the difference between a class and a component? Not much! Two things distinguish components. First, components are generally 'bigger' than classes; but this is not a distinction in principle. More importantly, components are delivered in the context of a framework within which they can interact: a 'component kit'.

Figure 2.2 shows part of the type specification of a queue component[3].

We can easily think of several ways to implement this type: as an array, as a linked list, etc. Sticking to arrays, there are still choices to make. We could use the implementation illustrated in Figure 2.3, where we maintain one pointer called 'last' and shuffle the values up to the front of the array and decrement the pointer by 1 when a 'leave' occurs. When there is a 'join' event, all we have to do is increase the 'last' pointer value by 1. Thus, $length = last + 1$.

---

[3]We are indebted to Alan Wills for this example.

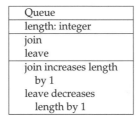

Figure 2-2   A specification.

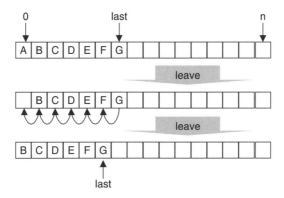

Figure 2-3   Implementation as an array with one pointer.

Alternatively, we can utilize the implementation shown in Figure 2.4, where we have to maintain two pointers but save some time on the shuffle operation. In this scenario, $length = last - first\ (mod\ n)$.

Here, n is the maximum queue length in both cases. The first element in the array is element 0.

So, we can interpret the queue as a component that can be implemented in multiple ways; but we could also interpret it as a component offering three services. A queue allows queuers to join and leave the queue and offers a service to retrieve the length of the queue at any time (except in the middle of a join or leave operation). Each implementation has its own algorithm for computing this retrieval of length, but each of these must satisfy the two rules in the specification. So, components look very much like service interfaces.

Thus, SOA can be viewed as a philosophy that drives the development of components by defining their interfaces clearly and in a way that relates to real needs. CBD then packages the services for development and maintenance, often using technology such as J2EE, .NET, CORBA and so on; although CBD is not necessarily about component middleware of this type. SOA and CBD both encourage the separation of specification and implementation.

Also, note that component specifications are almost always described using rules, as above. This is equally true of services. Rules of the type given above

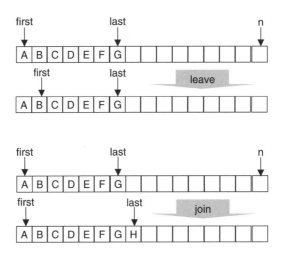

Figure 2-4   Implementation as an array with two pointers.

constrain the relationships among services; joining or leaving a queue changes its length.

Components, when delivered, must be documented and provided with a test harness. The documentation must state at least the following:

1. What the component expects of the environment into which it is placed: other components and services that must be present; their QoS parameters; etc.

2. Which services the component can be expected to provide: its specification.

3. Which business rules the component must conform to.

Another observation, coming both from work on component design methods and from the exigencies of current component frameworks, is that it is useful to classify components and organize the architectural layers around the classification.

Date (2000), Cheesman and Daniels (2000) and Andrews (2007) all identify a difference between general components and **core components**: objects or concepts that 'really' exist in the domain. Consider the potential components needed for building administrative systems for public libraries.

Clearly, Book is a core component, although we might profit from including a generalization of it such as Lendable_item. How about Member? No! Membership is a **rôle component**; the core object is Person. Membership is an association between people and libraries. Perhaps we should generalize the concept of library too, perhaps using Fowler's (1996) party pattern. A library is a kind of organization which is, in turn, a kind of party. People are also parties. Another apparent core concept is the idea of a loan but, here too, there

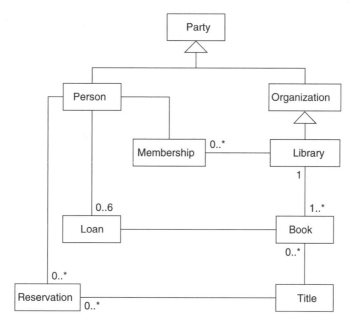

Figure 2-5 Some components for a library system.

are advantages in realizing that loans represent not things but a key business process of the library; a **process component**.

Figure 2.5 offers a UML type diagram representation of some of the components in a library. The cardinality constraints represent a particular kind of business rule. 1..* against Book is interpreted as the rule 'A library owns at least one and possibly many books'. 0..6 against Loan means that 'A person need have no loans but is not permitted more than 6 (at any one time)'. But there is another rule that is not shown on the diagram. We certainly do not want people who are not members to be able to borrow. This kind of rule is very common; whenever there is any kind of cycle in a UML class diagram then there is a potential rule lurking. Here are some of the rules that might be implicit in this diagram:

- The person borrowing a book must be a member of the library that owns the book.

- A reservation must be for a title that describes a book owned by the library.

Note that neither of these rules need be true (i.e. apply): interlibrary loans; purchase on reservation. So, perhaps the rules are more complex:

- The person borrowing a book must be a member of the library that is a member of the same interlibrary loans organization as at least one library that owns that owns a copy of that book.

- A reservation must be for a title has describes a book owned by the library unless there are four of more reservations for the same title, in which case the library will order one copy of that title.

There is a pattern here, our first in this book. The idea of patterns will be covered fully in Chapter 7, but bear with us whilst we present a thumbnail sketch of it.

Pattern 11	ASSOCIATION LOOPS CONCEAL RULES
Context	You are trying to DISCOVER BUSINESS RULES (5) and have completed part of BUILDING A TYPE MODEL (4). You know that you must WRITE THE CARDINALITY CONSTRAINTS AS RULES (12).
Problem	**How can you be sure that you have not missed any rules implicit in the type model?**
Example	Refer to Figure 2.4. Start with a person. Do they have a loan? If yes choose one. Every loan is for a unique book that has a unique title. Does the title have an outstanding reservation against it? If yes, go back to the person you started with. Does that person have a reservation? If so, is it for the same title? Perhaps the rule is: 'A member may not reserve a title which they have already borrowed a copy of'.
Solution	**Look for cycles (loops) in the type diagrams. Start at every type in the loop, choosing a generic instance of that type, and follow the associations to another type. Ask if each route brings you to the same instance. Write down the rule that says it does.**
Resultant context	The rules you have written down may not be true, so now ASK THE BUSINESS (13) and ASSIGN RULES TO COMPONENTS (14).

Words set in small capitals represent other patterns: patterns that we shall encounter later in this text.

So, working with component models reveals business rules. In the same way, service specifications reveal rules and are incomplete without them. Component models are a good way to round out the specification of services.

Component modelling is a crucial step on the road to good service oriented architecture. Modelling should encompass business matters and not just data and functional models of the software encouraged by many current UML tools and practices. As we shall see in Chapter 7, models must look beyond the system boundary and encompass all stakeholders, although models often need to map to the platform architecture (.NET, J2EE, etc.) also. Models must always include business rules and constraints.

Business goals are supported by use cases. The type model is the vocabulary needed to express the goals of use cases. The pattern language of Chapter 7 begins with patterns that express this. We first ESTABLISH THE BUSINESS OBJECTIVES (1), then build a BUSINESS PROCESS MODEL (2) using use cases and focusing on their goals or postconditions rather than any notion of 'steps'. The use case goals **are** the services. As part of this we ESTABLISH THE USE CASES (3), DISCOVER BUSINESS RULES (5) and BUILD A TYPE MODEL (4).

Our requirements model needs to supply the software service specification:

- What business goals does it meet?
- What does it do?
- What information does it provide and require?
- What are the business rules?
- What are the quality requirements?
- What constraints and rules must be obeyed?
- Are there any interface dependencies?
- Who can use each service or component?
- What will it cost?

2.3 Agents and Rules

Agent technology has its roots in the study of distributed artificial intelligence, although the popularity of the approach has had to wait for more mundane applications in mobile computing, mail filtering and network search. Along with this plethora of new applications there is a great deal of very confusing terminology facing anyone attempting to understand the technology of intelligent agent computing. We read many conflicting and overlapping terms such as Intelligent Agents, Knowbots, Softbots, Taskbots and Wizards. Also, there are writings on network agents that are not true agents in the sense of most of the above terms. Furthermore, there are several competing definitions of an intelligent agent in the literature.

Russell and Norvig (1995) characterize an agent as 'anything that can be viewed as perceiving its environment through sensors and acting upon that environment through effectors. A rational agent is one that does the right thing'. A report from Ovum (Guilfoyle and Warner, 1994) tightens this slightly: 'An agent is a self-contained software element responsible for executing part of a programmatic process, usually in a distributed environment.' Luck and McBurney (2005) say that agents are 'autonomous, problem-solving computational entities' that can operate in 'dynamic and open environments'.

From this viewpoint, agents are components that, rather than being invoked directly, can make choices among their permitted actions and interactions, as assigned by their designers and owners. An **intelligent** agent makes use of non-procedural process information – knowledge – defined in and accessed from a knowledge base, by means of inference mechanisms. But a more compelling definition comes from Genesereth and Ketchpel (Riecken, 1994): 'An entity is a software agent if and only if it communicates correctly with its peers by exchanging messages in an *agent communication language*.' This is a most important point if agents from different manufacturers are to meet and cooperate. Kendall *et al.* (1997) say that agents are objects 'that proactively carry out autonomous behaviour and cooperate with each other through negotiation', which further supports this view.

Agent communication languages (ACLs) perform a similar rôle to object request brokers or web services protocols like SOAP, and may be implemented on top of them. ACLs are necessary so that agents can be regarded as distributed components that need not know of each other's existence when created. There are two kinds of ACL, procedural ones such as General Magic's Telescript, and declarative languages such as the European Space Agency's KQML/KIF.

One might add that an agent is an entity that can sense, make decisions, act, communicate with other entities, relocate, maintain beliefs and learn. Not all agents will have all these features, but we should at least allow for them. One way to do this is to classify agents according to the level of features they exhibit; in order of increasing complexity and power these are:

- Basic software agents;
- Reactive intelligent agents;
- Deliberative intelligent agents, and
- Hybrid intelligent agents.

It is common to apply the description 'agent' to quite ordinary code modules that perform pre-defined tasks. This is an especially common usage in relation to macros attached to spreadsheets or database system triggers and stored procedures. Such 'agents' are usually standalone and have no learning capability, no adaptability, no social behaviour and a lack of explicit control. The term is also applied to simple email agents or web macros written in PERL or Tcl.

Reactive intelligent agents represent the simplest category of agent where the term is properly applied. These are data-driven programs; meaning that they react to stimuli and are not goal oriented. They perform pre-defined tasks but may perform symbolic reasoning, often being rule-based. They are sometimes able to communicate with other agents. They may have learning capability. At a macro level they may sometimes exhibit explicit control, but there is no explicit micro-level control. They cannot reason about organization. Homogeneous groupings of such agents are common. Examples of reactive intelligent agents include monitor/alert agents encoded as a set of knowledge-sources or rules with a global control strategy. Service-oriented BRMS components often fall into this category

Deliberative intelligent agents are mainly goal-driven programs. They can have the ability to set and follow new goals. They typically use symbolic representation and reasoning; often using a production rule approach. They typically maintain a model of their beliefs about their environment and goal seeking status. They may be mobile and able to communicate and exchange data (or even goals) with other agents that they encounter. Deliberative agents may have learning capability. They can reason about organization and are able to perform complex reasoning. Their intelligence is programmed at the micro level at which there is explicit control. Heterogeneous grouping of these agents is possible. Data retrieval agents that will fetch and filter data from a database or the internet are typical examples of this kind of agent.

According to some authorities (Kendall *et al.*, 1997) this is the weakest permissible use of the term AGENT. **Weak agents** on this view are autonomous, mobile, reactive to events, able to influence their environments and able to interact with other agents. **Strong agents** have the additional properties of storing beliefs, goals and plans of action, learning and veracity, although there is some dispute over the meaning of the latter property.

Hybrid intelligent agents are a combination of deliberative and reactive agents. Such agents can be mobile and may try actively and dynamically to cooperate with other agents. If they can also learn, they are **strong hybrid intelligent agents**. Such agents usually contain (or may access) a knowledge base of rules and assertions (beliefs) and a plan library. An interpreter enables the agent to select a plan according to its current goals and state. When an event occurs a plan is selected (instantiated) to represent the agent's current intention.

It should now be easy to see that there are three prerequisites for agent computing: components, business rules and an ACL.

2.3.1 Agent Architecture

Adding rules to the interfaces of components has the useful side-effect of enabling us to model many intelligent agents and multi-agent systems without any special purpose agent-based modelling machinery. Agents are autonomous, flexible software objects that can respond to changes in their environment or context, engage in 'social' acts via a common agent communication language and be proactive in the manner of the Intellisense agents in MS Office, for example.

Intelligent agents are intelligent in the sense that they embody some kind of expertise or the ability to learn. This expertise may be encoded as business rules, in which case the agent must have access to an inference engine to process them. Learning algorithms are usually, of course, procedural in nature

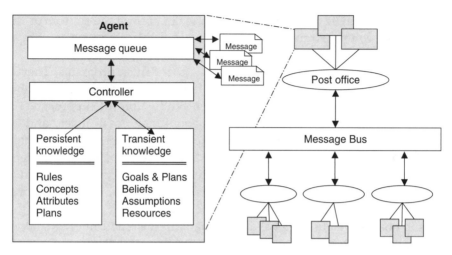

Figure 2-6   One possible architecture for an agent.

and may be based on decision branching (e.g. ID3), neural nets or genetic algorithms.

Agents need to communicate with users and with each other. As we have mentioned, the best way to do this is via a standard agent communication language. Unfortunately, such a universal standard is not yet agreed, so that designers are often forced to create one or work within a proprietary environment. The promise of SOA, especially in the light of web services, as we shall see, is that the ACL can be based on accepted industry standards such as SOAP and WSDL.

We can generalize about the basic architecture that most agent systems share. Figure 2.6 shows a typical architecture. Here, each agent has a controller that stores or can access an inference engine and problem solving strategy. The agent encapsulates two kinds of knowledge in its knowledge base: persistent and transient. The persistent knowledge often takes the form of attributes and methods that represent its ontology or type model, but the methods may be coded non-procedurally; Prolog perhaps or a BRMS rule language. The agent may also store knowledge about the rôles that it plays in the overall agent organization and about its plans. Plans, which are fixed, are to be distinguished from those that vary during execution, the latter being part of the agent's transient knowledgebase along with its current assumptions, beliefs, acquaintances and short-term goals. Agents communicate via a message queue and deliver messages to post offices on the network which, in turn, deliver to other agents, systems or users. Actual agent-based systems vary considerably but share this basic approach in outline at least.

One of the main reasons for the adoption of component technology is the move to distributed architectures. But *n*-tier architectures are often beset with severe network bandwidth problems. Using mobile agents can reduce the amount of network traffic. The mobility of agents means that, when it is more efficient, we can send the program across the network rather than a request to retrieve unfiltered data. Smart agents can be used to personalize systems for individual needs and skills, which has the effect of reducing the cognitive and learning burden on these users. Agents that can learn, adapt and exchange goals and data can be used to speed up information searches, especially across networks or the internet.

The agent model is a model of distributed problem solving. There are several approaches to the co-ordination of distributed co-operating agents. These include centralized control, contracting models, hierarchical control via organizational units, multi-agent planning systems and negotiation models. These are not discussed further here, but one type of strategy is especially important for systems involving multiple, co-operating agents that each apply specialized knowledge to help solve a common problem. A common architecture for such applications is the 'implicit invocation' or blackboard architecture (Buschmann *et al.*, 1996). This becomes important for BRMS, as we will see in Chapter 7.

It should be apparent that adding rulesets to components is all that is necessary to make them into agents. Forward chaining (data-driven) rulesets enable reactive agents and backward chaining (goal-driven) régimes support deliberative agents. Because each object can contain more than one ruleset and each ruleset may have a specified régime, hybrid agents can also be built. Of course, learning abilities would not normally be represented as rulesets but, more likely, by operations – or a mixture of the two.

Repositories of business objects become, effectively, the domain ontology, extending the concept of a data dictionary, not only by including behaviour in the form of operations but by encapsulating business rules in an explicit form.

Intelligent agents may have to operate in the presence of uncertainty, and uncertainty comes in many guises: probability, possibility and many more. Modelling systems that restrict the logic in which rules or class invariants are expressed to standard predicate logic or first order predicate calculus (FOPC) are too restrictive. A better approach allows the designer to pick the logic used for reasoning: FOPC, temporal logic, fuzzy logic, deontic logic (the logic of obligation or duty), etc. Just as a ruleset has an inference régime, it has a logic. In fact the régime and the logic are intimately related. For example, standard fuzzy logic implies (usually) a one-shot forward chaining strategy that treats the rules as if they all fire in parallel. Unfortunately, current BRMSs offer scant support for uncertainty.

2.3.2 Applications of Agents

Agents have been used to monitor stock markets and trade shares automatically, to find and buy cheap flights and to collect data on a user's use of a computer. They have evident uses in e-commerce where there are purchasing agents that can find the best price for a product, such as a book, across multiple web sites. An agent system handles malfunctions aboard the space shuttle. The White House uses e-mail agents to filter thousands of requests for information. MIT has built agents to schedule meetings. Sample applications of agent technology to date include data filtering and analysis, process monitoring and alarm generation, business process and workflow control, data/document retrieval and storage management, personal digital assistants, computer supported cooperative working, simulation modelling and gaming.

Agents in current systems perform information filtering, task automation, pattern recognition and completion, user modelling, decision making, information retrieval, and resource optimization based on negotiation (e.g. in air traffic control), routing.

Other current applications include:

- planning and optimization in supply-chain management;
- program trading;
- battlefield command and control simulation and training;
- network management and process monitoring (of networks and of business processes).

Another area where agent computing is becoming influential, at least as a modelling metaphor, is in business process modelling and re-engineering. The focus in most work on BPR is on process and this is as it should be. However, as Taylor (1995) has pointed out, an exclusive obsession with process can be dangerous because business depends on the management of resources and the structure of the organization as well as on effective processes. Thus, any approach to business process modelling needs to be able to model all three aspects: resources, organization and processes. It turns out that the agent metaphor when combined with an object-oriented perspective on systems analysis provides an effective solution to this modelling problem. Furthermore, modelling a user's responsibilities with an intelligent agent can often reduce the cognitive dissonance between the user's mental model of a system and its actual structure.

Components with rulesets support the modelling and design of intelligent agents and systems, but agents are also key to modelling business processes and reducing the cognitive dissonance between models of the world and system designs – an aim shared (we hope) by anyone implementing SOA.

Any agent worthy of the name provides a service. In the context of SOA, these services must relate to *business* services. But agents may also be consumers of services. In that sense, agent-based computing *extends* the ideas of SOA. Now let us look at some technologies that exist today and can be used to construct SOAs, and that may one day be the basis for a universally accepted standard for ACLs.

2.4   Service Oriented Architecture and Web Services

Web services provide a standardized way of interoperating amongst applications, regardless of the platforms they are running on. They realize SOA in a very practical way, using concrete agents that communicate by passing messages that conform to the standard protocols. The environment is open, in that agents can leave or join at will without disrupting the whole. Agents can act on behalf of service owners, to ensure contracts are met and relevant business rules enforced, or subscribers, to locate relevant services, negotiate contracts or deliver the results of service invocations.

Web services provide one possible infrastructure for SOA and indeed agent-based computing. Just as one can use SOAP without understanding SOA, one can adopt SOA without using SOAP, etc., but one cannot do SOA without good services.

Services are about using other (other peoples' and your own) systems as part of your own, these other systems offer functions, services, that you can use – your system will collaborate with these systems to achieve a goal. If disparate, distributed systems written in different programming languages are to communicate and collaborate with each other, they will need some sort of communication medium and a way of speaking to, and understanding, each other: a common language. A global communication protocol already exists: the internet, which is a mechanism for moving bits around. The first layer of abstraction built on top of this basic mechanism is for moving data around using TCP/IP. On top of this abstraction we can build web services; here the stuff that is moved around is XML and the mechanism used is intranet/extranet/internet. Building on top of this has many advantages; to use web services, there is no need to change the way that the infrastructure is used, web services represent just another application, and the existing internet protocols and infrastructure can easily be used; security applications, such as firewalls, will not become a problem.

Having got a pipe, some basic infrastructure, the web and XML, we need a language to describe the format of the messages and a mechanism to manage the interchange of messages. Since we have a distributed system, we also need to know where to look for things; these services are supplied by the following:

- WSDL (Web Services Description Language);
- SOAP (Simple Object Access Protocol);
- UDDI (Universal Description, Discovery and Integration).

A simple model will explain the functions of these various elements of web services. If we think back to before computers and the internet were central to communication, business could be done with letters carrying information

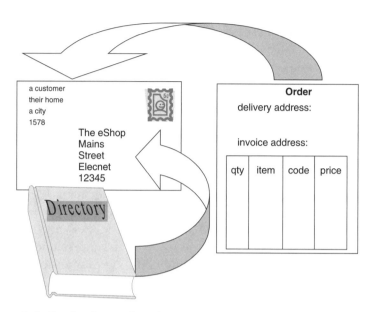

Figure 2-7   A simile of web postal services.

(the XML bit) and a PTT to deliver the letters (the web bit). To make business easier we might add some additional rules and services.

The postal service may define valid envelope sizes and where the stamp is placed, where the 'to' and 'from' addresses are written on the envelope, and where you post a letter – such standard will enable them to efficiently process your letter and speed its delivery to the correct address. To do business with another company, we can look up details of the company in either the yellow or white pages. Yellow pages classify businesses by type, white by their name.

To do business efficiently by post it would also be useful to have details of how to do business with the company. Information that describes what envelopes you should use, details of any forms you will need to complete (for example what needs to go on an order), any replies you might expect to get (the format of their invoice and delivery note) – an advanced postal service might publish these in a different coloured directory, say green pages. As a user using the directories, you fill out the necessary form or write the appropriate letter, put it in the envelope and post it to the address found in the directory and possibly await a reply if the rules tell you to expect one. The simile is illustrated by Figure 2.7.

UDDI is about the rules of the business including its whereabouts and how you contact it and what information needs to be exchanged to do business. WSDL is about the information you need to supply using various forms and letter formats in an exchange with the business; this is described in the business directory green pages. SOAP is about defining the rules of the post office. SOAP is a very simple postal service, if you need a more services such as recorded delivery, proof of posting, tracking of your letter, insurance and receipt of delivery you need more rules; this is what ebXML or BIZTALK are about – but these are not part of this discussion.

XML

In addition, we may well use XML, the acronym for eXtensible Markup Language, which is designed to structure data by marking individual items with tags that hint at what each item represents. The format of a particular XML document is described by a Document Type Definition (DTD) or in an XML schema (leading to the claim that XML is designed for defining XML documents). Thus an XML document with its DTD or XML Schema is designed to be self-descriptive.

XML is a language for communicating instances of abstract syntax (and for defining those abstract syntaxes). The concept of abstract syntax has been around for nearly 40 years; this is where the information being captured is separated from the concrete syntax used to write the information down. Of course, we need to write the abstract syntax down, but it is at a higher level of abstraction – we represent the information as a tree. XML is a flattened representation of a tree. Consider a simple example, in Figure 2.8, representing an if-then-else statement using abstract syntax.

This description will work for any language that has a traditional if-then-else statement; the keywords are left out; but we still have a representation of the information content of the statement. In XML we could represent an if-then-else statement, thus:

```
<ifThenElse>
  <BooleanExpression>
    . . .
  </BooleanExpression>
  <then>
     <statement> . . . </statement>
     <statement> . . . </statement>
    . . .
  </then>
  <else>
    . . .
  </else>
</ifThenElse>
```

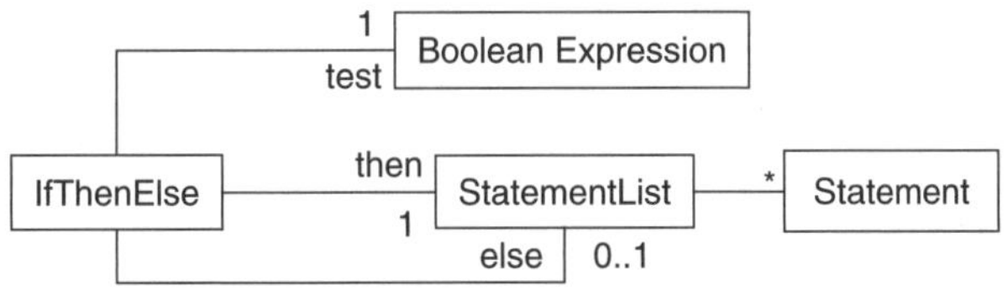

Figure 2-8 If-then-else as a UML type diagram.

It can be seen that XML can be used to encode objects, attributes and links, to flatten a collection of objects, their attributes and links into a form suitable for sending around the internet. Using XML, we can pass data around the internet as character strings that encode objects; and with SOAP we can call methods in distributed objects passing the structured data as arguments.

Note that an XML document does not do anything, it is just information marked with XML tags; do not run away with the idea that there are any semantics embedded in this information – that is encapsulated in the software that sends or receives the XML document; the software will have an understanding of what the information is about. The following example is a name and an address written using XML:

```
<address>
  <person>
    <firstname>Derek</firstname>
    <surname>Andrews</surname>
  </person>
  <no>356</no>
  <street>Main Road</street>
  <town>Glen Magna</town>
  <county>Leicestershire</county>
  <postalcode>LE34 7NH</postalcode>
</address>
```

An address has information about a person and where they live. An address has the house number, street, town and county – a fairly standard layout for an address in the UK, and fairly self-explanatory: it is self-descriptive. However, there are limitations. If you believe that this XML document does have some semantics, consider the dilemma faced by someone asked to supply address information to an American company. They may be asked to supply the following data:

```
<address>
<person>
 <givenname>Derek</givenname>
 <familyname>Andrews</familyname>
</person>
<buildingno>356</buildingno>
<street>Main Road</street>
<city>??Leicester??</city>
<state>??England??</state>
<zip><state code>LE</statecode>
<zipnumber>??34 7NH??</zipnumber>
</zip>
</address>
```

We have little problem with the person part, but is the city 'Leicester', the postal city for 'Glen Magna'? What do I supply for the state? Is it

'Leicestershire', but that is a county, and I know there are counties in the USA…Is it 'The East Midlands', the area I live in, or is it 'England' which could be considered a rough equivalent to state as it is the next thing up from a county, and the state of the UK is made up from the countries of England, Wales, Scotland and the province (not a country) of Northern Island. There are even more problems with the zip code; I will assume that I can use LE as the equivalent of the state code, but the rest of the post code is not numeric, and is meaningless as far as the UK encoding goes. The American company and I do not agree on the interpretation of the XML tags. It is not enough just to invent tags and hope that their names provide a meaning, the semantics must be given as well.

A subtler example is the following information interchanged by two hotels in a hotel chain about room occupancy:

```
<roomdetails>
  <roomno>34</roomno>
  <roomtype>double</roomtype>
  <occupant>Jo Smith</occupant>
</roomdetails>
```

Further investigation reveals that the message format only allows a room to have only one occupant no matter how many people can sleep in it – in this example we have a double room. What is the explanation? You need to know that the hotel chain doesn't care how many people are staying in a room; it only wants to know who is responsible for paying for it, the occupant. Providing both the sender and the receiver of this message are aware of this, there is no problem, but this information cannot be deduced from the XML alone, you need to know about the business and its rules.

XML can be used to exchange data between two incompatible systems. In this case it will be used a standard format that both ends of the transaction can understand and can translate their representation of the data to and from. In fact a message standard can be expressed in XML for many systems to exchange data, though they all will need to agree on the tags and the meaning of the data associated with those tags. As XML is character based, there is an additional advantage that one of the machines that can understand the data is the human brain. One of the advantages of XML is that we can extend a message format by adding additional tags to mark the additional information carried in the message. Existing applications will ignore the additional information; new applications can recognize and use it. Since the information is encoded using text, with XML, plain text files can be used to store data. XML can also be used to store data in a database. Applications can be written to store and retrieve information from either text files or database, and generic applications can be used to display the data – for example the XML can be translated into XHTML and displayed using a browser.

When deciding how information is to be encoded with XML, users of that particular piece of XML must agree on the names of the tags, their structuring (nesting) and most important the meaning of the data marked with a particular tag. From the above example it should be noted that the name of the tag is not enough for this, though it does help. Any one taking part in the interchange must have a shared (possibly dynamic) vocabulary, which includes the meaning of any terms (tags) used in a conversation.

SOAP

Middleware software such as CORBA, .NET and J2EE supply some sort of Remote Procedure Call mechanism (RPC), but it is not secure and there are compatibility problems communicating between different programming languages and different middleware, each must be supported by the mechanism. There is a requirement for a mechanism that avoids these problems: one based on HTTP would work since this is supported with browsers and servers and by the internet. SOAP is a communication protocol for exchanging information between applications; it wraps up a document and moves it over the internet. A SOAP document is encoded using XML. A SOAP method call is a HTTP request-response that conforms to the SOAP rules; think of it as being the procedure call mechanism for a service that uses a WSDL definition that gives the name of the service and describes any parameters that are needed.

A SOAP message looks approximately like this, leaving out some of the more complex parts.

```
Information to help with understanding and routing the
   request to the server:
<soap:Envelope
   xmlns:soap="http://www.w3.org/2001/12/soap-envelope"
   soap:encodingStyle="http://www.w3.org/2001/12/soap-
encoding">
<soap:Header>
...
...
</soap:Header>
<soap:Body>
  ...
  ...
  <soap:Fault>
  ...
  ...
  </soap:Fault>
</soap:Body>
</soap:Envelope>
```

If the Header element is present, it is the first part of the Envelope. This header contains application specific information which is about any bureaucracy surrounding the service such as details of the transaction it belongs to where two or more services need to be processed together (or not at all). Other services such as authentication, encryption used, any payments that are due and any other additional information that may be needed can also be placed here. This allows additional information to be added over time without breaking the original specification. The Body element is required and contains the actual SOAP message intended for the ultimate destination; it contains the name of the procedure and the arguments of the procedure call in programming terms. An error message is carried inside the optional Fault element. It is the contents of these three fields that are described in the UDDI using WSDL. It should be noted that because of the way SOAP is designed, its use is not restricted to use over the internet, it can also be used over other transport mechanisms such as email and message queues.

WSDL

WSDL is the acronym for Web Services Description Language. WSDL is an XML-based language which is used to describe a web service's capabilities by providing information about the business including its internet address, services provided and the message formats. In programming terms WSDL is the procedure declaration and SOAP is the procedure call mechanism. WSDL is an integral part of UDDI, an XML-based worldwide business registry. WSDL is the definition of the procedure call parameter names and types, but more general and expressed in XML; structured data can be used as parameters, rather than just simple data values.

Web services can use business services, but not necessarily the other way around; they are at different levels of abstraction. Just because you expose an API to the world as a set of web services, it does not mean you have SOA.

The format of a WSDL document follows:

```
<definitions>
<types>            Definitions of the data types that will be used in the
                   messages – these are machine- and programming
                   language-independent.
...
</types>
<message>          Definitions of the messages that will be transmitted; these can
...                be parameters with input separated from output or document
                   descriptions (parameters in a procedure declaration).
</message>
```

```
<portType>          What operations and function will be performed by the web
...                     service; these will refer to message definitions in
                        the<message>section to describe function signatures: the
                        operation name, input parameters, and output parameters.
                        (C.f. the procedure name and parameters – the WSDL
                        equivalent of a Java interface.)
</portType>
<binding>           Specifies binding(s) of each operation in the portType section,
...                     describes how the messages will be transmitted – the
                        communication protocols to be used by the web service and
                        further information about the operations defined in
                        portType – these will be specific to the underlying web
                        protocol used for exchanging the SOAP messages (there are
                        three recommended protocols: HTTP, HTTP GET/POST,
                        SOAP/MIME).
</binding>
</definitions>
```

UDDI

UDDI is short for Universal Description, Discovery and Integration. It is an XML-based directory that enables businesses to list themselves on the internet so they can be found by other businesses. A UDDI entry for a business providing web services consists of three main components that define what the businesses are, where they can be found on the internet and how the businesses can interact with each other over the internet. It is the web equivalent of a telephone directory with both yellow and white pages, together with additional information store in 'green' pages.

An entry in the white pages provides the basic contact information about a company, such as the business name, address and contact information. These may also provide a unique business identifier, such as Dun & Bradstreet's D-U-N-S number; these are unique nine-digit sequences for uniquely identifying a business. The white pages allow customers and business partners to discover business services based upon the business name.

An entry in the yellow pages describes the business services using different categories (e.g. being in the manufacturing or the software development business, as per a yellow pages telephone directory). This information allows others to discover business services based upon its category. For example, a service might be categorized as an 'Online Store' service and at the same time be categorized as a 'Book Store' service.

An entry in the green pages provides technical information on the behaviour and use of the business services that are offered, and any support functions supplied. Green pages in UDDI are not limited to describing XML-based Web services used over the internet, but any (electronic) business service offered by a business. This includes phone-based services such as call-centres, E-mail based services such as technical support for a product, fax-based services such as a fax to E-mail service, etc. Information such as the service location, the category to which this service belongs, and the specification for the services can all be found in the green pages.

A UDDI directory is designed to be interrogated by SOAP messages to provide access to WSDL documents that describe the protocol bindings and message formats required to use listed web services. These descriptions are encoded using XML. It should be noted that UDDI does not necessarily have its services described in WSDL for use by a SOAP call, other protocols can be used – for example a fax service would have described the protocol used by the fax, and email the type of messages supported (plain text or HTML for example).

Of the few companies that have pioneered service oriented architecture, fewer still have succeeded. Often they have proceeded by wrapping their existing systems so that they present themselves in the form of lots of web services. They end up with a business process (or application) layer that makes hundreds of very low level calls through the bus to the web service interfaces of the legacy systems. These point-to-point connections give immediate payback and get the job done, but at the expense of the creation of a vast amount of 'spaghetti' – far, far worse than when the same was accomplished by running wires between boxes.

This approach leads to:

1. Thousands of low level interfaces;

2. Brittle topology;

3. Poor extensibility;

4. Poor understandability and maintainability;

5. No reuse; and

6. Absolutely none of the promised benefits of SOA.

What is needed is an abstraction layer of business services (typically realized by components) that sit in the no-man's land between business and IT – and are understandable to both. These can then be reused and extended in line with changing business goals and priorities.

These services must be specified rigorously, not just in terms of XML schemata but also in terms of their process behaviour.

A possible acid test for SOA might be this. Give an executive director a pen and the back of an envelope, and ask her to draw boxes to represent the major services she uses to deliver the organization's business goals, to say which boxes are services provided by people and which by IT, and to describe how the services talk to each other – all at the highest level. We suspect that few companies are at that level of SOA maturity.

If SOA is limited to bottom-up, convenience grouping of low level API services, understood only within the IT department, business people will understand none of it; nor will the IT dept be any clearer on overall business goals and strategy.

SOA, done properly, will both provide and be based on a common language for business and IT. Then, existing and future systems can be discussed readily – using the names of the business services – the names of the boxes on that envelope. Service orchestration can then be done in business terms at the highest levels: I want this login service, this stockcheck service, etc.

2.5   Adoption Strategies

How does one build a world class rule-based, service oriented architecture? Moving from your current approach to software development to one geared towards an SOA approach will involve some changes. Building a business model is too often avoided as it is seen as extra, non-productive work. RUP (Kruchten, 1999) suggests writing lots of descriptive use cases as part of the requirements process. Both of these attitudes need to be changed. To find services, you need to understand the business, and a quick way to understand the business is to build a business model. Use cases are usually interpreted as being about developing the user interface, and the real user of the system is frequently not the person in front of the keyboard and screen. Thus we are interested in finding the real users of the system and their goals; then we can supply the services that will help them achieve those goals.

Moving from a business model to a working CBD/SOA system is a new skill to be developed, and using existing resources in a SOA involves careful development work. An architecture has to be designed and developed, and modified as experience is gained. Higher quality will need to be built into the software, as it may be seen outside the business or originating department. All these considerations will affect the way systems are developed and maintained. Our approach is broadly as follows.

As a first step, build high-level, abstract models of the business goals, business processes and business entities and concepts with the aim of:

- integrating different parts of the business;
- identifying reusable components that provide services;
- identifying the business rules that must be obeyed by these components;
- identifying common services and specifying them; and
- identifying the reuse of legacy systems.

Think about re-engineering the business, contracting out some services, contracting in others and especially doing new things by using other peoples' services. The slogan should be 'stop doing old, unprofitable things'.

Next, turning to the question of architecture, try to match your technology to the services defined. Then focus on business processes. Look for easier and new ways of doing business – reduce the number of business rules. Adopt agile development processes. Standard processes are not adequate. You will need additional or different tasks in the process, a different type of specification.

Adopting a BRMS will assist in the transition to SOA because service-based and legacy applications can be coupled using the BRMS as the common decision engine. In the transition period, decision logic is gradually extracted from the legacy and replaced with calls to the rule service (together with some code to interpret the responses). In this way, the legacy can be incrementally replaced by services. Most major BRMS vendors provide wizards for setting up a rule service using web services.

2.5.1 After SOA

'We have SOA, what are the benefits we should be seeing?' SOA, if done properly, should lead to more efficient business process, better process modularity and even business process reuse, but you must focus on the business and not the software.

'We have adopted SOA and have developed one or two successful systems; now what?' Are there any additional advantages? Since the services are about the business, and the business rules have been isolated in an appropriate component, it is easier to change the way the business works. Services supplied by other businesses can be absorbed into our own, if appropriate, and services we supply can be given to other businesses. Business rules can be simplified, and the way the business does its work can be changed for the better. Building SOA based systems encourages an understanding of the business and the way it works, this can lead to changing the business.

Existing legacy systems can be analysed and wrapped to supply services and, using some well-understood techniques, evolved into the new business structure. There are also techniques for replacing legacy systems over long periods so as to not impact the business.

As the emphasis is on modelling the business, by building a business (analysis, requirements) model (a Computation Independent Model using OMG terminology), the development team are in a position to investigate and exploit MDA, leading eventually to even cheaper and faster software development.

We can illustrate the importance of getting the interface right and the importance of emphasizing *business* services with the following example. Consider the problem of refuelling an airliner between flights at an airport. A clerk will use information about the flight (number of passengers, destination, cargo, plane type etc.) to calculate the optimal fuel load and send an order to the fuel company to refuel the plane with the necessary amount of aviation fuel when the plane arrived. Even if the order is placed electronically, it is likely to be placed some time before the refuelling is actually needed as the airline company has no idea of the availability of the fuel trucks; this is the problem of the oil company. In order for this to happen, the airline company will need to use estimates of the aircraft load from passenger and cargo bookings. Their requirement is to know fuel requirements ahead of time so they can schedule the trucks and necessary staff. There are two problems here: the software will be written for the clerk to use to work out the necessary fuel needs (the clerk may be automated and send an email order, but this does not change the problem). However, the real user of the system is not the clerk, it is the guy refuelling the plane, he needs to know how much fuel to load, this is what this part of the airline business is about. A service oriented interface will be about loading the correct amount of fuel onto the plane, nothing else; it is not about a conversation with the clerk as to airline type, destination, load, etc.

The message here is that you need to get outside of the system boundary to identify services. The system boundary tells you the services the interface designer wants, not the real user (who may not be the person using the computer – think call centre, the real user is the customer on the end of the telephone, not the call centre clerk!).

By writing detailed use cases we are concentrating on the user interface rather than what is happening in the real world, we are focussing on the solution rather than on the problem. Frequently this traditional approach leads to lots of documentation of the use cases, and little understanding of the business; detailed use cases are about the design of the user interface – this is an activity that we can leave until later. There is a need to do the description at a level that provides both understanding and provides a basis for detailed development of the HCI later. We need to move our perception up a level – at an abstract level we are interested in the goals of the business so we can supply business services that help in achieving these calls. The real user will need to be supported with services; the system user is supported by a user interface – low level stepwise use cases are about defining the system user interfaces.

Use cases define the interaction of the actors with the system, but the real user of the system may be far outside the system boundary. For example, in a library example: the library users want a reservation to be fulfilled when it is their turn in the queue of members waiting for a particular book. When they return a book, they want the transaction recorded so they are no longer responsible for the book they were loaned. Our library members are not that interested in the actual loan being recorded – though the library is very interested in that particular transaction. Thus the purpose of the system is to make certain that the business of the library is run properly. We should be interested in the goals of the real-user who can vary between the customer and the business, the goal of any actors using the system are not usually relevant for finding system services. There is a further advantage,

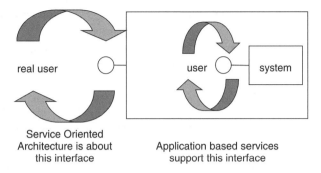

real user

user   system

Service Oriented
Architecture is about
this interface

Application based services
support this interface

Figure 2-9   The provenance of services.

if we write the system with services in mind we can consider all sorts of interesting changes. Sometimes the real users are actors – customers buying goods online – and it is still better to find their goals, not the system's. As suggested by Figure 2.9, there needs to be a change of emphasis – we need to understand the needs (goals) of the real user and supply services that help to satisfy those needs.

The way to identify business services is not by analysing the use of the system by an actor, but by analysing the business. As Graham (2001) points out, a transaction in a business is usually carried out as a conversation between two or more parties who are interested in some sort of joint goal – making a sale, obtaining a book on loan. It is the goal of the conversation that is of interest to us, this is the service and it is this that we will supply machine help with.

With a service oriented approach, the move from the real user using the system through an intermediary to using the system directly should be straightforward; just changing the user interface should be the maximum amount of work that needs to be done. More exciting changes can be made with a service approach, there is a possibility of changing who does what. Suppose you request services from a supplier. For example, returning to the problem of refuelling an aeroplane at an airport. The current approach is likely to be ordering the requisite amount of fuel from the fuel company. An extreme approach would be to get the oil company to fill the plane as necessary with a bonus of the oil company sharing any cost saving with the airline. This could lead to just in time refuelling, where the optimal amount of fuel is loaded on the plane by the oil company, and the airline managing the optimum cargo/passenger mix. In a more general case, we move from a client/supplier approach to a partnership approach or even a consumer/supplier approach with the supplier driving the business with the incentive of profit sharing. The migration from one approach to the other is easily managed if we have services which are about the business rather than services that are about the interfaces. We can also see with the migration of control that there are cost savings that can be made, and these can be shared with partners as an incentive to move in this direction.

Generalizing, we are moving along the following delegation of control: from the client being in control to the service provider being in control, with these intermediate possibilities:

1. Do exactly this for me.
2. Will you do this for me? Here is the information you will need to work out what I want.
3. Will you do this for me? Here is access to the information you will need to work out what I want.
4. Do this for me when I need it – I will tell you when. Ask for any information you need to work out what I want.
5. Do this for me when I need it; ask for any information you need to work out what I want and when I want it.

If the original system was set up correctly to supply services, this migration of control from the client to the service provider is reasonably straightforward. The service provider can move to a just in time service with some negotiation with the client about fuel *versus* plane load.

One way of testing for SOA at a global scale has already been given, on a smaller scale we can look at the messages that pass between actors to confirm a conversation, these are the messages we need to model in our system, since one of the participants in a conversation is likely to be replace by a machine.

If you have a paper system with clear understanding of the information flowing around, it is much easier to re-organize things to improve productivity or to take advantage of new business opportunities. The same principle holds for computer based systems.

In a nutshell, low coupling and high distribution give the service provider control; high coupling and low distribution (SOA) give the client control. Ultimately, if SOA is implemented well, the real user may be willing to do more work; and share the cost saving with the IT function.

2.6   Summary

We looked at the nature of SOA and its connexions with BRMS. They have in common the aim of raising the level of abstraction closer to the concerns of real business users; the real user not the IT department or administrative users; systems for the business, for employees, for customers or for suppliers; systems for the real user not the 'user'. SOA provides services that help people perform tasks that deliver them value. BRMS goes further and separates the rules from the code. Without BRMS, SOA is less effective and harder to maintain. SOA starts with business objectives and processes and focuses on a reusable service level abstraction layer. Rules are parts of its specification. Components are grouped into services during design.

We saw that CBD was a very natural way to design for SOA and met some analysis patterns that are relevant to SOA, CBD and BRMS. SOA, CBD and BRMS are complementary technologies. We also saw that rule based components could be regarded as intelligent agents.

SOA is not the same as web services but the latter is one way to implement it. Beware of low level calls in the middleware, leading to a spaghetti of low-level point-to-point connexions. Don't start with wrappers; don't start with technology.

Let us put all this together. SOA, BRMS and CBD, used together offer potentially tremendous business benefits. In future we may see the technology broaden out into intelligent agent architectures that unite and enrich all these technologies. Web services have an important rôle to play as an implementation technology and may provide the basis for future ACLs.

Lastly, we considered the issues facing adopters of SOA.

2.7 Bibliographical Notes

The fundamental ideas of component-based development were described, from different points of view and emphasis, by Sims (1994), Szyperski (1998), D'Souza and Wills (1999), Cheesman and Daniels (2001) and Graham (2001). Andrews' forthcoming book (2007) focusses on the design of component-based systems and service oriented architectures and, in particular, extends the ideas of John Daniels and Alan Wills in the form of the Catalysis™ II method.

There is a large literature on agent-based computing and intelligent agents. Notable works, from our present point of view, include Farhoodi (1994), Ferber (1995) and Graham (1998; 2001).

The internet is a source for many discussions on and (competing) definitions of service oriented architecture.

CHAPTER 3

Approaches to Business Rules

Who shall decide, when doctors disagree?

Alexander Pope (*Moral Essays*)

There have been three fundamental schools of thought on business rules. As we saw in Chapter 1, the most prevalent comes from the database tradition, but the oldest springs from work on artificial intelligence. More recently, people interested in object modelling and formal methods have begun to pay attention to business rules in the context of UML specifications. This chapter takes a brief look at these competing but overlapping approaches, and tries to establish a workable synthesis and some guidelines on how to select an approach and a product supporting it.

Which approach is best? There is no simple answer; it depends on the nature of the problem. So, who shall decide? The users, guided by the nature of the problem, sound architectural vision and patterns based on experience and best practice: they should decide.

3.1 Database-centric Approaches

Looking back at some of the articles written in the late 1980s and early 1990s in journals such as *Database Newsletter*, one is tempted to suspect that the only business rules of interest to the database community are very simple ones involving cardinality constraints and simple arithmetic computations; inference is hardly mentioned. However, this narrow view has matured and broadened as business rules management systems have evolved into mature products.

The most consistent and compelling argument for the database-centric approach comes from Chris Date (2000). He argues that business rules are there to ensure that the facts represented in the database cannot be corrupted by updates that violate the rules. Whenever, an update is performed the rules, including all inferences from them, are checked and, if violated, the update is aborted.

Date argues that progress in computing is about raising the level of abstraction. I agree. Both business rules, object modelling and – as we saw in Chapter 2 – SOA are all about raising abstraction levels. Next he argues that declarative is better than procedural description. Again, I mostly agree. But then he goes on to conflate declarative descriptions with executable specifications. I think this is a misunderstanding. There is no reason why an executable specification cannot be described procedurally. In fact, when dealing with computations in domains such as engineering or actuarial work, it is often more natural for the business users (engineers, actuaries, scientists, etc.) to express themselves procedurally. It is also a moot point whether certain UML problem descriptions are procedural or not, especially when the approach to executable specification is based on MDA or other approaches to code generation. For example, are finite state machines declarative or not? The scholastically inclined could argue this point alongside the activity of placing angels on the head of a pin. We shall not do so here.

So let us stick with this rather beguiling view of incorruptible databases as a justification of business rules. Date's position depends entirely on what is known as the Closed World Assumption (CWA); this is the assertion that every tuple or instance in a database represents a true fact. If it's in the database, it's true; and if it isn't, then it is false. One consequence of adopting this view of databases is that, as Date has argued elsewhere (1983), one must not allow null values in databases. Not only are there multiple interpretations of the meaning of a null value (unknown, missing, etc.), but a null indicates a truth value other than 'true' or 'false' and the CWA no longer makes sense without substantial modification.

As I have said, the CWA is beguiling; if we add business rules to the update mechanism, there can never be an error in our business records. This will please any red-blooded data administrator who no longer has to fret about those pesky users sticking duff records in the database. However, from the viewpoint of the requirements engineer, the situation is less clear. As Michael Jackson has pointed out over and over again (1995; 1998; 2001), one of the challenges in specification is allowing for the situation when the computer model of the world (the database) gets out of synch with the actual world. Anyone who has been the victim of identity theft or who has been given a faulty credit rating will attest to the importance of this problem. The trouble is that, in the best of all possible worlds, the CWA is rarely valid. 'Ah yes,' I hear you protest, 'but if we have all the rules in place then no dodgy data can ever get past them to soil our pristine records.' My response is merely to say that, however good a specifier you might be, you will *never* know all the rules, except for domains where the human factor is severely absent. No, we need a business rules environment that acknowledges that the database may contain falsehoods.

On the other hand, preventing gross update errors is certainly a worthwhile benefit; business rules should be part of the data or object model.

Date, like most authors on the subject, offers a classification of rules (based on one proposed by Jim Odell) into various kinds of constraint and two kinds of 'derivation': computation and inference.

There are some dangers here. First, whilst it is often inadvisable, it is always possible to recast constraints into if/then form. Once that is done, inferences can be executed and the constraints chained. I think that it is better to drop the distinction between inference rules and constraints and to concentrate on differences between what a rule or constraint refers to. For example, the age range constraint that we met in Chapter 1 refers to a single attribute (date of birth), and is best represented by restricting the domain of the attribute (to dates that give ages over 16). This is no different in principle to restricting the domain to non-negative reals, for reals that we need to perform square roots upon. On the other hand, constraints that refer to more than one attribute are often best thought of as rules, e.g. 'If the delivery address is different from the invoice address then . . . '

The distinction between computations and inferences is important, but not for the reasons that Date, and others like him, give. He regards computations as declarative statements, but this is not so in general. He conveniently gives examples with no brackets; but even the simplest formula for the straight line, $y = m.x + c$, cannot be understood without seeing its implicit procedurality; the reader must know that the TIMES function must be applied before the ADD function – otherwise the formula has a different meaning.

> Calculations are inherently procedural.

The whole point about business rules is that we are trying to make life easier for the user. Obfuscating the procedurality of computations does not help one iota with this. Sometimes, for example it helps understanding to compute and deliver computations in stages (showing the 'working'). In this way, we might show monthly spend in a spreadsheet above a row showing cumulative monthly spend. Clearly the top row must be (logically) computed first. For a more complex example, consider the symbolic solution of integral equations. When I learnt this at school at the age of 16 or 17, we had to grasp that some equations could only be solved using the substitution of a (usually trigonometric) function for one of the variables. It goes like this: first guess at a suitable function, then try it, applying standard antidifferentiation formulae; if this fails, try another function. This cannot be done except if it is done procedurally.

Now, there is nothing in this view that says that computations cannot be handled as part of a BRMS solution. But it seems to me sensible to make a strong distinction between knowledge that is fundamentally procedural and rules that are entirely declarative. We shall return to this point in Chapter 4.

Given the view that business rules are primarily there to guarantee database integrity, Date is tempted to assert that rules should be part of the database. Indeed, the rules for domain constraints almost always are, and things like range constraints (single row rules) should probably be. However, as Date concedes, there are advantages in keeping business rules quite separate from the database engine. The first is what he calls DBMS independence: the rules can be applied to data stored by DB2, Oracle, Sybase, etc. But more importantly, keeping the rules in a separate central repository means that the rules can be maintained independently of data, applications and infrastructure.

From the SOA angle, a database management system can be regarded as a service. It is a better service if all updates are mediated by business rules, but there is no reason why the application of the rules cannot be hived off as a separate service which is called on update.

One final methodological point characterizes the database-centric view on business rules. Designers taking this view will, as Date recommends, start with the data model or, more generally, an object model. That is to say, they create an object model or start with an existing one before writing the rules. These rules can then refer to any entities in that model. Some BRMS products, such as ILOG JRules, encourage this by allowing the user to import a data model from existing Java code. As we will see in the next chapter, rules do not make sense unless they are based on an object model. However, as we shall also see, it is possible to write the rules and *then* extract the implicit model.

In general, the database-centric approach plays down the rôle of inference and emphasizes the non-expert nature of rules. It encourages designers to base the rules around the data model and, thus, assumes that such a model is constructed prior to explicating the rules. It is most appropriate in domains where automated decision making is not important but data integrity is. However, the risk here is that it may be difficult to predict whether automated decision making will or will not be important in the future.

Of all the products in the BRMS sector, it seems to me that Sapiens and Versata are the ones most closely aligned with this viewpoint, although this is not to say that other BRMS products cannot be used to build database-centric applications nor that products like Versata cannot be used outside the database-centric paradigm.

3.2   GUIDE and the Business Rules Group

Starting up between 1989 and 1993, the GUIDE project set out to define and categorize business rules. Like Date, GUIDE includes computations as a kind of derivation rule. The final project report (Hay and Healy, 1997) presented a metamodel of business rules. The GUIDE approach extended the database-centric approach by placing more emphasis on rule independence (relative to databases) and on inference. It has provided a benchmark for all existing BRMS products.

The mantle of the GUIDE project was taken over by the Business Rules Group from 1997. The group evolved from a project team within GUIDE. Its initial focus was on business rules that could be implemented directly in IT systems; i.e. row 3 of the Zachman Framework (Zachman, 1987).

Later, the focus broadened to include the business perspective as well as the information system and technology perspectives. In 2002, it published its most influential work: the Business Rules Manifesto, a pithy statement of the principles of rule independence, reproduced here as Appendix A.

In 2000, it published a second work dealing with one important aspect of business rules from the business (Zachman 'row 2') perspective: the motivation behind the rules. The group has contributed to the OMG Business Semantics of Business Rules (BSBR) initiative. In 2005, the group's Semantics of Business Vocabulary and Business Rules (SBVR) was accepted by the OMG to move into the finalization stage of the OMG standardization process.

The Business Rules Group continues to provide a benchmark for work on business rules and BRMS products.

3.3   Using UML and OCL to Express Rules

Since the earliest days of object modelling, sagacious methodologists have acknowledged that business rules must be recorded. Building on the same entity-relationship modelling techniques as the database-centric approach, they all insist that cardinality constraints should be recorded on class diagrams. More general constraints, however, are usually consigned to separate documentation or written as free text on diagrams. In UML, 'notes' are often used, but the idea is essentially the same: scribble the rules on the class diagrams.

From a business rules perspective, this will not do.

For one thing, it violates the key design principle of object encapsulation, which is necessary to maximize reuse; objects should encapsulate everything they need to be reused – including the rules that apply to them. But here is a dilemma. We also want rules to be reusable as independent entities, which indicates that rules and objects should be stored separately. A related point is that, thinking of SOA and viewing components as providing services, we must insist that components come equipped with the rules that they conform to. The very first article of the Business Rules Manifesto insists that rules are first class citizens.

This is the same dilemma that Chris Date wrestled with: do we store the rules 'in the database' or do we opt instead for rule independence? Certainly, all BRMS products go for the latter. So, do we thus abandon all hope of component reuse? I present one possible answer to this question in the form of a pattern in Chapter 7, where I show that it is possible to encapsulate 'references' to rules while still maintaining the actual rules in a central repository.

There is a further problem with rule encapsulation: some rules refer to many objects. Again the solution is given as a pattern in Chapter 7: POLICY BLACKBOARD (18).

In their seminal work on Catalysis, D'Souza and Wills (1999) emphasize that many business rules may be discovered by examining 'loops' in UML type diagrams. We saw this already in Chapter 2 (Figure 2.5), but let us consider another example, as shown in Figure 3.1.

Airlines operate regularly scheduled routes, such as BA735, and these occur as multiple flights; an instance of such being 'BA735 on 2008/02/29'. They also employ pilots who, in turn are qualified to fly only certain models of aircraft, such as the Airbus A720E or Boeing 777. There are two loops in this diagram. As a result we can identify at least three potential business rules. To find the first, consider the aircraft identified by the code G-LAPM. Map this to one of the flights that uses it, say 'BA735 on 2008/02/29'. Now map this flight to its assigned pilot, which might be Jane Bloggs. Now go the other way round the loop: G-LAPM is a Boeing 777. Mapping along the remaining association, is Jane qualified to fly this type of plane? This suggests the potential rule:

- Every flight must be captained by a pilot who is qualified to fly the plane

This can be rewritten in OCL as:

- Flight :: captain.qualified_to_fly –> includes (plane.model)

Note the rather ugly syntax of '–> includes'; ugly, that is, if you are not a C++ programmer. It stands for set membership and can be thought of as a backwards epsilon: '∋'.

The other rules might include:

- The captain must be employed by the same airline that operates the flight.
- The take-off and landing airports must be different (no joy rides).

The question now is which type specifications (components) should encapsulate the rules. My instinct suggests that the first rule belongs to a description of Flight (as indeed the OCL quantifier suggests) because Flight already encapsulates the information needed to check the rule's validity: plane and captain. The second rule seems to belong to Airline, on the same grounds. For the third rule, it is as plain as a pikestaff that the rule must belong to Route; otherwise each airport would have to store knowledge of other airports.

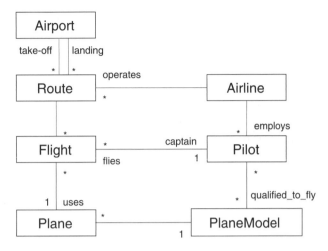

Figure 3-1   A type diagram with three loops.

We can use a pattern to help make this kind of decision: PUT RULES AT THE MANY END of associations.

While rules discovered in this way are usually multi-attribute constraints, it is possible that they might be better regarded as business rules and made subject to inference. For example, suppose that we know that CheapoJet has a policy of only employing 747-qualified pilots and only using 747s on Irish routes. Then we can *deduce*, or *infer*, that flight CJ142 from Brest to Cork is an OK flight with respect to our first rule. It is extremely uncommon for UML and OCL practitioners to think in this way and cast their rules accordingly.

While we can always express constraints and rules in OCL and rules in OCL are at least guaranteed to be well-formed and thus be implemented, expressing them in this way may present a barrier to business people understanding them. Expressing the rules in (a subset of) natural language is generally the preferable approach, although it is sometimes a good idea to check that each rule can be expressed in OCL or some other formal language. Implementing and testing the rule in a BRMS also can provide a check on 'well-formedness'.

3.4   Business Rules Management Systems and Expert Systems

The third and oldest approach to business rules management is that associated with so-called 'expert' or 'knowledge-based' systems. As discussed in Chapter 1, such developments are ultimately descended from the EMYCIN shell. During the 1980s a number of expert system shells appeared as products and there was a flurry of interest in the technology, partly fuelled by the

Japanese state's investment in what they called their Fifth Generation Computing project and the reactive programmes in other parts of the world, such as the British Alvey Project and Europe's ESPRIT.

After some early commercial successes, interest in the technology waned and, by the 1990s, 'expert systems' was a label to be most studiously avoided by anyone in sales or marketing. It was widely reported that expert systems had not 'lived up to expectations', and many believed that this was due to lack of visibly successful applications. Nevertheless, from that time to this, expert systems technology has crept in to hundreds of everyday IT applications and consumer devices.

Expert systems are used in controllers for railway trains, washing machines, 'shake-free' video cameras, vacuum cleaners, software wizards, program trading systems, email spam filters, video games, and many more mundane and familiar items. But, of course, you never hear about it.

So, if valuable applications do exist, why the stigma? In working with this generation of the technology, I found that the architecture of most commercial products was monolithic and, ultimately, unstable. Most shells required that an application ran entirely within the shell or its run-time system. The commonest approach then required developers to write rules that were then compiled, thereby generating the variables and other data structures needed by them. When object technology emerged into the commercial arena, it proved difficult or impossible to integrate rule processing with object-oriented programming. Interest therefore shifted away from expert systems as a development technology. A few pioneering vendors, like the French company ILOG, did come up with rule engine architectures that were compatible with the object-oriented approach but, at that point in history, they had to struggle against generally negative market perceptions. Other companies whose products had emerged from a LISP culture, such as Neuron Data, were able to deal with objects due to their similarity with the 'frames' of artificial intelligence (AI) (Bobrow and Winograd, 1977). However, it was a battle and we have had to wait for the business rules movement to see this technology return into the daylight.

ILOG and Neuron Data focused on componentizing their products and we now see their direct descendents as full-blown, mature, repository-based BRMSs in the form of ILOG's JRules and Fair Isaac's Blaze Advisor.

So, is there a difference between an expert system and a business rules management system?

Barbara von Halle (2002) answers 'yes'. She argues that expert systems only address esoteric or complex decision problems – like the medical diagnoses of MYCIN – and that rule execution is not 'tied to database activities'. Both these statements are untrue in general. Many of the expert systems that I built, helped build or was privy to in the 1980s were quite unesoteric and sometimes database-centric. A tourist board offered a decision aid to help visitors select a restaurant for the evening. A white goods retailer scheduled its customer service visits. A bank scanned its database for potentially fraudulent credit card transactions – a typical rule was 'if there are multiple purchases of similar power tools over a short period then fraud is indicated'. Hardly esoteric or complex knowledge! An insurance office used an expert system to assess fire risks using rules that involved checking such arcane things as whether there were enough fire extinguishers in the staircases. Credit authorization, compliance in unit trust dealing, sales forecasting, computer capacity planning, loan advice; the list goes on. I never worked in a single domain that required the knowledge of anyone with a Ph.D.

Halle identifies three other characteristic features that distinguish expert systems from BRMSs:

- Expert systems use an inference engine that can chain rules together.
- In an expert system, there are usually 'hundreds or thousands of inference rules' that may need to be executed to arrive at a decision.
- Expert systems can handle uncertainty.

The first two of these are clearly related, so let us look at them together. Nearly all modern BRMS products include an inference engine nowadays: Blaze Advisor, Haley Rules, JRules, Versata, to name but four leading ones. And, as Fair Isaac's Paul Vincent (private communication) stresses: 'We compete strongly on our ability to process thousands of rules per second in high transaction environments.[1]' Other vendors tell me the same thing.

Thus, I assert, four of Halle's five distinctions do not stand up to scrutiny, although I admit that there are expert systems that operate in esoteric domains and which would not be within the focus of the average BRMS vendor. I also concede that many business rules may be applied without the need for inference. But her last point is right – well, almost right.

None of the leading BRMS products available today and known to me has any sophisticated facilities for managing uncertainty. Blaze Advisor uses a proprietary technique called 'scorecards', which we will look at later in this book, but uncertainty management is not a feature of any of the other products. It seems that the customer just doesn't need it. We will return to uncertainty management in Chapter 4 but, for now, there is one point worth making. While the *raison d'etre* of BRMS is not uncertainty using mathematical probabilities or fuzzy logic, all current systems *can* handle one form of vagueness. Consider the following business rule (paraphrased from Ross, 2003):

> *An order must be shipped by premium service if*
> *the order is a rush order and*
> *the order includes hazardous materials and*
> *the customer is a platinum customer and*
> *the order destination is remote.*

---

[1]My paraphrase.

This rule (or its syntactic equivalent) could be executed by any BRMS. But it brims with uncertainty. What is a 'rush' order? What does 'hazardous' mean? How far away is 'remote'? There are two ways to resolve such vagaries; either the user puts in an estimation of the order as rush or not, or the database includes some arbitrary definition of rush such as 'delivery requested within three days of order'. In the former case, the uncertainty is captured by the crisp category 'rush', based on the user's vague perception and crisp decision of the boundary between urgency and normality. In the latter case, the same conversion of vague to crisp is done when the three-day definition is laid down in the database. Similar remarks apply to the terms hazardous, platinum and remote; they all capture the uncertainty of human perception in a crisp form that first order predicate logic (or SQL) can cope with.

It may be worth noting that, when fuzzy terms are defuzzified by making arbitrary definitions of applicable ranges, such as 'platinum if disposable income greater than $60,000', then we can expect such definitions to be volatile over time.

Apart from this point about uncertainty, Halle's main distinction is about the nature of 'expert' knowledge. In the early days of expert systems it was argued that the main barrier to building such systems was that of eliciting expert knowledge: the so-called knowledge engineering bottleneck; a term coined by Ed Feigenbaum. This bottleneck is not so much to do with the esoteric nature of the knowledge as the phenomenon of tacit knowledge: knowledge that you don't know you know.

One of the key points about BRMS and SOA, as I have argued, is that we need to move the control of business systems into the hands of business people. We need to engage users in the definition and maintenance of business rules. The overriding assumption is that the users know the rules. In many cases this is true, but even in seemingly mundane domains, like stock control, much knowledge remains tacit or buried in inaccessible legacy code or out of date documentation. I came across an interesting demonstration of this quite recently. An acquaintance of mine works for a company that had implemented a sophisticated stock control system and considered it such a success that, after a year or two, the company decided that the system was so reliable that they could dispense with the services of the human stock control clerks who operated it. The result was that the system pared the inventory down to statistical optimality – at levels below what the now-redundant users had ever permitted – resulting in improved margins. However, the lack of 'slack' led to several late or unfulfilled orders and the customers deserted in droves to the 'less efficient' competition. The lesson? The stock controllers knew something (and something fairly obvious at that) that had not been formulated in the rules of the system.

Tacit and expert knowledge is present in many everyday domains: stock control, credit chasing, customer relationship management, regulatory compliance, and many more. Why should we value the expertise of a clerical or manual worker any less than that of an industrial chemist or a physician? When I'm sick I need the doctor, but when my central heating goes on the blink the plumber's knowledge and skill is just as valued. A friend of mine, the late Rob Milne, built a very successful business by encapsulating the knowledge of skilled artisans into expert systems that could diagnose faults in vibrating machinery.

Although some would argue that early expert systems were designed to emulate individual human decision-making and that business rules for an operational business process need technical support, that is more definitive and institutional. I conclude that there are no significant technical differences between expert systems and BRMS, although the application domains and uncertainty management features may distinguish the two. If there is a difference it is chiefly one of 'mindset'. As a result, I think that the techniques of knowledge acquisition developed in the context of early expert systems work remain immensely valuable, especially in dealing with tacit knowledge. We will deal with these techniques in Chapter 6. However, the business rules movement has added considerable value; their architecture is more flexible and robust; their emphasis on repository-based centralization of rules is invaluable; their focus on non-esoteric domains is timely; it is good that they have reminded us of the importance of using rules to control database updates. The main differences, therefore, are those of emphasis and terminology.

Having said all this, I will close by making a genuine distinction between some knowledge based systems and BRMS. Despite the exaggerated claims of some theoreticians (e.g. Chomsky, 1980; but several others) not all knowledge is rule based. Indeed, Collins (1990) shows that some skilled domains are not amenable to the rule-based expert systems approach at all. Indeed, neural networks are not built using explicit rules, but definitely contain knowledge[2]. An object-oriented model contains much knowledge that is not rule-based. Some problems are entirely computational, and it is nonsensical to recast them as rule-based systems. A good example might be modelling the evolution of the cosmos based on various assumptions about the amount of dark energy in the universe, or modelling what happens in a piston chamber when a spark ignites the petrol. We shall return to the questions of different types of knowledge in the next chapter. For now, I want only to say that BRMS are characterized by being based on *rules*. This limits the domains and problems to which they can be applied.

3.5 Other Developments

The final piece of background that we need, before embarking on a technical description of business rules management systems, is the work that has been

---

[2]Actually a trained neural net is equivalent to a set of fuzzy rules, but this is not widely understood in practice.

done on methods and process for business rules development and on stylistic conventions for writing rules.

The most profound contribution on method comes from Barbara von Halle (2002), whose book remains the definitive work on the subject. Despite my quibbles with her (above) on expert systems, I cannot fault much of her methodological work, except to say that (precisely because of her attitude to expert systems and focus on the database-centric view) she misses out many of the methodological guidelines that are needed for effective knowledge acquisition and requirements engineering in the context of a BRMS project. Chapters 6 and 7 represent my attempt to fill this gap. I refrain from presenting organizational patterns that duplicate Halle's work, although it would be an interesting project to recast and rework her ideas in the form of patterns.

Halle's method recommends a phased approach reminiscent in some ways of RUP; there are five phases and each one addresses four needs, to separate, trace, externalize and position rules for evolution. The scoping phase involves developing a plan for rule management, establishing the business context and purpose and laying down an IT architecture. The planning phase includes tasks for analyzing, designing, implementing, integrating and testing rules and establishing standards and a repository. The discovery phase includes extremely useful guidance on such matters as how to run facilitated workshops, how to write rules, how to interpret use cases, where to look for rules in existing documentation, and so on. The analysis phase looks at existing and alternative business processes and revisits objectives; it also refines the rulebase. Finally, the fifth, design, phase implements the rules and applications using them; usefully, natural language versions of the rules are used as the basis for error messages. The method focuses strongly on data analysis as well as business rules. As yet, Halle's work is the only major contribution to methodology for business rules management systems.

Apart from Halle, two other authors have made major contributions to the question of how to phrase rules to make them clear. Ross (2003) presents a very detailed classification of rules types and extensive guidance on how to formulate and express rules in English. Morgan (2002) also gives much useful guidance on rule formulation. Although the guidance in these works is undoubtedly valuable, practical considerations lead me to think that I would not always have time to apply the methodological guidelines with any rigour on a real project. What one *can* do is absorb the principles implicit in the guidelines; principles such as:

- Rules must be declarative.
- Rules must not contain 'noise' (or 'fluff' to use Ross's term).
- Logical connectives ('and', 'or' and even more especially 'not') should be used with great care or eliminated.

- Ambiguous terms are not allowed.
- And so on.

One pattern that emerges most strongly from this work is that it is almost always better to WRITE THE CONSEQUENT FIRST. That is to say, rather than writing the rule in IF...THEN...format (with the antecedent clause first), write it with the conclusion (the consequent clause) first. So rather than 'if rain is forecast then take an umbrella', we would prefer something like 'take an umbrella when rain is forecast'.

3.6   Standards, Directions and Trends

The area of business rules management is evolving rapidly. The BRMS product vendors continue to play leapfrog with respect to performance, usability and features. We can expect to see strong competition based on each product's ability to process thousands of inferences more rapidly than its counterparts. Similarly, vendors will want to ensure that rules can be created easily by non-technical business analysts – or even users – as well as programmers.

It has been suggested that business rules engines, instead of being standalone product offerings, may become incorporated directly into J2EE or .NET application servers. There is some evidence for this trend; BEA built a rule engine for security and personalization; IBM has a simple engine in WPS, Microsoft has rules in WWF, Oracle has a rule engine based on Jess; JBoss is packaging Drools; etc. However, no application server vendor has yet done a convincing job of broadening their offering to cater for business users. Nor do they seem to have a very deep understanding yet of the business rules lifecycle, as opposed to the traditional IT development cycle. Such developments may not mature until the 2010s. They will need to offer mature products that can probably only be gotten through acquisition, the barrier to entry being set fairly high by existing products, especially in terms of performance.

At the time of writing there are several initiatives aimed at producing and agreeing standards for business rules. In 2005, the Business Process Management Initiative (BPMI.org) and the Object Management Group (OMG) announced the merger of their business process management standards activities. The combined group, the Business Modelling & Integration Domain Task Force (BMI DTF), continues work on the BPMI's Business Process Modelling Notation (BPMN) standard for business modelling, and the Business Motivation Model (BMM) contributed by the Business Rules Group. Separately, a standard defining the Semantics of Business Vocabulary and Business Rules (SBVR) is underway.

It may, in passing, be worth mentioning another proposed standard for webservice-based descriptions of business processes. BPEL4WS (or just BPEL) is the result of collaboration between IBM, BEA Systems, Microsoft, and others.

It provides a language and notation for the formal specification of business processes and business interaction protocols. In doing so, it extends the Web Services interaction model and enables the latter to support business transactions. However, BPEL does not recognize the notion of activities performed by users or any kind of independent activity; everything in BPEL is a web service operation, not an activity or work unit. Given the view of SOA presented in Chapter 2, this seems to be a serious restriction.

The SBVR metamodel specification is designed to support interchange of business vocabularies and rules amongst organizations. SBVR is designed for use by business people and for business purposes independent of information systems designs, although the actual specification is dauntingly large and complex. It is also intended to provide the business vocabulary and business rules underpinned by first order predicate calculus (FOPC) with a small extension into what it calls alethic or 'modal' (actually deontic) logic for transformations by IT staff into MDA PIM system designs. In most cases, such transformations will not be fully automated. Ross's RuleSpeak is an example of a rule notation that complies with SBVR. Rule authoring products such as RuleArts' RuleXpress support the SBVR directly. The emphasis on FOPC tends to situate the SBVR in the database-centric camp, although there is nothing in it which prevents a broader interpretation. On this broader interpretation, SBVR is intended to offer a business vocabulary for defining business vocabularies and business rules in completely technology-independent fashion.

Another OMG standard concentrates on the type models that must underpin business rules management systems. The Ontology Definition Metamodel (ODM) aims to provide a common metamodel for a variety of knowledge representation techniques, with a key objective of supporting the semantic Web. It includes MOF metamodels for RDFS, OWL, Topic Maps, Entity-Relation Diagrams, generic Description Logics in several formats, and Simple Common Logic. The SBVR group has been coördinating with the ODM group for some time and SBVR supports a superset of the logic supported by ODM, and there are plans eventually for interchange between ODM/OWL and SBVR based on an MDA mapping. OWL (Web Ontology Language) is a web-standard language, written in XML, for processing information on the web designed to be interpreted by computers rather than people. The term 'ontology' refers here to a machine-processable representation of knowledge, designed for automated inferencing. The chief audience for the ODM is the developers of rule engines or other tools that capture and prepare ontologies for inference engines from other declarative forms, such as UML models and structural business rules. In ODM ontologies, knowledge is assumed to be monotonic; i.e. over time knowledge can be added but not removed or contradicted. We discuss the notion of ontology further in Chapter 4.

The ODM is being developed concurrently with SBVR. The draft proposed ODM includes metamodels of several popular knowledge representation languages, with mappings between them.

SBVR covers vocabularies (ontology) and business rules. It makes a strong distinction between a concept and its expression. It does not standardize expression but does illustrate business rule expression in three ways: SBVR-SE (a structured English form that the standard itself uses), BRS RuleSpeak, and ORM. Other languages and notations are encouraged.

These standards provide quite different viewpoints. ODM is to OWL as SBVR is to things like RuleSpeak. SBVR deals with business rules, which ODM does not cover. ODM is for ontologists (business thing analysts) and SBVR is for business users or business rule analysts. OWL is a semantic web standard, whereas SBVR is a business modelling standard.

It has been suggested that the definition of a reference architecture for BRMS would be useful, but it has yet to be agreed exactly what this term signifies.

Another topic of much discussion is the issue of whether it is possible to share rules across businesses. Although the SBVR supports this semantically, it doesn't have anything to say about the practical difficulties. Clearly, if rules are stored in a repository, then they may be shared across an organization if they are carefully crafted enough. Another way that rules may be shared (with users) is through explanation facilities. In this way customers can consume rules internal to the business: 'We are rejecting your order because . . . ' The technology to do this has been around since MYCIN and is buried in many of the leading products; especially those that use rete for inference. Having said this, a bit of 'hand crafting' still seems advisable – to make explanations readable. The BRMS vendors report that, at present, explanation facilities, as used in KBS-type conversational interfaces, are little used in business rule engine deployments, except perhaps for testing, auditing and debugging rules. When business rule engines are used for high-performance process automation or decision-making, complex logging at run-time of the rule executions must usually be customized to the audit requirements of the rule service; there is a trade-off between performance and logging detail. Therefore, most tools provide some mechanism for turning on a logging mechanism that can later be interpreted off-line or in a separate process. Or one may add some side-effects to rules, to record important decisions explicitly.

The third way in which rules could be shared is one organization offers its rules to another. 'You can embed *our* rules in *your* process.' The thought may make you shiver a little. Doesn't it correspond to the oh-so-common product line vendor's wisdom: 'Our product does it right; you have to change your business to fit our best practice.' And there are slightly Orwellian overtones too.

Rule sharing is an interesting area that may benefit from some standardization in the future.

I think that uncertainty management will become increasingly important as products mature and the range of applications to which they are applied is extended. The range of techniques available in older expert systems products included uncertainty management using Bayesian probability and MYCIN-like certainty factors. Very few expert systems shells permitted fuzzy rules (rules using the linguistic variables of fuzzy logic) although such rules are embedded routinely these days in consumer electronics and household durables. The fact that the SBVR rules out fuzzy rules makes it unlikely that the major vendors will move in this direction in the foreseeable future. Perhaps, therefore, there is an opportunity for a small vendor in this niche market.

The most immediate changes are occurring as the BRMS vendors play technical leapfrog with each other, improving performance, adding new features, making it easier for non-technical staff to write rules and so on – and eating each other up through mergers and acquisitions.

3.7   Summary

This chapter surveyed the chief different approaches to business rules. We considered the dominant database-centric view and its evolution into the broader church of GUIDE and the Business Rules Group. We noted *en passant* that although calculations are rules, they are inherently procedural and so need to be treated slightly differently in some circumstances. We also noted the dependency of this view on the CWA: a flawed assumption in many real-world situations and a dangerous one with respect to requirements engineering.

Next, we looked at UML and the formal methods tradition and their take on rules. We saw that rules and constraints could be found by looking for loops in type diagrams and that rules should be encapsulated by components. Several useful patterns emerged from this.

Thirdly, we considered the expert systems tradition and its contribution, including its emphasis on inference rules. We demolished the prejudice that says that expert systems are different in principle from business rules management systems although, of course, the technology and the emphasis on *management* are different.

I drew attention to the work of Barbara von Halle on the development process and that of Tony Morgan and Ron Ross on rule writing style.

Lastly, I discussed directions and trends, including emerging standards such as SVBR and OWL, rule sharing and the controversial issue of uncertainty management.

3.8   Bibliographical Notes

Tony Morgan (2002) and Ron Ross (2003) both give useful guidance on how to write rules in a clear and standard way. Barbara von Halle's 2002 book is *essential* reading in conjunction with this text if you want to understand how to scope and run a business rules project. Chris Date's highly readable monograph (Date, 2000) is well worth reading for its profound insights into relational database theory and practice and the rôle of business rules in that context.

Business Rules Management Technology and Terminology

Say first, of God above or man below,
What can we reason but from what we know?

Alexander Pope (*Essay on Man*)

This chapter presents the key scientific and technical ideas and terms needed to understand the rest of this text. We cover several techniques for representing and discovering knowledge and the main techniques for reasoning with it.

The knowledge representation techniques include rules, semantic networks, object models, decision tables and decision trees. We also explain the basic forms of inference used in BRMSs, including techniques of rule induction and data mining. Finally, we examine the modern notion of ontology and its significance for BRMS.

In the next chapter we will use this knowledge to gain an understanding of current BRMS technology.

4.1 Rules and Other Forms of Knowledge Representation

Most of us are familiar with the notion of data; that is, unstructured sets of numbers, facts and symbols. These data can convey information only in virtue of some structure or decoding mechanism. In the limiting case, this distinction can be illustrated by two people who may communicate via a channel that may only carry one message consisting of a single symbol. The datum, the symbol itself, carries no information except in virtue of the presence of the channel, whose structure determines that the receiver may learn from the absence of a symbol as well from its transmission. This structure is, in turn, determined by the shared knowledge of the sender and receiver. Two points emerge from this example. Information always has a context while data may be context free; thus if I say 'she shot up' that is a datum for which I would need to explain whether the person in question was an astronaut or a heroin addict to convey unambiguous information. Knowledge is usually seen as a concept at a higher level of abstraction, and there is a sense in which this is true. For example, '1000' is a datum, '1000 millibars at noon' could be information about the weather in some situations, but 'Most people feel better when the pressure rises above 1000 millibars' is knowledge about barometric information and people. The realization that much knowledge is expressed in the form of heuristic descriptions or rules of thumb is what gives rise to the conception of knowledge as more abstract than information.

Apart from asking what it is, epistemologists have traditionally raised several other problems concerning knowledge, including:

- How it may be classified;
- How it is obtained;
- Whether it has objective reality;
- If it is limited in principle.

As a preliminary attempt at classification we might note that there are several evidently different types of knowledge at hand; knowledge about objects, events, task performance, and even about knowledge itself. If we know something about objects such as tomatoes we will probably know that tomatoes are red. However, we are still prepared to recognize a green tomato as a tomato; so that contradictions often coexist within our knowledge. Object knowledge is often expressed in the form of assertions, although this is by no means the only available formalism and OO-style objects or frames are particularly well suited to this purpose. Here are a few typical assertions:

1. Tomatoes are red.
2. Zoë is very lively.
3. This house is built with bricks and mortar.

Knowledge of causality, however, is expressed typically as a chain of statements relating cause to effect. A typical such statement might be 'If you boil tomatoes with the right accompaniments, chutney results.'

Such knowledge is well represented by sets of rules that can be chained together or by logical propositions within a particular logical calculus.

To perform a task as commonplace as walking requires a very complex interacting system of knowledge about balance, muscle tone, etc.; much of which is held subconsciously and is deeply integrated with our biological hardware. Knowledge about cognition, often called meta-knowledge, also needs to be represented when such questions as 'What do I know?' and 'How useful or complete is a particular knowledge system or inference strategy?' are raised. This, I hope, shows that there is no clear boundary between knowledge and inference, as practices. Each interpenetrates the other; we have inference with knowledge and knowledge about inference.

There are various dimensions along which knowledge can be evaluated:

- Scope   —What does it cover?
- Granularity   —How detailed is it?
- Uncertainty   —How likely, certain or plausible is it?
- Completeness   —Might we have to retract conclusions if new knowledge comes to light?
- Consistency   —How easily can we live with its contradictions?
- Modality   —Can we avoid its consequences?

The above dimensions are all connected with some form of uncertainty. This arises from the contradictory nature of knowledge. Knowledge presents itself in two basic forms as absolute and relative. To understand this, consider the whole of the history of science, which is an attempt to arrive at a knowledge of the environment we inhabit and change our relationship with it. The scientist develops various theories that explain the experimental evidence and are further verified in practice. She never suspects that any theory is comprehensively correct, at least not nowadays. Newton's models overthrew the theories of earlier times and were in their turn arguably overthrown by Einstein's. If nature exists beyond, before and apart from us then it represents, in all its complexity, an absolute truth which is (in principle) beyond knowledge, because nature is not in itself human and knowledge is. To assume otherwise is to assert that nature is either a totally human construct or that the whole may be totally assimilated by a fragment of itself. This is not to say that the finite may not know the infinite, only that the knowledge may only be relative. Otherwise the finite would contain the infinite and thus become infinite itself. Thus all truth seeking aims at the absolute but achieves the relative, and here it is that we see why all knowledge must perforce be uncertain. This is why the correct handling of uncertainty is one of the primary concerns for builders of knowledge-based systems of any sort.

The dimensions of knowledge mentioned above all will have some bearing on the techniques used to represent knowledge. If we choose logic as the representation then, if our knowledge is incomplete, non-monotonic logic will be required in preference to first order predicate logic and, in the presence of uncertainty, a logic capable of handling it will be required. Similar remarks apply to inconsistent knowledge where contradiction must be handled either by the logic or the control structure or metalogic. Modality will require the use of a logic that can deal with necessity and possibility.

If, on the other hand, we choose objects, frames or semantic network representations, the scope and granularity will affect the amount of storage we can expect to use. For this, it is useful to have some metrics. Granularity is often measured in **chunks**. Anderson (1976) defines a chunk to be a learnt configuration of symbols which comes to act as a single symbol. The passage between levels of representation is an important theme in AI research and has great bearing on the practical question of efficiency of storage and execution. Generally speaking, you should choose a granularity close to that adopted by human experts, if this can be discerned, and use chunking whenever gains are not made at the expense of understandability.

4.1.1   Rules and Production Systems

The concept of reducing systems to a few primitives and production rules for generating the rest of the system goes back to Post, who with Church and Turing all worked on the idea of formal models of computers independently. Post's original work was concerned with the theory of semigroups, which is of interest in algebraic models of language. Newell and Simon (1963) introduced them in the form in which we find them in knowledge based systems as part of their work on GPS, the general problem solver, which was an attempt to built an intelligent system which did not rely for its problem solving abilities on a store of domain specific knowledge, but would *inter alia* generate production rules as required. For example, Marvin the robot wants to go to Boston. He is faced with an immediate problem before this goal can be satisfied: how to get there. He can fly, walk/swim, ride a bus or train, and so on. To make the decision he might weigh up the cost and the journey time and decide to fly, but this strategy will not work because he is not at an airport. Thus he must solve a subproblem of how to get to an airfield which runs a service that takes him close to Boston. In production rules his reasoning so far (he hasn't solved the whole problem yet) might look like this:

1. If I want to go to New York then I must choose a transport mode.
2. Flying is a mode of transport which I will choose.
3. If you are at an airport then you can fly.
4. I am not at an airport.
5. If I want to be at an airport then I must choose a transport mode.

Incidentally, we should note the distinction between Marvin's goal, being in Boston, and his tasks, the steps to be taken to get there. All reasoning of this nature can be equally well viewed as goal decomposition or task decomposition. It can easily be expressed in a UML use case model.

The five statements above consist of assertions and productions, and together these represent some of the knowledge Marvin needs to begin reasoning about his problems. There are many reasoning strategies or inference methods he can employ. For the time being, we are interested in the representation of knowledge by production rules, as these IF/THEN constructions are known.

The left hand side, A, of a production rule of the form 'If A then X' is called its **antecedent** clause and the right hand side, X, its **consequent**. It may be interpreted in many ways: if some condition is satisfied then some action is appropriate; if some statement is true then another can be inferred; if a certain syntactic structure is present then some other can be generated grammatically. In general the A and X can be complex statements constructed from simpler ones using the connectives AND and OR and the NOT operator. In practice only the antecedent is permitted this rich structure so that a typical production would look like this:

> IF (animal gives birth to live young AND animal suckles young)
>   OR location is mammal-house
>   THEN animal is mammal

The parentheses disambiguate the precedence of the connectives and avoid the need to repeat clauses unnecessarily. Production systems combine rules as if there were an OR between the rules; that is between the antecedents of rules with the same consequent. A production rule system may be regarded as a machine which takes as input values of the variables mentioned in antecedent clauses and puts out values for the consequent variables. Clearly, it is equivalent to a system with one machine for each consequent variable unless we allow feedback among the variables. When feedback is present we enter the realms of inference.

Production rules are easy for humans to understand and, since each rule represents a small independent granule of knowledge, can be easily added or subtracted from a knowledge base. For this reason they have formed the basis of several well known, large scale applications such as DENDRAL, MYCIN and PROSPECTOR. They form the basis of nearly all BRMS products. Because the rules are, in principle, independent from each other, they support a declarative style of programming which considerably reduces maintenance problems. However, care must be taken that contradictory rules are not introduced, since this can lead to inefficiency at best and incorrect conclusions at worst. Another advantage that has been exploited in rule-based systems is the ease with which a production system can stack up a record of a program's use of each rule and thus provide rudimentary explanations of the systems reasoning. Lastly, productions make fairly light demands on a processor, although relatively large amount of memory or secondary storage will typically be required.

Precisely because they are memory intensive, production systems can be very inefficient. Also it is difficult to model associations among objects or processes. This makes the taking of short cuts in reasoning difficult to implement.

The declarative style makes algorithms extremely difficult to represent, and flow of control is hard to supervise for a system designer. Lastly, the formalism – as described so far – makes no allowances for uncertain knowledge. For these reasons, it is now becoming more common to find that knowledge based systems use several different kinds of knowledge representation, usually a mixture of rules, objects and procedures.

4.2   Knowledge and Inference

The question of how human beings store and manipulate knowledge is a question we can only touch upon here. The questions of how knowledge comes about and how it may be substantiated, what philosophers call the problem of cognition, or epistemology, is sufficiently neglected in the existing literature of knowledge engineering to deserve a little attention, though. We also ask how the interconnection between knowledge and inference is mediated. In my view, it is this relationship that leads to the need for uncertainty management in expert systems.

Consider two important questions about the representation of knowledge. First there was the question of how knowledge is represented in the human or animal brain, and now there is that of what structures may be used for computer representation. The biological question is the concern of cognitive psychology and psychoanalysis, and will not exercise us greatly here. However, the theories of psychologists and psychoanalysts have much to offer in the way of ideas for knowledge discovery techniques. The interdisciplinary subject of artificial intelligence has been defined as 'the study of mental faculties through the use of computational models' (Charniak & McDermott, 1985); exactly the reverse of what interests builders of knowledge based systems. Perhaps this is why there has been such confusion between the fields of AI and KBS. One important point to make categorically is that no one knows how the human brain works, and no one could give a prescription for the best computer knowledge representation formalism even if they did. Until some pretty fundamental advances are made, the best bet for system builders is to use whatever formalism best suits the task at hand, pragmatically.

Apart from its ability to be abstract at various levels, knowledge is concerned with action. It is concerned with practice in the world. Knowing how people feel under different atmospheric conditions helps us to respond better to their moods, work with them or even improve their air-conditioning (if we have some knowledge about ventilation engineering as well). Incidentally, it also assumes the existence of various socially evolved measuring devices, such as the barometer, thermometer and so on. Knowledge is a guide to informed practice and relates to information as a processor of it; that is, we **understand** knowledge but we **process** information. It is no use knowing that people respond well to high pressure if you cannot measure that pressure. Effective use of knowledge leads to the formation of plans for action, and ultimately to deeper understanding. This leads to a subsidiary definition that knowledge is concerned with using information effectively. The next level of abstraction might be called 'theory'.

From this point of view, inference is to knowledge as processing is to information. Inference is the method used to transform perceptions (perhaps via some symbolic representation) into a form suitable for re-conversion into actions. It may also be viewed as an abstraction from practical activity. In our experience of the world we observe, both individually and collectively, that certain consequences follow from certain actions. We give this phenomenon the name causality, and say that action A 'causes' perception B. Later (both in ontogenesis and philogenesis[1]) we generalize this to include causal relations between external events independent of ourselves. From there it is a short step (one originally taken at the end of the Bronze Age) to the idea that ideas are related in a similar way; that symbol A can 'imply' symbol B. This process of abstraction corresponds, according to Piaget, to the process of child development. Historically, it corresponds to the development of the division of labour. In other words, just as tool making and social behaviour make knowledge possible, so the interdependencies of the world of nature are developed into the abstract relations of human thinking; part of this system of relationships corresponding to inference.

Of course, computers do not partake of social activity, nor yet do they create tools (although they may manufacture and use them if we include robots in our perception of computing machinery). As far as inference is concerned, we cannot expect computers to encompass the richness and depth of human reasoning (at least not in the foreseeable future). For many thousands of years it has been convenient, for certain applications in the special sciences, to reason with a formalized subset of human reasoning. This 'formal logic' has been the basis of most western technological developments and, while not capturing the scope of human informal reasoning, is immensely powerful in resolving many practical problems. Thus, we are converging on a definition of inference which will serve the purposes of knowledge engineering. Inference in this sense is the abstract, formal process by which conclusions may be drawn from premises. It is a special kind of metaknowledge about the abstract relationships between symbols representing knowledge.

Many philosophers have questioned whether true artificial intelligence is possible in principle. In my view the question is merely maladroit. Clearly,

---

[1]Ontogenesis is the origin or developmental history of the being (the individual in this sense) and philogenesis the origin of the species. I deliberately choose these terms to remind the reader of the ancient and famous Greek aphorism: "Philogenesis recapitulates ontogenesis".

if we are able in future to genetically (or otherwise) engineer an artificial human being there is no reason (excluding spurious religious arguments) why the constructed entity should not be 'intelligent' by any normal criteria. If, on the other hand, the question is posed as to whether electronic computers of the type currently existing or foreseeable can pass the Turing test, then matters are a little different. Human cognition is a process mediated by both society and the artefacts of Man's construction. It may well be that no entity (be it a computer or a totally dissimilar organism from outer space) could ever dissemble its true non-social, non-tool making character sufficiently to deceive the testers. My belief is that artificial intelligence in this sense is impossible, but that useful results are to be obtained by trying to achieve an approximation.

4.2.1   Semantic Networks

A semantic network consists of a set of nodes and a set of ordered pairs of these nodes called 'links', together with an interpretation of the meaning of these. Terminal links are called 'slots' if they represent properties (predicates) rather than objects or classes of objects. A frame is a semantic net representing an object (or a stereotype of that object) and will consist of a number of slots and a number of outbound links. Frames correspond to both classes and instances in object modelling. This unification is explained below.

Semantic networks and object models are both used to represent knowledge about objects and the static relationships among them rather than knowledge about the dynamic relationships expressed by rules. Object models can express knowledge such as 'all healthy dogs have two eyes'. Rules can express knowledge such as 'if a dog starts to bark then an intruder may be present'. These are two quite distinct kinds of knowledge. *Both of them are essential* in dealing with any problem.

Semantic nets generalize object models. Classes and their instances are represented uniformly in the former whereas, in object-oriented programming, there is a profound distinction. In both representations, we have associations (links) between classes. But in object-oriented programming inheritance between classes and classes and between classes and instances is treated differently. We can say that a Dog is *a kind of* Mammal but, when we encounter Fido, we have to say that Fido *is a* Dog. Furthermore, once created, Fido is a dog forever. He can't ever migrate to the class of GuardDogs during his lifetime; he's destined to be just plain old Dog till he dies. Obviously, this is not the way most people think or express themselves in natural language. Because of this limitation, it is tricky to model rôles, such as guard dog or retired person. In fact, patterns are used to get round the problem (STATE and VISITOR usually).

The semantic network approach corresponds far more closely to common sense. In Haley Authority, using an example supplied by Haley Systems, we can say 'an applicant provides an answer to a health question'. Health questions are a kind of question. Questions have instances like 'What is your name?' whilst health questions have instances like 'Do you smoke?' or 'Question 17'. We can also, in the same underwriting application, talk readily about dangerous occupations specifying, perhaps, 'Iraq security consultant' as an instance.

Semantic networks are thus far more expressive. Nevertheless they can be readily (and automatically) mapped onto the Java object model.

Let us now descend from these abstract considerations and ask how computers can be made to simulate reasoning.

4.3 Inference in Business Rules Management Systems

Given that knowledge is stored in a computer in some convenient representation or representations, the system will require facilities for navigating through and manipulating the knowledge if anything is to be achieved at all. Inference in the usual logical sense is this process of drawing valid conclusions from premises. In our wider sense it is any computational mechanism whereby stored knowledge can be applied to data and information structures to arrive at conclusions which are to be plausible rather than valid in the strict logical sense. This, of course, poses problems in relation to how to judge whether the conclusions are reasonable, and how to represent knowledge about how to test conclusions and how to evaluate plausibility. Thus, we can see that knowledge representation and inference are inextricably bound together, though as opposites.

4.3.1 Forward, Backward and Mixed Chaining Strategies

Up to now we have only considered the problem of how to infer the truth value of one proposition from another using a rule of inference in just one step. Clearly however, there will be occasions when such inferences (or proofs) will involve long chains of reasoning using the rules of inference and some initial suppositions (or axioms). We now turn to the inference methods that feature strongly in all rule-based systems and are often supplied as standard in BRMS products.

Forward Chaining

To fix ideas, consider a system whose knowledge is represented in the form of production rules and whose domain is the truth of abstract propositions: A, B, C, . . .

The knowledge base consists solely of rules as follows:

Rule 1: A and B and C   implies D
Rule 2: D and F   implies G
Rule 3: E   implies F
Rule 4: F   implies B
Rule 5: B   implies C
Rule 6: G   implies H
Rule 7: I   implies J
Rule 8: A and F   implies H

To start with, assume that the system has been asked whether proposition H is true given that propositions A and F are true. We will show that the system may approach the problem in two quite distinct ways. Assume for the present that the computer stores these rules on a sequential device such as magnetic tape, so that it must access the rules in order unless it rewinds to rule 1.

What I am about to describe is a basic forward chaining inference strategy. This itself has several variants: we may pass through the rules until a single rule fires, we may continue until all rules have been processed once, or we may continue firing in either manner until either the conclusion we desire has been achieved or until the database of proven propositions ceases to be changed by the process. A little thought shows that this gives at least four different varieties of forward chaining. This will become clearer as we proceed.

The assumption is that A and F are known to be true at the outset. If we apply all the rules to this database the only rules that fire are 4 and 8 and the firing of rule 8 assigns the value true to H, which is what we were after. Suppose now that rule 8 is excised from the knowledge base. Can we still prove H? This time only rule 4 fires, so we have to rewind and apply the rules again to have any chance of proving the target proposition. Table 4.1 shows what happens to the truth values in the database on successive applications of the rules 1 to 7.

So, H is proven after five iterations. Note, in passing, that further iterations do not succeed in proving any further propositions in this particular case. Since we are considering a computer strategy, we need to program some means by which the machine is to know when to stop applying rules. From the above example there are two methods; either 'stop when H becomes true' or 'stop when the database ceases to change on rule application'. Which one of these two we select depends on the system's purpose; for one interesting side-effect of the latter procedure is that we have proved the propositions B, C, D and G and, were we later to need to know their truth values, we need do no more computation. On the other hand, if this is not an important consideration we might have proved H long before we can prove everything else.

It should be noted that we have assumed that the rules are applied 'in parallel', which is to say that in any one iteration every rule fires on the

Table 4-1   Naïve forward chaining.

Proposition	Iteration number							
	0	1	2	3	4	5	6	7
A	T	T	T	T	T	T	T	T
B		T	T	T	T	T	T	T
C			T	T	T	T	T	T
D				T	T	T	T	T
E								
F	T	T	T	T	T	T	T	T
G						T	T	T
H						T	T	T
I								
J								

basis that the data are as they were at the beginning of the cycle. This is not necessary, but we would warn of the confusion that would result from the alternative in any practical applications; a knowledge-based, and thus essentially declarative system, should not be dependent of the order in which the rules are entered, stored or processed unless there is some very good reason for forcing modularity on the rules. Very efficient algorithms, notably the rete algorithm, have been developed for this type of reasoning.

These strategies are known as **forward chaining** or data directed reasoning, because they begin with the data known and apply the rules successively to find out what results are implied. This strategy is particularly appropriate in situations where data are expensive to collect but potentially few in quantity. Typical domains are loan approval, financial planning, process control, scheduling, the configuration of complex systems and system tuning.

In the example given, the antecedents and consequents of the rules are all of the same type: propositions in some logical system. However, this need not be the case. For example, for the industrial control applications the inputs might be measurements and the output control actions. In that case it does not make sense to add these incommensurables together in the database. Variations on forward chaining now include: 'pass through the rules until a single rule fires then act'; 'pass through all the rules once and then act'.

Backward Chaining

There is a completely different way we could have set about proving H, and that is to start with the desired goal 'H is true' and attempt to find evidence for this to be the case. This is **backward chaining** or goal directed inference. It is usual when the only thing we need to do is prove H and are not interested in the values of other propositions.

Backwards chaining arises typically in situations where the quantity of data is potentially very large and where some specific characteristic of the system under consideration is of interest. Most typical are various problems of diagnosis, such as medical diagnosis or fault finding in electrical or mechanical equipment. Most first generation expert system shells were based on some form of backward chaining, although some early production rule languages such as OPS5 used forward chaining.

Returning to our original eight rules, the system is asked to find a rule that proves H. The only candidate rules are 6 and 8, but 6 is encountered first. Let us ignore rule 8 for the present. At this point we establish a new subgoal of proving that G is true, for if we can do this then it would follow that H were true by *modus ponens*. Our next subgoal will be to prove that D and F are true. Recall that we have told the system that A and F are true, so it is only necessary to prove D. The whole proof proceeds as shown in Figure 4.1.

The observant reader will have noticed that we could have proved H in one step from rule 8. The point is that rule 8 was not reached and the system could not know in advance that it was going to be quicker to explore that rule than rule 6. On the other hand, if the original line of exploration had failed (suppose rule 4 was deleted) then the system would have had to backtrack and try rule 8. Figure 4.2 illustrates the proof strategy more pictorially.

Backward chaining can thus be viewed as a strategy for searching through trees built in some solution space. The strategy we have described is usually called depth-first search in that context. We now look at other strategies.

Mixed Strategies

We have looked at two fundamental forms of inference, forward and backward chaining. In practice, most reasoning is a mixture of at least these two.

Trying to prove H
Try rule 6
Trying to prove G
Try rule 2
F is true, trying to prove D
Try rule 1
A is true, trying to prove B
Try rule 4
It works. B is true
Backtrack to trying rule 1
Trying to prove C
Try rule 5, it works C is true
Apply rule 1, D is true
Apply rule 2, G is true
Apply rule 6, H is true
Goal achieved; stop.

Figure 4-1   Proof by backward chaining or recursive descent.

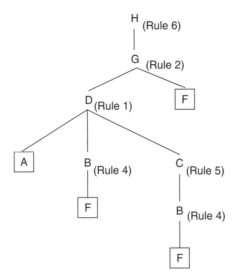

Figure 4-2 A proof tree. Propositions in boxes are those found in the database (i.e. those known to be true).

Given some initial assumption, we infer a conclusion by reasoning forwards and then apply backward chaining to find other data that confirm these conclusions. Alternatively, we start with a goal, backward chain to some plausible reason and then forward chain to exploit the consequences of this new datum. This is often called **opportunistic chaining** or, less succinctly, 'backwards reasoning with opportunistic forward chaining', because the data directed search exploits the consequences of data as they become available 'opportunistically'. This method is commonly found in the better BRMS products. Another way of looking at it is to observe that every rule becomes a demon.

Rete

There have been several attempts to construct computer languages specifically for knowledge representation. The best known, early languages were probably KRL (Bobrow and Winograd, 1977) and OPS5 (Forgy, 1982). The basic form of representation in OPS5 is production rules. OPS5 first achieved notoriety because it was used in the highly successful XCON system, which was used by Digital Equipment Corporation (DEC) to configure orders for VAX™ computers. The fact that a large chunk of XCON, concerned with database access, was written in the procedural language Bliss32 is rarely mentioned, but that does not change the fact that the knowledge incorporated in the system is the key to its success. DEC's success rate in the configuration task increased by a factor of more than two, resulting in huge savings. Even more important is that XCON enabled DEC to maintain its distinctive policy of delivering just what the customer asks for, however non-standard. The maintenance of the OPS5 rulebase was in fact a vastly costly operation, because of the continual updates in the product range.

Rete is a very efficient mechanism for solving the difficult many-to-many matching problem in artificial intelligence. Rete is an algorithm that evaluates a declarative predicate against a changing set of data in real time. Consider an SQL select statement that executes a WHERE clause to find matching rows. Rete uses a progressive relational join to update a view of matching rows. As rows are added to any table, it's evaluated against the predicate and mapped into or out of the matching view.

Rete is much more efficient at determining the relevance of rules, given particular data, than the equivalent nested if/then/else or select/case constructs. The greater the number of rules, the greater rete's advantage over procedural code. This applies to rule execution. Of course, *writing* the rules is also far more efficient in a BRMS. These two points are critical in leading modern corporations to considering BRMS technology as a viable next step.

When a rulebase becomes large, the naïve algorithm for forward chaining illustrated in Table 4.1 can become very slow because few changes are made to the facts in working memory at each cycle. Rete compiles the rules into a network of predicate tests, inferences and actions. The rete network modifies itself after each rule firing, so that unneeded rules do not fire. For further details of rete see, for example, Russell and Norvig (1995). Each product reviewed here has a proprietary improvement on the basic published algorithm. These improvements are largely responsible for the variation in performance of the three rule engines. The three engines all also modify basic rete to permit backward and mixed chaining.

4.4   Data Mining and Rule Induction

The other principal mode of inference is **induction**. Broadly, induction enables us to infer new rules from collections of facts and data. The word 'induction' has two senses: the Aristotelian sense of a syllogism in which the major premise in conjunction with instances entails the generalization, or the sense of empirical generalization from observations. A third sense, the principle of mathematical induction, need not concern us here. It is with the second sense we shall be concerned. Most authorities talk about induction in terms of probabilities; if we observe that sheep on two hundred hillsides all have wool and four legs, then we may induce the generalization 'all sheep have wool and four legs'. Every observation we then make increases the probability of this statement being true, but never confirms it completely. Only one observation of a shorn, three-legged merino is needed to refute the theory. From our point of view, this cannot be correct. There are many kinds of uncertainty, and it can be said equally that our degree of knowledge, belief or the relevance of the rules is what is changed by experience rather than probability. The obsession with probability derives (probably) from the prevailing empiricist climate in the philosophy of science; experience being seen only as experiments performed by external observers trying to refute some hypothesis. Another view is possible. The history of quantum physics shows that we can no longer regard observers as independent from what they observe. Experience takes place in a world of which we humans are an internal part but from which we are able to differentiate ourselves. We do this by internalizing a representation of nature and checking the validity of the representation through continuous practice. However, the very internalization process is a practice, and practice is guided by the representation so far achieved. From this point of view, induction is the process of practice that confirms our existing theories of all kinds. The other important general point to note is that the syllogism of induction moves from the particular to the general, whereas deductive and abductive syllogisms tend to work in the opposite direction; from the general to the particular.

The probabilistic definition of induction does have merit in many cases, especially in the case of new knowledge. It is this case that current computer learning systems always face. In nearly every case, computer programs which reason by induction are presented with a number of examples and expected to find a pattern, generalization or program that can reproduce and extend the training set.

Suppose we are given the training set of examples shown in Table 4.2. The simplest possible algorithm enables us to infer that:

```
IF female
   THEN analyst
IF male AND (blue eyes OR grey eyes)
   THEN programmer
IF brown hair AND brown eyes
   THEN operator
```

Table 4-2 Training set.

Name	Eye colour	Hair colour	Sex	Job
J. Stalin	blue	blonde	male	programmer
A. Capone	grey	brown	male	programmer
M. Thatcher	brown	black	female	analyst
R. Kray	brown	brown	male	operator
E. Braune	blue	black	female	analyst

However, the addition of a new example (brown eyes, brown hair, female, programmer) makes the position less clear. The first and last rules must be withdrawn, but the second can remain, although it no longer has quite the same force.

The first attempts at machine learning came out of the cybernetics movement of the 1950s. Cybernetics, according to its founder Weiner (1948), is the science of control and communication in animal and machine. Several attempts were made, using primitive technology by today's standards, to build machinery simulating aspects of animal behaviour. In particular, analogue machines called homeostats simulated the ability to remain in unstable equilibrium; see Ashby (1956). Perceptrons (two-layer neural nets) are hinted at in Weiner's earliest work on neural networks, and, as the name suggests, were attempts to simulate the functionality of the visual cortex. Learning came in because of the need to classify and recognize physical objects. The technique employed was to weight the input in each of a number of dimensions and, if the resultant vector exceeded a certain threshold, to class the input as a positive example. Neural network technology has now overcome an apparent flaw discovered by Minsky and Papert (1969), and impressive learning systems have been built.

Rule based learning systems also exist. Quinlan's interactive dichotomizer algorithm, known as ID3, selects an arbitrary subset of the training set and partitions it according to the variable with the greatest discriminatory power using an information theoretic measure of the latter. This is repeated until a new rule is found, which is then added to the rule set as in the above example on jobs. Next the entire training set is searched for exceptions to the new rule and if any are found they are inserted in the sample and the process repeated. The difficulties with this approach are that the end result is a sometimes huge decision tree which is difficult to understand and modify, and that the algorithm does not do very well in the presence of noisy data, though suitable modifications have been proposed based on statistical tests.

One of the problems with totally deterministic algorithms like ID3 is that, although they are guaranteed to find a rule to explain the data in the training set, if one exists, they cannot deal with situations where the rules can only be expressed subject to uncertainty. In complex situations, such as weather forecasting or betting – where only some of the contributory variables can be measured and modelled – often no exact, dichotomizing rules exist. With the simple problem of forecasting whether it will rain tomorrow it is well known that a reasonably successful rule is 'if it is raining today then it will rain tomorrow'. This is not always true, but it is a reasonable approximation for some purposes. ID3 would reject this as a rule if it found one single counter-example. Statistical tests, however useful, require complex independence assumptions and interpretative skills on the part of users.

A completely different class of learning algorithm is based on the concept of adaptation or Darwinian selection. The general idea is to generate rules at random and compute some measure of performance for each rule relative to the training set. Inefficient rules are deleted and operations based on the ideas of mutation, crossover and inversion are applied to generate new rules. These techniques are referred to as **genetic algorithms**.

Genetic algorithms are also closely related to neural nets as pattern classification devices. Genetic programming is a form of machine learning that takes a random collection of computer programs and a representation of some problem and then 'evolves' a program that solves the problem. It does this by representing each program as a binary vector, or string, that can be thought of as a chromosome. The chromosomes in each successive sample can 'mate' by crossing over portions of themselves, inverting substrings of their bodies and mutating at random[2]. Programs that score well against some objective function that represents the problem to be solved are allowed to participate in the next mating round and, after many generations, there is a good chance that a successful–but not necessarily optimal–program will evolve.

None of the products considered herein offer any sort of rule induction facility. However, there are several products on the market that do and we envisage some benefit from taking the output from such systems and offering the resultant rules to a BRMS.

4.5   Techniques for Representing Rules

In all BRMS products, rules are represented as sentences, usually containing the words IF and THEN. Morgan (2002) recommends a better style aimed at removing ambiguity, making relationships explicit, avoiding obscure terminology, removing wordiness, and so on. His style is remarkably close to natural language. He ends up preferring forms such as

> *A loan may be approved*
> *if the status of the customer is high and the loan*
> *is less than 2000*
> *unless the customer has a low rating*

to

> *if the customer status is high and the loan is less than*
> *2000 and the customer does not have a low rating*
> *then approve the loan*
> *if the customer status is high and the loan is less than*
> *2000 and the customer has a low rating*
> *then don't approve the loan*

---

[2]Given two binary strings (representing chromosomes) 110101 and 111000, their crossover (at the fourth place) could either be 110000 or 111101. Crossing over at the first place corresponds to choosing one of the original strings.

In some products there are representations alternative to rules. We now consider two of these.

4.5.1 Decision Trees and Decision Tables

Decision Trees

Behavioural science has evolved several theories as to how people reach decisions. Such descriptive theories usually conclude by stating that managers do not make decisions on a purely rational basis. To help managers improve their decision making, however, a normative theory such as decision analysis is required. Decision analysis consists of three principal stages:

1. Determine problem structure and objective function (desirable outcome and measure thereof);
2. Assess uncertainties and possible outcome states and their consequences;
3. Determine a 'best' strategy for achieving a desirable outcome.

A decision problem is characterized as one of selecting one from several options so as to maximize some function of possibly many variables, attributes or criteria. The naïve formulation is to organize these into a table of options against attributes. Many methods are available to achieve the requisite selection: maximizing, minimaxing, regret and so on. The disadvantage of decision analysis of this kind is that complex problems are sometimes oversimplified by it, a method of overcoming this will be considered in due course. The so-called modelling school of decision analysis would attempt to construct a more explicit model of the relationships, usually as a decision tree such as the one in Figure 4.3.

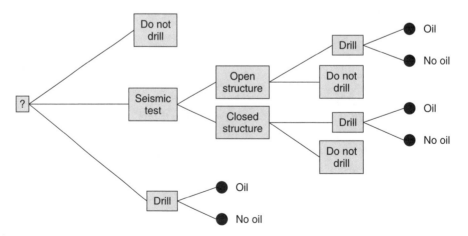

Figure 4-3 The oilman's problem.

In most professions and businesses, decision making takes place in an environment where the cost of obtaining precise information is unjustifiably high. In recognition of this fact the classical theories of decision analysis, operational research and decision theory make extensive use of normative statistical techniques. The decision problem is either a question of choosing an optimal course of action, such as the ideal mix of ingredients in animal foodstuffs, subject to constraints such as lowest cost and some requisite nutritional value, or it is concerned with generating a plausible set of alternatives. It is the first case, which has received most attention. A decision problem, in this latter sense, is given by stating a set of options, a set of states, a transformation which to every pair consisting of a state and an option returns a new state representing the consequence of choosing that option, *ceteris paribus*. Since the null option (do nothing) is always included, this provides a model of the evolution of the system to which may be added feedback and/or feedforward control of options.

Thus, we see that cybernetics becomes a special case of decision theory, and indeed many of the mathematical techniques are held in common. In addition, decision models include a utility function, which represents the ranking of outcomes with regard to their desirability in a given context. This function is analogous to the metrics required for homeostasis in cybernetic systems. In the cases where decisions can be made in the presence of certain data, the techniques of operational research, such as linear and dynamic programming and systems dynamics, are the most commonly used. This leaves us with essentially only one tool: the decision tree. A decision tree is merely a hierarchy showing the dependencies between decisions. It is a shorthand description of some aspects of the general decision model whose chief value is to clarify our thinking about the consequences of certain decisions being made. However, with the introduction of probabilities the decision tree becomes a powerful tool.

To see this, consider a very simple example. If one wishes to open a sweet shop, one must decide where it is to be located. There are, let us suppose, three options: near a school in an expensive suburb, in the busy high street or opposite a playground in a deprived inner city area. Let us call these options A, B and C. To each of these we can assign a probability of financial success, based on basic cost/revenue calculations and the history of similar ventures. In each case, however, there are other decisions to make, such as how much to invest in stock. Suppose the options and probabilities of success are as displayed in Figure 4.4, where X, Y and Z represent these other decisions.

Combining the probabilities shows that option C is the most likely to succeed, despite the fact that on the basis of the first level of decision it was the worst option. Exploring the decision tree further might change the position again. Enhancements of this application of probability theory have proved most effective in attacking a wide range of decision problems. It is

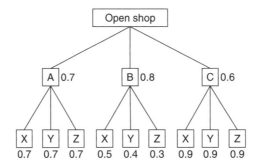

Figure 4-4   A decision tree with probabilities.

also possible to use certainty factors in place of probabilities, in which case the arithmetic is different.

In many cases the branches of a tree will be annotated with and followed when particular ranges of values hold for a variable. For example we might set a particular credit limit for a client with annual income in the range 50,000 to 100,000.

Decision Tables

Decision tables represent the same knowledge and rules as decision trees in a tabular format. For example, Table 4.3 is equivalent to a ruleset stating:

```
If card type is ''Standard''
      then discount code is 1
      unless age is between 18 and 30
If card type is ''Standard'' and age is between 18 and 30
      then discount code is unknown
If card type is ''Gold''
      then discount code is 2
      unless age is between 31 and 40
If card type is ''Gold'' and age is between 31 and 40
      then discount code is 1
If card type is ''Platinum''
      then discount code is 3
      unless age is between 31 and 40
If card type is ''Platinum'' and age is between 31 and 40
      then discount code is 1
```

We can see that the techniques of rule induction discussed above may be applied to extract the rules from the table automatically. We can also generate a table from a ruleset.

The main problem with decision tables is that they grow unmanageably large when there is a large number of conditions in the rulebase. Even in the example above, where this is not the case, six rules translate to 72 table entries.

Table 4-3 A decision table.

Min age	Max age	Card type	Discount code
18	30	Standard	
18	30	Gold	2
18	30	Platinum	3
31	40	Standard	1
31	40	Gold	1
31	40	Platinum	1
41	50	Standard	1
41	50	Gold	2
41	50	Platinum	3
51	60	Standard	1
51	60	Gold	2
51	60	Platinum	3
61	70	Standard	1
61	70	Gold	2
61	70	Platinum	3
71	120	Standard	1
71	120	Gold	2
71	120	Platinum	3

Their advantage arises when the organization already holds the knowledge in this form: pricing charts, rate tables, etc.

There is a cruder approach that regards each row in the table as a separate rule; so that row two would correspond to a rule stating:

```
If card type is ''Gold'' and age is between 18 and 30
then discount code is 2
```

Clearly this approach gives as a larger number of rules – one for each row – and the rules will be hard to read and understand. We characterize the approach as **row-oriented decision tables**. Rule subsumption checks may allow the author to tidy up the resultant rulesets, but we think the induction approach is far sounder. It is better to use a data mining system to extract rules from decision tables and feed them into a BRMS.

4.6 Uncertainty Management

To arrive at a decision in the presence of absolute certainty with respect to all the relevant facts and considerations is a luxury rarely afforded to human beings. Assumptions must be made about data values that are not available, about events which may or may not have occurred, and about consequences likely to flow from a given decision. Many of these assumptions may be made unconsciously or subconsciously. Some may be made explicitly, with whatever degree of justification may be adduced. Mathematics may be prayed in aid of some assumptions made on statistical bases. Otherwise, rules of thumb and accrued experience serve as a guide.

In business, there are many sources and kinds of uncertainty including random events, experimental errors, errors of measurement, uncertainty in judgement, lack of evidence or lack of certainty in evidence.

Classic expert systems used three methods of handling uncertainty:

- vague terms (linguistic labels) in the type model;
- Bayesian probabilities; or
- certainty factors.

More rarely, some used a fourth method: fuzzy logic. Current BRMS offerings do not major on uncertainty management. For most of them the only method is that of using vague terms in the type model. In this crudest of methods, we ascribe true of false values to terms that are inherently vague. For example, if my physician knows a rule that states 'Prescribe a pain killer if pain is severe,' then she might ask me 'Is the pain severe or slight?' Alternatively, she might press on the affected region of my body and judge the severity of the pain from the intensity of my reaction. Either way she will have to assign a truth value to the attribute 'severe'. There is judgmental uncertainty, but it is concealed by the labels and left up to the humans to estimate.

In systems based on Bayesian probability, inference is predicated on Bayes' theorem:

$$\text{Prob}\{X \text{ is A}\} = \frac{\text{Prob}\{Y \text{ is B}|X \text{ is A}\}.\text{Prob}\{X \text{ is A}\}}{\text{Prob}\{Y \text{ is B}\}}$$

One interpretation of this formula is to say that new evidence modifies the previously believed probability of some event or hypothesis. The revised (or *a postiori*) probability in the hypothesis is the prior (or *a priori*) probability, multiplied by the ratio of the conditional probability of the event occurring given the hypothesis as true to the overall probability of the event occurring. This is the method used by most email spam filters.

The key point of the Bayesian approach is not that its results differ from classical probability theory in situations where both approaches may be taken, but rather that it allows us to form *a priori* probabilities for hypotheses in situations where detailed knowledge does not allow us to establish strict, objectively determined odds. In this sense, the Bayesian approach is about *belief* in the likelihood of outcomes rather than mere probability.

Certainty factors are also about belief but not about likelihood. The technique was at the core of MYCIN, but there have been several variants of it. The simplest assigns a numerical measure of belief in any fact or rule between − 1 (false) and +1 (true). Uncertain terms in the premise are combined: ANDs are computed as minima and ORs as maxima. This is essentially the same mechanism used in fuzzy set theory as well. These numbers may be combined under inference too. For example, suppose we know these rules:

1. If the engine will not turn over
    then the battery is flat {0.6}
2. If the horn will not sound
    then the battery is flat {0.9}

Assuming both pieces of evidence to be present, Shortliffe's formula, as used in MYCIN, would give an accrued belief in the hypothesis of a flat battery of 0.96.

Fuzzy logic enables us to conceive of rulesets such as the following:

1. Our price should be low
2. Our price should be about 2*direct.costs
3. If the opposition.price is not very high then
    our price should be near the opposition.price

The machinery of fuzzy logic allows this formal language to look very much like English, but this is not natural language; it is compilable code. To make it work we need to set up definitions of fuzzy sets like 'low' and 'high' for the 'linguistic variable' Price as illustrated in Figure 4.5 (a and b). The fuzzy sets

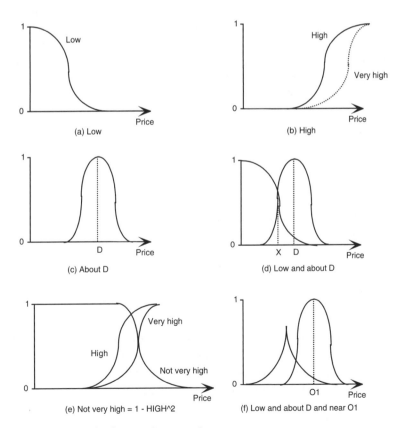

Figure 4-5 Fuzzy sets, hedges and connectives.

are defined as vectors over the scale of relevant prices for, say, washing powders. 'Very' is an operator that takes the square of every point of the curve representing the fuzzy set. The result 'very high' is shown in 4.5 (b) too. The words: 'our', 'should' and 'the' are noise words and ignored by the compiler. 'Be' is a synonym for 'is'.

As the variable Price increases from zero, the truth value of 'low' falls off; eventually 'high' begins to become true, until we reach maximum truth at some point. The rules also contain the hedges: 'about', 'near', 'not' and 'very'. The set 'very high' is usually computed as the square root of 'high'. To get 'not', subtract the truth value from one. 'Near' and 'about' are synonyms and are usually represented as a bell-shaped or triangular fuzzy set either side of the crisp number concerned; D in the Figure 4.5(c).

The above rules are quite realistic in the context of fast moving consumer goods marketing. We want the good to be cheap and affordable; but we also want to cover costs and make a profit (rules 1 and 2). Given a direct cost of 13, the fuzzy mathematics of this would take the intersection (i.e. the minima) of 'low' and 'about 26'; this is marked as X in Figure 4.5(d).

Statement 1 in the policy means that the price should be as compatible as possible with 'low'; i.e. the price ought to be exactly zero. This contradicts the assertion that it should be twice direct costs; a result of the need to turn a profit based on experience. The remarkable thing is that the fuzzy policy will automatically resolve this contradiction by taking that price that gives the maximum truth value for the intersection of the fuzzy sets. This is labelled X in Figure 4.5 (d). The peaked intersection now represents an elastic constraint, or feasible region, for price. Figure 4.5 (c) shows the fuzzy set 'about 2*direct.costs'.

Rule 3 must now be interpreted. We take an actual value for opposition price, O, and compute how true 'not very high' is for it. This truth value is T. The fuzzy inference rule is interpreted as truncating the output fuzzy set 'near opposition' at the level T. We now arrive at the result by taking the union of 'low and about D' with this truncated set. D stands for '2*direct.costs' here. Finally, if we want an actual value for Price rather than a fuzzy set, we must defuzzify. In this case, we choose the mean of maxima method to do this. Figures 4.6 (b) and (c) illustrate that there are two cases. As the value of T exceeds the maximum truth in the feasible region there is a sudden jump in output from R2 to R1. This models exactly what happens in real life; decision output is discontinuous. In process control, smooth output is required and the centre of moments defuzzification rule would be used.

The purpose of this example is to show how fuzzy rules, used to capture business policy, can be made to provide quite precise, although perhaps non-linear and complex, models of behaviour.

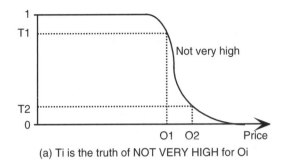

(a) Ti is the truth of NOT VERY HIGH for Oi

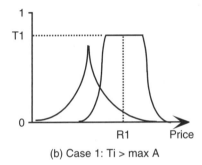

(b) Case 1: Ti > max A

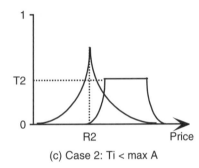

(c) Case 2: Ti < max A

Figure 4-6   Fuzzy inference.

Sometimes, even when a BRMS cannot deal with uncertainty, it may be used in conjunction with other software that can. For example, predictive models (e.g. score models, neural net models, generated decision trees, etc.) can be generated by Fair Isaac's Model Builder analytics tools and either mapped to rules (e.g. as a decision tree) or plugged into a ruleflow (e.g. a neural net model). In this way, the decision lifecycle may be stated, for example, as follows:

1. Create a decision tree for defining a business strategy as a part of a decision ruleflow.

2. Execute this multiple times in production.

3. Use the production data (decisions and their later consequences) in Model Builder to define a new or refined decision tree.

4. Replace the original tree with a new one and test against old data; run it alongside for comparison, or just replace it.

5. Iterate as needed.

The only other way that a BRMS can *appear* to deal with uncertainty is to rely on the uncertainty inherent in natural language.

4.7   Ontology and Epistemology: the Rôle of Object Modelling in Natural Language Processing

There are, arguably, four basic branches of Philosophy: Epistemology, Ontology, Ethics and Aesthetics. All other branches of Philosophy, such as the Philosophies of Politics or Language, draw on these disciplines to some extent. All of them are relevant to system development.

Epistemology concerns what we know. Some knowledge can be expressed as procedures, rules and relationships. Epistemology includes the science of method: Methodology. Ontology, sometimes called Metaphysics, concerns what exists: what are the objects in our world. Aesthetics is clearly relevant to ergonomics and usability. Ethics or Moral Philosophy enquires into whether the systems we build are useful, legal or morally sound.

Business rules management systems cannot be built without paying attention to both rules (epistemological facts) and the objects that these rules refer to. In recent years, computer scientists have come to use the uncapitalized word 'ontology' to mean the objects and concepts within a domain of discourse; thus the **domain ontology**. There has been much research on the topic of ontologies, but all we need to know here is that a type model or a semantic network can be used to represent any domain ontology that we are likely to need in the context of a business rules management system.

Like many other people in the field, I believe that getting a computer to understand completely free-form natural language is impossible. This is so because understanding a sentence requires context and much context is socially generated; e.g. it may rely on such thought processes as sympathy or 'putting oneself in someone else's position'. Until computers become social creatures, therefore, they cannot be intelligent enough to understand natural language. In particular, any attempt to represent rules in natural language will fail unless there is a well-constructed model of the objects and concepts in the domain, their attributes and relationships. This type model or domain ontology provides the business **vocabulary** that the rules can use to talk about a problem. Furthermore, there must be a link between the type model and the rule language. As a matter of fact, the same applies to use cases, which cannot be interpreted with a type model to provide the vocabulary.

All BRMS products require that you build such an object model or database. The only questions are the order in which you create the models (rules first or objects first) and the degree of integration of the models. In practice, this is best done iteratively. If you already have a database or object model, you can express the rules (and indeed the use cases) in terms of it. But you may also elicit rules that use terms not yet in the vocabulary; this will lead to changes to the type model.

One approach, used in early expert systems shells, is to create the objects automatically by parsing or compiling the rules. This leads to an impoverished, flat object model that often can't distinguish objects from their attributes and makes it difficult to attach methods or rulesets to objects, and is complex to interface to existing business data. A better approach is to create a good, packaged and layered component model separately from the rules. This is usually not a trivial task, and many organizations do not yet have sufficiently advanced component modelling skills.

Date, Halle, Morgan, Ross and the Business Rules Management Group all talk about ontologies as 'fact models'. In their terminology, **terms** are objects (i.e. classes or instances) or attributes of objects and **facts** are associations amongst objects, including specialization or aggregation associations. We will stick with the term 'type model'. In particular, Halle legislates that such fact models should be 'devoid of methods'. This is an error. While we do not want the business rules buried deep in the object model, there is no way that we want the more mundane procedures that define types elevated to the level of business rules. For example, we would not wish to promote the rules of arithmetic that define real numbers of dates to the level of business rules.

If natural language processing is to be attempted, we need to do two additional things. The model needs to reflect the way people think about objects and the way they construct sentences to talk about them.

The way normal people think about objects is not quite the same as the semantics of a C++ or Java object model. For example, in rule-based applications, rôles are important concepts and, in real life, instances often change rôles or adopt multiple rôles; I can be a student *and* an employee. For this reason a modelling approach based on semantic networks is more appropriate than one based on the semantics of programming languages. Such a model, however, must be translatable into code.

To capture the rich and varied way people construct sentences to talk about objects, we have a choice: either restrict the syntax or teach the machine how to understand a wide range of phrasing. Both approaches have advantages. A well-designed formal syntax can look like English and is quick and easy to type once you know it. A parser can warn you if you have violated the syntax or referred to an object that doesn't exist. However, the rules may look strange to the untutored eyes and it is impossible to just pick up rules written by business experts and just drop then into the application. On the other hand, natural language phrasings need to be made explicit by the knowledge base creator and this takes time and effort. The reward for the extra effort is that practically anyone can now add or change rules with the domain.

That last caveat is important; the system has to *know* about a particular domain. The object model and the phrasings constitute the limits of the system's knowledge. An old joke illustrates this point well. A clever artificial intelligence programmer taught his system to use metaphor, so that it understood the sentence 'Haste is needed because time flies like an arrow.' The first user he demonstrated it to typed 'A screen is needed because fruit flies like a banana,' and crashed the system.

4.8 Summary

This chapter presented the basic theories of knowledge representation, inference and uncertainty in knowledge and rule-based systems.

4.9 Bibliographical Notes

Hayes-Roth *et al.* (1983) provide a good introduction to expert systems. Morgan (2002) gives a simple introduction to first order predicate logic. Both he and Ross (2003) give extensive advice on how to formulate and phrase rules. Graham and Jones (1988), though long out of print, is one of the very few works to provide extensive coverage of the use of fuzzy logic to express business rules.

Features of Business Rules Management Systems

It is a capital mistake to theorize before you have all the evidence.

Sir Arthur Conan Doyle *(A Study in Scarlet)*

I have already quoted Tony Morgan's succinct definition of a business rule. It is worth repeating: 'A compact statement about an aspect of a business [that] can be expressed in terms that can be directly related to the business, using simple, unambiguous language that's accessible to all interested parties: business owner, business analyst, technical architect, and so on'. Morgan, because he has a long track record in artificial intelligence, assumes that these rules are embedded in a régime that can link them together; a key component of any BRMS.

In much other work, the implicit definition is much more fuzzy. Many writers, coming – as they usually do – from a database background, see business rules as little more than database constraints or even simple formulae.

The formula margin = revenue – direct.costs is *not* a rule. It is a statement of identity. It could even be regarded as a procedure for computing margin, as can many algebraic equations of this sort. Rules in BRMSs are characterized by being non-procedural; they state what is true, not how to compute it. Having said this, it is quite right that a modern BRMS should allow formulae to be stored alongside the rules in the repository. I merely want to make the distinction because there are many cases where it is both clearer and more efficient to implement calculations in conventional source code.

The mavens of UML mostly see business rules as coextensive with the idea of OCL-type statements and, of course, they are not completely wrong in this. Indeed, I would agree that a business rule is exactly a logically valid statement concerning the objects in the domain that must always be true[1]. However, what this view misses is the idea that rules interact. Even simple facts can interact. If I, for example, tell you that the writer of this book has grey eyes and that Ian Graham is the author of this book, now you know these two facts. But what if I were to ask you 'What colour are Ian Graham's eyes?'

Of course, you know the answer. But I haven't told it to you. You *inferred* it!

Similarly, from two rules that say 'if you overeat then you are likely to become obese,' and 'obese people often die young,' you may infer the obvious, dismal, if reassuringly probabilistic conclusion.

So, a BRMS has to support automatic inferencing, as well as rules and facts. Rules and facts are the easiest to formalize.

A rule is a statement that has, or can be transformed into, the form IF x THEN y, where x and y can be of the form A is P and—or B is Q and—or . . . but y can also be an instruction to do something: an action. An example might help.

> *If an applicant's socioeconomic group is A and the applicant is not married then send the luxury dating brochure*

This is written in fairly plain English. In a conventional rule language it is likely to be a little more opaque of expression – something like

> *If Applicant.SEG is "A" and Applicant.married is FALSE then "Send luxury dating brochure" is indicated.*

As we have already seen, business rules need not always follow the if/then form, but may be specified in different formats that are not as closely linked to the underlying rule-engine implementation or syntax. Business rules often tend to use the deontic (must or must not) form to express constraints or inferences. For example:

- An order must not be invoiced before dispatch.
- The luxury dating brochure should be sent to an unmarried applicant whose socioeconomic group is A.
- An applicant for credit must be at least 18 years of age.

Morgan (2002) gives a great deal of useful guidance on how to phrase rules, preferring the above form to the 'if . . . then . . . ' form imposed by many products. Ross (2003) gives similar guidance in the context of his RuleSpeak.

---

[1] The Object Management Group is, at the time of writing, in the process of extending UML to address business rules, with standards such as Business Semantics for Business Rules and the Production Rule Representation (the latter being co-developed by IBM, Fair Isaac and ILOG amongst others).

In this chapter, we will look at the features of business rules management systems, the technical terms and issues and some of the leading BRMS products. The features we are interested in include the following.

- Architecture.
- Integrating with enterprise applications.
- Knowledge representation.
- Inference strategies.
- Forming rules into independent but chainable rulesets.
- Creating intelligent applications that interact with users through natural, understandable and logical dialogues.
- Allowing business analysts and even users to create, understand and maintain the rules and policies of the business.
- Rule repositories, versioning, etc.

We also apply three of these products to a simple application.

5.1   The Components and Technical Features of a BRMS

BRMSs are related (both intellectually and commercially) to the expert systems products of the 1980s. To understand them it helps to know a little about their origins, although current BRMS products have come a long way since then and are equally influenced by database considerations, as we saw in Chapter 3.

Rule-based or 'expert' systems, sometimes called knowledge-based systems, are computer systems that can give advice or make decisions in a narrowly defined area at or near the level of a human expert. There are two kinds of such systems: systems that take decisions, which are chiefly process controllers and applications such as financial program trading systems, and systems that act as decision support systems, giving advice but not making autonomous decisions. This definition is couched in terms of what expert systems do. More importantly, rule-based systems are defined by how they do it: by their architecture. The most important architectural feature is that knowledge about a problem (in the form of rules, say) is stored separately from the code that applies the knowledge to the problem in hand. This applies equally to BRMSs. Some early expert systems jumbled up facts, data, procedures and rules in the knowledge base whereas modern BRMSs usually maintain a cleaner demarcation between business rules and business data. The rulebase is seen as acting upon the database (including metadata).

The repository of chunks of knowledge in a BRMS is referred to as the **rule base** or **knowledge base** and the mechanisms which apply the knowledge

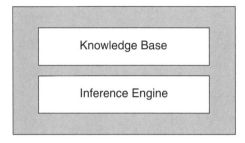

Figure 5-1   The architecture of a business rules service.

to the data presented to it as the **rule engine** or **inference engine**. This characteristic architecture is illustrated in Figure 5.1.

It is now widely accepted that there are essentially four components of a business rules management system. Firstly, the underlying environment of symbol and value manipulation which all computer systems share and which can be thought of as the programming languages and support environment; editors, floating point processors, data structures, compilers, etc. The grey area in Figure 5.1 represents this. Secondly, we have the structure of the knowledge base itself, including methods of representation and access, and then there must be some techniques for applying the knowledge in a rational manner to the problem at hand. This third element is the inference engine, which chains the rules together to reach valid conclusions. Usually, this is done non-procedurally, but some BRMS also provide other methods whereby, for example, ruleset execution can be handled by a faster approach such as procedural rule firing. The fourth element is the repository, in which the rules are stored and from which they may be manipulated, versioned, shared, managed and so on. Figure 5.2 shows the rule (or decision) service in a broader architectural context, emphasizing the separate character of the repository (from which rules may be imported into the rule service) and the probable presence of a database or databases that must be coupled with the business rules in applications. Note also that, nowadays, we may use a separate rule authoring package. We will see examples of this later in this chapter.

The knowledge base and the inference engine are separated from one another to facilitate maintenance. After all, in most cases rules and policies will change over time and one does not want to rewrite the inference engine (the program code) whenever a new rule is added.

The knowledge base usually contains different kinds of knowledge; typically these include knowledge about objects, procedures and causal relationships. Knowledge about objects is usually stored in the form of an object model, XML schema, data model or semantic network. We discussed object knowledge in Chapter 4 under the heading of ontologies. Procedural knowledge may be represented as rules but could be Java methods, Excel macros and so on. Some business procedures can also be represented with rules.

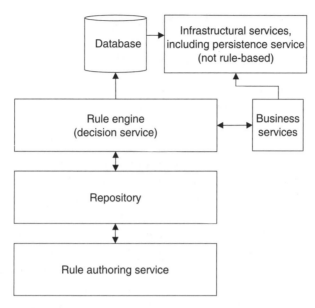

Figure 5-2   The architecture of a business rules management system.

5.1.1 Rules

Knowledge about causal relationships is usually stored in the form of **rules** of the form 'IF A THEN X'. Unlike the if/then statements found in conventional languages like Java, COBOL or C++, rule languages in are typically **declarative** or equivalently **non-procedural**; that is, the order in which the rules are written is not important. These rules work on knowledge about entities or objects. As we have said, another important way to represent knowledge is as **procedures**, as found in conventional languages. There are various other ways to represent knowledge, but rules, procedures and objects are the main ones used in business rules management systems at present.

In all BRMS products, rules are represented as sentences, usually containing the words IF and THEN. Morgan (2002) recommends a better style aimed at removing ambiguity, making relationships explicit, avoiding obscure terminology, removing wordiness, and so on. His style is remarkably close to natural language. He ends up preferring forms such as

> *A loan may be approved if*
> > *the status of the customer is high*
> > *and the loan is less than 2000*
> > *unless the customer has a low rating*

to

> *if the customer status is high and the loan is less*
> *than 2000*

> *and the customer does not have a low rating*
> *then approve the loan*
> *if the customer status is high and the loan is less*
> *than 2000*
> *and the customer has a low rating*
> *then don't approve the loan*

Most commercial BRMS products support the second style of rule writing; only a few, such as HaleyAuthority, provide completely natural support for the first. Blaze Advisor, as we shall see, offers a completely different approach in the form of its Rule Maintenance Applications. These allow the creation of custom rule maintenance forms that allow users to interact using any format of rule presentation considered appropriate to the business situation. Another approach used, for example in JRules, is to let the developer create 'verbalizations' for the object model to make rules more readable. Default verbalizations allow one to use phrases like 'the contract is completed' rather than just 'contract is completed'.

5.1.2   Rule Templates

Rule templates are design patterns for rules. In many circumstances, a rule might be applicable to several data. In such cases, rule templates allow for the creation of rules with empty slots to be filled in later. A business rule template represents a partially defined business rule that contains placeholder slots for missing information. Templates can be used to create multiple rules with a similar structure, where only the value filled in the slots varies. Rule templates save time when writing rules and help to enforce a standard, readable rule writing style.

5.1.3   Rule Syntax Checking

A good BRMS will offer facilities for checking the rule syntax in real time, as the rules are entered. With structured rule languages, it is useful if the syntax checker highlights keywords, variable and values using different colours. There should be clear links between the object model and the rules. All the modern products that I have tried have excellent syntax checking and debugging facilities.

5.1.4   Procedures and Algorithms

Some knowledge is distinctly procedural. For example, we cannot compute our tax liability unless we first know our income and expenditure.

Rule representation can be very cumbersome when the knowledge to be stored is procedural. Examples include mathematical and financial computations. A good BRMS will offer the ability for rulesets to invoke procedures and for procedures to call upon rulesets to execute and return values.

5.1.5   Ruleflows

Ruleflow mechanisms within BRMSs let the designer specify that knowledge modules or tasks be carried out in a particular order. These tasks may be rulesets, functions or entire ruleflow modules. Such a feature is essential for a good BRMS.

5.1.6   Decision Tables and Decision Trees

In some products, there are alternative representations to rules for if/then knowledge. We consider two of these: decision trees and decision tables. Decision trees represent the rules pictorially, as a tree structure. This may be a useful aid to debugging or communication between users and developers or analysts, but is not usually how business users visualize their knowledge. Decision tables represent the same knowledge and rules as decision trees in a tabular format.

The main problem with decision tables is that they grow unmanageably large when there are a large number of conditions in the rulebase. The approach gives a larger number of rules – one for each row – and the rules will be hard to read and understand. We characterize the approach as **row-oriented decision tables**. Rule subsumption checks may allow the author to tidy up the resultant rulesets, but we think a rule induction approach is far sounder. It is better to use a data mining system to extract rules from decision tables and feed them into a BRMS.

We looked at decision trees and tables in more detail in Chapter 4. The main advantage of decision tables arises when the organization already holds the knowledge in this form: pricing charts, rate tables, etc. However, this advantage largely evaporates when the rules can access the same data in the form of lookup tables.

5.1.7   Inference

An inference engine offers one or more means of applying knowledge to data. The most common strategies are known as **backward chaining** and **forward chaining**. Backward chaining or **goal-directed** reasoning is typical of product selection, diagnostic or advice giving systems. It involves deriving a plausible reason for some given fact. For example, given the fact 'the patient has spots' a medical expert system might reason that the patient could have been among young children recently since young children often have measles and measles causes spots. Forward chaining or **data-directed** inference takes all data present and attempts to discover as much as possible by applying as many rules as possible to them, or filling as many frame slots (object attributes) as possible. This is typical of process control and scheduling applications. It is also typical of many 'form filling' applications, such as tax credit or loan approval. Most rule-based systems involve a mixture of backward and forward chaining and other strategies to reduce blind search.

Implementing forward chaining efficiently is hard since, when a rulebase becomes large, naïve algorithms for forward chaining become very slow because few changes are made to the facts in working memory at each cycle. **The rete algorithm** is a very efficient mechanism for solving this problem. Rete (Latin: net) is much more efficient at determining the relevance of rules, given particular data, than the equivalent nested if/then/else or select/case constructs. The rete network modifies itself after each rule firing, so that unneeded rules do not fire. The greater the number of rules, the greater rete's advantage over equivalent procedural code. This applies to rule execution. Of course, writing the rules is also far more efficient in a BRMS. Refer back to Chapter 4 for more details on rete and inference strategies.

Most of the leading commercial rete-based products offer support for backward, forward and mixed chaining using the rete algorithm. Each product has a proprietary improvement on the basic rete algorithm. These improvements are largely responsible for the variation in performance of rule engines. The engines must all also modify basic rete to permit backward and mixed chaining.

5.1.8 Uncertainty and Explanation

Two other features, which separate rule-based systems from other computer systems, are that they can often

- incorporate qualitative or judgemental reasoning and manage uncertainty;
- provide an explanation of their reasoning.

If the last two features are both present, rule-based systems can offer multiple conclusions ranked by a measure of confidence. Both features, if required, tend to increase the cost of system building and may, in some circumstances, imply additional complexity in defining the business rules. Built-in explanation facilities are useful debugging aids, but are rarely suitable for user enquiries. Useful facilities for explanation of the system's reasoning to users must usually be hand crafted.

Reasoning about uncertainty adds to the complexity of a system, and the knowledge acquisition associated with specifying it, but permits it to tackle more complex problems.

There are several techniques for managing uncertainty, the most common being:

- Reasoning explicitly using verbal labels for uncertain terms
- Truth maintenance systems
- What-if facilities
- Certainty factors
- Bayesian probability
- Fuzzy sets

No current major BRMS product offers sophisticated uncertainty management or the last three uncertainty management techniques. Blaze Advisor offers a scoring system based on the idea of scorecards, which can be regarded as a certainty factor variant.

HaleyAuthority relies on uncertain linguistic constructs, such as 'may be' and 'could'. With most other products, it is a matter of choosing attribute names that imply uncertain value ranges; e.g. terms such as 'risk averse'.

Most of the major BRMS products support truth maintenance well. A truth maintenance system keeps track of dependencies among sentences and allows the rule engine to retract assertions in a consistent way. This takes account of the kind of uncertainty we face when, over time, things we once believed true become false (*cf* Russell and Norvig, 1995). Truth maintenance can help improve the explanation facilities offered by a BRMS. What-if is handled in the testing environments of BRMS products or could be coded into any application that relies on a rule engine.

Chapter 4 discussed knowledge representation, inference, and uncertainty management in much more detail. It also included more detailed material on such topics as decision tables, rule induction and data mining, explanation facilities and semantic networks.

Explanation and Help Facilities

Imagine a conversation between a life assurance salesman and a potential client. The rep takes the customer's personal and financial details and enters them in to the BRMS application on her laptop. She then asks a few well-chosen questions. At the end of this, she announces 'Thank you for your frankness, Mr Suzuki. I think the best product that we can offer you is a life policy linked to an investment in gilt-edged government bonds. That will provide you with adequate death benefit to cover your wife's needs and provide for your son's education and marriage costs.'

'Thank you, Diana, but I don't understand why.'

'Well, you told me that you are only 27.'

'That's right.'

'That is quite young in this context and we have a rule that says – No, look, I can show you.'

She swivels her knees so that he can see the display on the laptop. 'See? This rule here.'

Mr Suzuki slides his spectacles up his nose and reads.

> *A bond linked policy is recommended for a client*
> *if the client is averse to risk and young*

'OK; but what made you think I'm averse to risk? I never said anything about that.'

'We think that people with young children are usually averse to risk, because they want to protect their interest in as safe a way as possible. Look, here's the rule.' Diana presses a function key.

> *A client is averse to risk if the client has children*

'Ah! So, I understand now. What will the growth projection look like?'

The sale is nearly closed and both Diana and Mr Suzuki are pretty sure that the recommendation is a good one.

On a technical level the BRMS has fired a 'best product' ruleset, given the recommendation (bond) and printed an elaboration of the benefits (stored as explanation text perhaps). When asked, it unwinds the rule stack and shows which rules have fired.

Several BRMS products I have looked at offer this kind of rule trace in test mode. The same information is available to the applications using the rules but, in each case, it requires some programming to create an interface such as the one used by Diana's company. This is a shame but it is really quite hard to design completely general-purpose user-friendly explanation and help facilities.

We will return to this 'best product advice' example later in this chapter.

5.2 BRMS Products

There are many products that allow users to develop rule-based systems. Not all of these may be classified as BRMS because some, such as the expert system 'shells' of the 1980s and their descendents, do not usually offer repository-based rule management. I am also tempted to exclude a number of popular open source solutions because they are not rule *management* systems. Examples include Jess and Drools, although they could be combined with a separate repository.

Jess is a rule engine and scripting environment written entirely in Java language by Ernest Friedman-Hill at Sandia National Laboratories in Livermore, CA. Jess was originally inspired by the CLIPS expert system language, but has grown into a complete, distinct, dynamic environment of its own. Using Jess, you can build Java software that has the capacity to perform inferences on declarative rules. Jess is small, light, and has a fast rule engine. The Jess language is still compatible with CLIPS, in that many Jess scripts are valid CLIPS scripts and vice-versa. Like CLIPS, Jess uses the rete algorithm. Jess adds many features to CLIPS, including backward chaining, working memory queries, and the ability to manipulate and reason directly about Java objects. Jess is also a powerful Java scripting environment, from which you can create Java objects and call Java methods without compiling any Java code. [http://herzberg.ca.sandia.gov/jess/] Oracle has adopted and adapted Jess as its rule engine.

Drools is an augmented implementation of Forgy's rete algorithm tailored for the Java language. Adapting rete to an object-oriented interface allows for more natural expression of business rules in respect of business objects. It is an engine for processing rete graphs and is therefore a purely forward chaining system. Drools wraps the semantics of the normal relational rete into an object-oriented model compatible with Java. Additionally, by mapping to objects, domain specific languages can be created that operate upon an application's own object model. [http://drools.org/]

With Jess and Drools there is the problem of lack of support. Neither are there any high-level authoring and management tools. These deficiencies may render such tools unsuitable in many commercial environments, although the Oracle version of Jess will clearly be supported.

Computer Associates' CleverPath Aion Business Rules Expert is a descendent of the Aion expert system shell. It is rete-based and offers a component-based development environment. However, it has a slightly monolithic character and the rule engine is not offered as an embeddable component. Nor is it repository-based; rules are stored as a collection of rulesets. CleverPath Aion BRE supports decision tables, dynamic rules, and a sophisticated inference engine. There are links to CA's neural-net-based machine learning (i.e. data mining) system, Neugent. [www3.ca.com/Solutions/Product.asp?ID=250]

Mindbox's ART*Enterprise* is another born-again shell and considered by me to be monolithic rather than component-based – for all its strengths. [www.mindbox.com]

ESI's Logist is a purely forward chaining rule-based expert system shell with a pseudo-natural-language interface. Typically, ESI claim, Logist is used by organizations to offer their clients customized services, to promote customer retention and avoid revenue leakage and billing errors. [www.esi-knowledge.com/BR_logis.asp]

As an aside, Netherlands based LibRT offers an interesting complimentary product to any BRMS. LibRT VALENS is claimed to be the first independent product targeted at verifying and validating business rules created in third-party business rules management systems. There is a known relationship with CA's CleverPath Aion and Blaze Advisor. [www.LibRT.com]

Corticon is a non-rete-based rule engine. It will generate web service, Java and J2EE applications on top off existing applications but does not offer a set of components for embedding in them. Nor is it repository based. In rete-based engines, the best performance arises when the objects are fairly simple (the number of attributes to be tested is small) and the number of rules is large. However, when the item of work moving through a business process is more complex (such as an insurance claim with all its attendant objects (policy, injury, employer, medical bills, and litigation motions) the number of possible variables that need to be examined by the rules becomes large. The number and depth of association paths to be traversed is also significant. In these scenarios, rete engines do not scale well – their agenda management phase consumes noticeable time. Corticon integrates with Staffware, a leading business process modelling tool and probably shines brightest for this kind of application rather than when applied to normal BRMS problems. It is certainly a product worth looking at. [www.corticon.com]

RulesPower from the eponymously named company co-founded in 2001 by Charles Forgy, author of the original rete algorithm, is intended to allow business management personnel to create and maintain the business logic that represents their business policies. However, the focus of RulesPower is on business process modelling and there is no focus on providing the rule engine as a component within a larger application, which is the focus of our interest. RulesPower offers instead a good but monolithic solution to the problem of building a BRMS. RulesPower was taken over by Fair Isaac in 2005 and its advanced rete algorithm (rete III) is being integrated into Blaze Advisor to enhance further the latter's performance.

It is not the intention of this work to review all available BRMS products but it is helpful to survey a few in order to illustrate the principles involved. A good BRMS should

- allow business analysts to create and modify the rules;
- use a fully-featured repository;
- support backward chaining;
- allow the rule engine to be a component or service within larger applications;
- allow applications to be deployed in a service oriented architecture;
- focus on business rules management (as opposed to just workflow) problems;
- provide good report generation facilities;
- provide evidence of successful commercial applications;

- be compatible with a component-based or service-oriented architecture; and

- offer commercial-standard professional support (thereby we eliminate the open source products).

All the products discussed below are rete-based and exhibit the above qualities.

5.2.1   Blaze Advisor

Fair Isaac's Blaze Advisor Version 6.0 provides the same BRMS on 2 main platforms, Java and .NET, with an option on the Java version allowing the generation of COBOL code. The Java requires a (freely available) JVM to be installed, and the latter requires Microsoft's .NET Framework to be installed (and recommends Visual Studio too).

The tutorial material is thorough and reveals Blaze Advisor as a mature product with complex features; although beginning users may well not understand the need for all of them.

Application development (viewed as 'rule service development') proceeds by importing or creating objects, rulesets, functions, event rules, questions sets, enumerations and ruleflows within a project repository. This can be done in any order but it is natural to start with the basic object model: classes and enumerations. These can be imported via wizards from Java, COM/.NET, XML, or a database – plus there is a mechanism for defining your own Business Object Model Adapter. You can create your own classes and instances too, although Fair Isaac stresses that this is usually done for prototyping and testing only. Once you have created the classes, you can type rules into a ruleset window. Backward chaining requires the creation of event rules or questions sets, which can be used to generate prompts for missing values, so that interactive testing is possible.

An application calls upon the rule server and engine to provide a service, such as classifying a situation or diagnosing some problem. In turn, the rule server accesses any needed data. Rules are maintained in a repository with features comparable with other leading products. It enables changes to be managed for multiple concurrent users and supports workflow in development with permissions for change management. This architecture is summarized in Figure 5.3.

The rule syntax has moved on a lot since the days of Nexpert Object, and we find a good compromise between natural language syntax and formal syntax, similar to that of JRules (see Section 5.2.3 below). Business users, though, are protected from the actual rule syntax as they use rule maintenance applications that access the repository directly in maintenance mode.

Blaze Advisor offers three different ways to address the rule authoring problem:

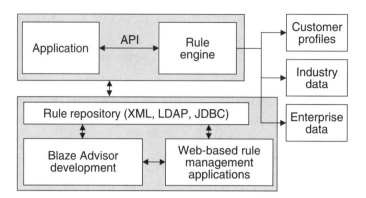

Figure 5-3   Blaze Advisor architecture.

- An English-like Structured Rule Language (SRL) for expressing the rules, as well as any data patterns or local classes and instances.
- Decision trees, decision tables and scorecard models, which are graphical or tabular ways of creating rules.
- Rule Maintenance Applications (RMA), which are customizable web-based rule authoring interfaces that can be generated directly from Blaze Advisor.

The SRL is an object-oriented programming language designed to make writing and reading business rules seem English-like. It has the features of a programming language, and is intended for use by programmers (as well as "technical business analysts" who are not averse to tasks like programming Excel macros) to create the entities, control the execution flow, and perform the operations required by the rule service. However, it also provides a syntax for authoring rules that is understandable (i.e. readable) by people with little or no programming background. The Blaze Advisor IDE (a proprietary interactive development environment) includes a set of editors that simplify the creation of SRL entities, and generate much of the syntax. Normally, programmers use the IDE to develop the data model and execution flow, and then provide the business user with access to edit specific rulesets. This access can either be through direct editing of the SRL, the use of ruleset metaphors, or through an RMA. Regardless of which is used, the business user's edits are compiled along with any other SRL to produce the executable rule service, which is either a project that is loaded by the runtime Rule Server, or in the case of COBOL output, compilable COBOL code. The SRL syntax falls a long way short of natural language, but I found it fairly easy to read. Writing rules in it requires knowledge of the object model's structure and variable names. Developers can also choose to write templates for rules, which are used by the RMA Generator wizard to provide an interface for business users. This interface follows the philosophy that typing any formal language is too much to expect a busy business person to achieve, and instead displays the parameters that make up the rule within any text – or indeed, HTML construct – that the user needs. This can obviously be much closer to natural language syntax. The assumption is that developers are available to learn how to create rule templates and RMA forms.

Building an RMA involves abstracting from the rules to create more generic rule templates within which the user may select values, ranges, objects and so on. A template contains value holders and contents. Each value holder specifies a particular type of value, or enumeration list of values. The contents contain standard rules and includes embedded placeholders. Each placeholder refers to a value holder. The value defined by the value holder will be inserted into the contents to replace the placeholder. Sets of values corresponding to the value holders are stored in separate repository items called instances. When an instance is resolved, the result is a set of rule entities.

A template can be as simple as a single statement that exposes a single value for editing such as "theCustomer.age > [minimum age]". Templates can get quite complex too. They can include multiple value holders, and can define complete rule entities or even multiple entities. In addition, a value holder can hold multiple values of the same type. A value holder can also refer to another template. In such a case, a placeholder for the value holder will resolve into a resolved instance of the referred template. This permits flexible, hierarchical structures that support precise control over what can and cannot be edited. For example, a ruleset template could contain a value holder referring to a rule template that defined a particular form of a rule. The rule template could in turn contain value holders pointing to various code templates that define particular conditions and actions that are valid for the rule.

RMAs are generated from the rule templates within a web browser.

Creating a rule template requires a careful reading of the tutorial and some practice. You can copy the text of a rule into the content section of the template and then replace the parts that need to be modifiable with placeholders. On the other hand, generating a crude RMA from the template was relatively straightforward.

Blaze Advisor provides good facilities for entering rulesets as row-oriented decision tables. It also has a useful graphical decision tree representation. The latter does not support probabilistic trees. Uniquely, Blaze Advisor offers 'scorecards': a special form of table that lets the system reason using additive scores. For example, in a credit scoring application, we may score professional and skilled occupations more highly than unskilled ones. These scores can be combined with other factors such as outstanding mortgage liabilities to arrive at a final score for credit-worthiness. This is the mechanism used by Fair Isaac for the credit scoring applications which the company is well known for, especially in the USA. Other applications include fault diagnosis and sales promotion targeting. Entering textual 'reason codes' for each score makes the method auditable. The score model metaphor provides a limited way of handling probabilistic rules.

There is a built-in library of mathematical and financial functions and there is a complete procedural language supporting most familiar programming constructs. This language is at a higher level than Java, giving Blaze Advisor (in my opinion) a slight edge on products that use unadorned Java for this purpose. Business rules are written in a structured if/then syntax. Rulesets execute under a rete-based inference engine, or may be selected to run in a procedural fashion ('sequentially') if the rules do not need to be declarative or to chain with one another. There is also a licence option for a "compiled sequential" mode, in which the rules are compiled to Java or .NET bytecode as appropriate, although this is transparent to the user and still allows for rule changes to be made to a running rule server as necessary. Another licence option is the aforementioned COBOL output. The rulesets, together with procedures and functions, can be chained procedurally or 'orchestrated' using ruleflows. Blaze Advisor lets you group your rules into functional rulesets, and then lets you control the sequence in which rulesets are called by using a ruleflow. Ruleflows are displayed using a proprietary, but clear, graphical notation.

The product supports different policy and rule expression formats: if/then, constraints, declarative definitions. Rules can use Java-style dot notation or more English-like, business-friendly constructs (aliases for attributes), or both interchangeably. Rule templates are supported well.

Effective dates and times can be stated for each rule.

Rule inheritance is Blaze Advisor's approach to rule subsumption. Any rule can refer to any other rule, in which case it inherits the referred rule's conditions. This is used, for example, in the decision tree metaphor. Rule inheritance saves development time and leads to cleaner rulebases, but it can be dangerous when used improperly. However, Blaze Advisor is a tool that, when used properly, can help companies focus on the important things in business life.

A good analysis tool supports conflict resolution: potential rule conflict. Rules whose actions do not change values in the same ruleset are identified as candidates for, more efficient, procedural execution. Infinite loops within the rules are detected automatically. An HTML conflict report can be produced and printed. The AnalyzeRuleService test picks up rulesets that do not cover the state space.

Blaze Advisor's Business Object Model Adapters (BOMA) provide a common business object representation against which to write rules. In this way, a rule that is written against a Java entity can also be used against a .NET entity. Then, at runtime, you pass corresponding Java objects, COM objects, COBOL copybook entries, database records, or XML documents to the rule engine, and the BOMA automatically maps them to the correct types of business objects.

Rule developers using SRL can use a full range of debugging facilities including stepping through rules, setting breakpoints on any internal or external data item referenced in the rules, viewing cross references and execution traces, and monitoring performance. The development environment can also be used to debug a rule service transaction taking place on a remote server.

There are localized versions of the IDE for Japanese, French, German, Italian, Korean, Portuguese, Spanish and Chinese (Simplified and Traditional), including all menu items, error messages, and pop-up help windows. Also, all strings support Unicode, so that item names can be in the appropriate language.

Blaze Advisor offers good compliance with standards, such as JavaBeans, EJB, COM+/DCOM, W3C XML and CORBA (the OMG's Common Object Request Broker Architecture).

It is relatively easy to deliver an application into most architectures, including thin clients. There are built-in wizards, called Quick Deployers, that generate the necessary client code to invoke the Advisor Rule Server. Options include vanilla J2EE as well as specializations for IBM Websphere, BEA Weblogic, Oracle and Sun application servers, as well as a variety of different deployment types such as EJB, Message-driven Beans, Web Services, as well as plain old embedded code. Naturally, the .NET version only deploys to .NET environments, but that includes C# and Visual Basic interface generation. All versions, including generated COBOL, share the same repository, for greater rule consistency. The Quick Deployer also configures the rule server's configuration file, as this component is not so much programmed via an API but configured via XML. Rule servers can manage multiple rule services, and in turn multiple rule engines (called 'agents') can be configured for rule services to provide multi-user scalability. A separate deployment component called a Deployment Manager can coordinate rule updates to a live rule server.

Blaze Advisor provides an internal versioning and access control mechanism. In addition to providing a rule check-in/check-out repository, Blaze Advisor allows you to have several versions of the rules for different applications and permits control over who has access to which rule or rulesets. New in Version 6.0 is improved ownership control, ruleset segmentation and release management. Customizable management properties and queries for both technical and business users further enhance rules maintenance applications. New "best practice" documentation helps guide repository design for best performance and maintainability. IBM has certified that Blaze Advisor is optimized across all of its major platforms, including IBM iSeries, pSeries, xSeries, and zSeries.

Another key feature of Version 6.0 is the integration of the Innovator Workbench with the rule builder product. This gives better integration of features such as decision tables and scorecards and makes the interface to RMAs more transparent.

The things I like most about this product are its interactive testing facilities, making backward chaining far easier to realize, good rule analysis features and its general level of tool integration and ease of use. Also, the RMA is a very sensible alternative to natural language rule authoring, in the right circumstances.

As someone with considerable experience of building systems using the older expert systems shells, I felt immediately at home with Blaze Advisor. I was able to use the product to get sample applications up and running within a relatively short time. A less technically inclined business analyst might have struggled more with the design interface. Therefore, Blaze Advisor is not really suitable for environments where business users need to get closely involved in the creation and maintenance of business logic unless there are development resources available to create a custom rule interface. The rules can then be presented to users in a non-technical way via generated browser pages. If one takes the view that natural language is not always the best way for busy users to enter rules, then Blaze Advisor's web-based rule interface (the RMAs) is a very attractive alternative. Such a view is reasonable in situations where the rules have complex interrelationships, or where the users have no desire to enter rules in their raw form.

Blaze Advisor is a mature product with good integration features and is capable of addressing many BRMS situations. Good tuning facilities can be applied to improve performance (for example, procedural rules execution is possible). Future versions will also benefit from the adoption of Forgy's fast rete III algorithm. Blaze Advisor shines in the number of tools it offers to programmers.

Related Fair Isaac Products

Founded in 1956, Fair Isaac is a company that focuses on the provision of decision support and analytics software. Blaze Advisor integrates with Fair Isaac's other tools. For example, Model Builder for Decision Trees helps define strategies such as for marketing campaigns, and once defined, the resulting decision tree can be imported into Blaze Advisor. Model Builder for Predictive Analytics is a data mining and analysis tool whose analytic models can be executed in a Blaze Advisor ruleflow. Decision Optimizer is aimed at resource allocation problems in the style of linear programming. Blaze Advisor can invoke these models when complex calculations are required. Blaze Advisor also provides rule-based services for Fair Isaac's vertical-market solutions for loan originations (TRIAD), fraud detection (FALCON), debt recovery (PLACEMENTS PLUS), and others. A custom Blaze Advisor solution for the ACORD insurance standard, already deployed in some insurance carriers in the US, and SmartForms – which adds a fourth deployment platform for business rules developed with Blaze Advisor: XML-based web forms (XForms) – have both been announced. SmartForms automates data validation by caching rules on the client using XForms technology, and is an important addition to Blaze Advisor's capabilities.

5.2.2   HaleyRules and HaleyAuthority

Haley Systems Inc. (formerly The Haley Enterprise) specializes in rule-based and case-based reasoning technology. Software from Haley is embedded in a variety of commercial software packages and applications. The company was established in 1989. Its core products are HaleyRules, which is a fast rete-based rule engine, and HaleyAuthority, a natural language rule authoring system that generates code for HaleyRules. HaleyAuthority was originally called Authorete (but always pronounced Authority) to emphasize its support for rete.

HaleyRules uses a rule language called Eclipse, a sophisticated descendant of the CLIPS language, which is in turn a descendant of OPS-5. Eclipse provides an extended version of the CLIPS rule language syntax using a proprietary version of the rete algorithm to support both forward and backward chaining. It is implemented in a layered architecture for maximum development and integration flexibility. It includes an extensive programming interface for ANSI C and Visual Basic to libraries at each level of its layered architecture, and is encapsulated in and integrated within C++ as Rete++. It is also available as Agent OCX for COM integration with OLE automation under Windows and as an ActiveX control that supports Microsoft COM, Visual J++ and Internet Explorer. There is no connection whatsoever with IBM's Eclipse IDE.

HaleyRules is embedded in every copy of HaleyAuthority but may be purchased separately. Haley's rule engine has a very small footprint when implemented (1,000 rules use less than 1Mbyte). The engine can run in less than 4 MB of RAM. It has even been ported to a Palm Pilot and other PDAs.

HaleyAuthority is a Windows application (thus no JVM is required), but it does have a Web Services component as well. HaleyRules is available both as a pure Java implementation and a C-based implementation with out-of-the-box interfaces for integration with Java, .NET, C++ and Visual Basic applications. The availability of native and Java implementations enables Haley to support a wide range of platforms and application scenarios.

The files that are deployed for testing are the same files that would be used within an application. Typically, HaleyRules is embedded in an application or server side process and API calls are used to initialize the engine and give it the HaleyAuthority generated files to load. HaleyAuthority does not produce applications; it generates the logic (rules) that can be accessed by applications through the use of the HaleyRules engine. HaleyRules has a clever knowledge base loader that only loads what has changed, thus reducing the impact of changes on users.

One powerful feature of HaleyAuthority is its automatic generation of integration or glue code. It also has code import functionality that allows you

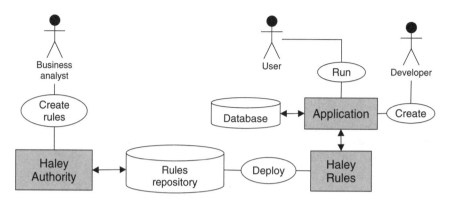

Figure 5-4   Haley architecture.

to import an XSD or, say, a Java object model and map the elements of the XSD or the object model to its concept model which is defined in business terms. HaleyAuthority then generates the glue code that enables the rule engine to invoke the object model at runtime. In the case of the XSD, XML requests conforming to the XSD can then be directly asserted into HaleyRules, which does the processing. This means that there is no need to write code to parse the XML – the engine does it. This facilitates the integration of existing applications with little programming. Another use of this capability is that you can write rules that orchestrate interactions among existing implementation objects.

The Haley product architecture is depicted in Figure 5.4

Unlike products that use multiple structured syntaxes, HaleyAuthority enables you to enter your rules in plain English. Uniquely, HaleyAuthority generates executable logic from business requirements and policies expressed in natural language (currently only English). This is very helpful in helping you avoid errors. I could not get away with entering any ambiguous rules: rules that other products will tolerate at the syntactic level. What you do is type a rule such as

> *An annuity is recommended for a client if the client is averse to risk and the client is retired*

or

> *An application should be referred if the applicant is a smoker*

Then you need to teach HaleyAuthority what the statement means by defining the ontology: the concepts and relationships (vocabulary) used in it. This is done in a quite non-technical way compared to other BRMS products; it does not require programming knowledge or a prior implementation of objects in Java or .NET. The disadvantage of this approach is that it may make linking to an existing database more complex. Of course, if there are multiple sources of business data, this complexity is ineluctable, as any data warehousing project will testify. When HaleyAuthority 'understands' a term, that part of the statement appears in bold type. Starting with the concept of an application, you create an entity with that name and another called applicant that is a specialization of a person. You also create smoker as a kind of person. The feel is much more like a semantic net than a Java object model, although a Java object model is generated automatically behind the scenes.

Now you have to define relationships for being referred and smoking. Simple pop-up dialogues guide you to create a referred relation with application as a 'rôle'. Notice that you do have to understand basic entity modelling concepts, like the difference between many-to-one and one-to one relationships, but this isn't too much to expect of a business analyst, I think.

Next, define any phrasings for the relation that you want to be able to use, in this case: an application should be referred. To do this, you specify that the phrasing uses the modal verb SHOULD and the past participle of TO REFER with the auxiliary verb BE. Not too hard, providing you have some inkling about English grammar. Now to populate the world with smokers you create a relation using IS as the verb and giving smoker the 'syntactic grammatical rôle' of direct object and applicant that of subject. And you're done. HaleyAuthority understands the rule.

The more rules you create, the quicker this process gets as the semantic model becomes more complete. Furthermore, it's much more natural than having to start with an object model, say in Java, and any attempt at sloppy thinking or ambiguity is soon detected by this tool. HaleyAuthority uses an internal expert system for parsing and semantic processing of statements in real time on a word-by-word basis. HaleyAuthority also suggests valid choices as a sentence is being defined.

As an example of the clarity of thought that HaleyAuthority insists on from its user, when I wanted to say 'if a client has any children' I had to decide if child was a concept related to client (a client has a child) or having children was a property of a person. This indicates that some training and practice would benefit most users.

One downside is the terminology that HaleyAuthority uses: 'grammatical rôle' seems to stand for case (in the grammatical sense) and (in other places) HaleyAuthority talks about the '–ing verb form' rather than what I have always called the present participle. On the other hand, you soon get used to it and the user interface is superb; I really like being able to drag one concept over another to create a relation between them. Like most native speakers of English, my only non-superficial knowledge of grammar was acquired by trying to learn *foreign* languages. HaleyAuthority assumes at least a basic skill level in this respect. On the other hand, it assumes no technical skills beyond elementary entity modelling.

The product supports different policy and rule expression formats: if/then, constraints, declarative definitions. In addition, HaleyAuthority lets you write general statements directly in natural language. HaleyAuthority supports the expression of archetypes, templates, overrides and specializations and exclusions, including the ability to specify the conditions under which an override or exclusion should apply using applicability conditions (see below), rule templates, and designation of statements as overrides for other statements

Although HaleyAuthority allows you to enter business rules in natural language, it does not allow the use of any kind of punctuation, like commas and even humble concluding full stops. If you add a stop, HaleyAuthority can't compile the rule. It does, however, understand the Saxon genitive apostrophe as in: 'A person's mother's niece is the person's second cousin'. The fact that I really could (and did) type in this last sentence and get it understood impressed me in some ways far more than the more focused tests I have done with this product. This definition of second cousin is hard to cope with for a human, never mind a machine. And of course the question of punctuation doesn't even *arise* with other BRMS products, none of which go anywhere near this level of natural language processing. So the mystery is this; if the Haley programmers are clever enough to get the product to understand the Saxon genitive, why can't they just strip out the commas and stops when it parses a rule?

Test cases can be defined using XML-based test data that represent incoming transactions. However, it does not have any equivalent of Blaze Advisor's useful interactive testing facilities. To test your rules, you have to create a set of instances of your concepts with different attributes. Since HaleyAuthority contains embedded within it a copy of HaleyRules, it can be used to simulate the execution of the knowledgebase – especially as it allows the use of XML patterns representing external transactions for these simulations. It also allows non-technical rule authors to compare test results so that they can carry out regression tests themselves. HaleyAuthority allows these test cases to be grouped so that automatic regression tests can be run as the rules evolve.

Debugging is supported both within HaleyAuthority at the rule level, and within the development environment for HaleyRules, where detailed tracing of rule execution and working memory changes is possible. HaleyRules also provides an API for passing knowledgebase execution information to external applications at runtime.

HaleyAuthority has very good effective date mechanisms, with the ability to create deployment polices with future effective and expiration dates. You can reason with concepts like TOMORROW and YESTERDAY.

The product has a repository which enables changes to be managed for multiple concurrent users. This supports workflow in development with rôle-based permissions for change management. The repository supports workflow features that can be used to implement an approval process for rule maintenance, tagging rules as 'proposed', 'reviewed' or 'approved'. Ruleflows are implemented by setting module (i.e. ruleset) priorities and writing rules to control branching among the modules.

There is automatic, real-time, multiple cross-referencing of rules and concepts (ontology).

With regard to the tabular representation of rules, the current version of HaleyAuthority supports look-up tables rather than decision tables. Look-up tables allow information to be presented to rulesets in tabular form and reasoned with. A look-up table relates up to two sets of variable ranges (such age ranges) to a set of actions (such as the medical tests required of an applicant for life assurance). This has the same effect as support for decision tables in that rule data can be captured in tabular form. It suffers from the same disadvantage of decision tables; i.e. a large table may be equivalent to only a few rules. However, it is a useful tool to have, and is easy to use.

HaleyAuthority includes a useful library of dates, units and quantities and phrasings for reasoning about them. These offer improved productivity and shorten the rule development cycle. For example, you can write rules that mention dates and temporal concepts such as before and after, without having to write any code to define such concepts. You can create polices with future effective and expiration dates – deployment parameters can be directly associated with modules. Many basic concepts are predefined and the concept sets are extensible. For example, DOLLAR and TON are predefined. Adding YEN and TONNE is easy because they still behave as money and weight. So we can write 'If the unladen weight of a vehicle is more than two tonnes then the vehicle is a heavy goods vehicle'.

Incremental development and selective deployment is helped by the ability to make incremental additions to modules and sentences.

HaleyAuthority provides a simple deployment mechanism whereby an authorized person can deploy the rules directly into test or production environments, without any downtime. As HaleyRules can be configured or instructed by an application to check for any updates to the rules, it can then examine the deployed files and only load the changes like data; that is, without needing the current process to be restarted. Code generation capabilities include integration code for invoking external object models and direct processing of XML requests.

There is built-in support for importing data and mapping it to the business vocabulary, usage, orchestration, and integration with external data representations and methods (XML, .NET, Java). HaleyAuthority has import wizards to support this process. Support for XML input is direct with no need for additional programming. It generates the integration code automatically.

There is support for dynamic or 'hot' deployment. The HaleyAuthority deployment button can invoke an external script. Support for multiple concurrent knowledge bases is good too. A single instance of HaleyRules can load multiple knowledgebases, and for each knowledgebase it can maintain an unlimited number of working memories subject to memory and CPU constraints of the host platform.

There is not currently an operation-level 'undo' (e.g. undoing the addition of a concept). However, rollback is supported on the knowledgebase, which enables 'undo' of all of the operations performed during a session.

Haley has multiple levels for the knowledge base, as well as change management and test results.

HaleyAuthority's nested logic syntax conforms to Morgan's rule style guidelines and can dramatically reduce the size of rulesets. In an IDC report, the following single HaleyAuthority nested statement was said to replace a conventional if/then equivalent with 12 complex rules:

```
A child meets the relationship test
   if the child is the taxpayer's child
   if the child is a descendant of a child of the taxpayer
   if the child is a relative of the taxpayer who cared for
the child
   if the child is an eligible foster child
      unless the child is married
            unless the child is a dependent of the
taxpayer
               if the taxpayer can claim the child as
an exemption
               if the taxpayer gave away the right
               to claim the child as an exemption
```

Here is an example of just *one* of the twelve equivalent rules (also in Haley syntax):

```
If the child is a relative and the taxpayer cared for the
child and the child is married and the child is a
dependent of the taxpayer and the taxpayer can claim
the child as an exemption
then the child meets the relationship test.
```

There is a point of controversy on this style of rule reduction. If you combine multiple rules into a single rule you save space, but are you effectively 'rule programming'? What happens if you need to add a side-effect: another action for one of the cases? You may need to rewrite your whole rule instead of just modifying a single rule. Of course, HaleyAuthority does not make the choice for you. You need to choose. In my opinion, the solution to this conundrum is to develop domain-specific analysis patterns to assist in matching the rule style to problem type, performance requirements, etc.

IDC also identified impressive reductions in the number of conditions and overall words. This 'applicability condition' style of rule writing is a powerful alternative to the more usual if/then style. Applicability conditions can be dragged to other modules to save retyping them.

Custom vocabularies for HaleyAuthority are available or being developed to support some vertical market sectors.

HaleyAuthority is significantly different from the other products in the market. The system can really understand natural language expressions, as opposed to systems that substitute pseudo-English in place of pseudo-code. It is especially easy to use when making changes to the rules once the knowledge base has been built. Features such as nested conditions and 'unless' clauses serve to both make applications more efficient and reduce the overall time it takes to develop and edit rules.

The HaleyRules rule engine offers good support for rete, forward, backward, and mixed chaining, automatic truth maintenance and conflict resolution. It has the ability to handle a large number of rules and large numbers of concurrent requests/transactions, users, and rule executions. HaleyAuthority also supports multiple evaluation and ruleflow control strategies. The product lets you define, maintain and organize rules into rulesets or modules. Applicability conditions can be shared across rulesets easily by defining these at the module level. Priorities and applicability conditions may be applied at both the module and statement levels.

I think HaleyAuthority fits best into development environments where business experts or non-technical business analysts need to (and are available to) create, maintain or test the business rules that reflect evolving business policy. This is absolutely necessary when policies change rapidly and time to market may not be sacrificed to the application backlog. Where the users are too busy to maintain the rules themselves, it is less suitable.

5.2.3 JRules

ILOG's JRules is a platform for designing, implementing and managing the business logic incorporated in enterprise applications. It is the Java version of an older (and almost certainly slightly faster) library of inferencing and rules management components written in C++. It has a long and respectable history and is by now a robust and reliable offering. It runs on any platform with an appropriate Java virtual machine.

The architecture integrates comprehensive environments for business rule authoring and management, business rule application development, managed rule execution and business rule testing and simulation. It caters to developers, by enabling them to develop Java applications using their existing application development skills. Developers can combine rule-based and object-oriented programming to add business rule processing capabilities to new and existing applications. It caters to policy managers, by letting them manage their rules, once these are developed, and resources as the business evolves, and without recourse to IT.

JRules 6 has four modules:

- **Rule Team Server** (RTS) is a scalable rule management server and repository with a collaborative web environment for authoring, managing, validating, and deploying business rules. It is designed for policy managers (non-technical business experts) and offers features to control permissions, rule level locking during editing, rule history and versioning, as well as the ability to freeze a set of rules and rollback rule versions to this saved state.

- **Rule Studio** is an integrated development environment (IDE) for rule applications that integrates directly into the Eclipse family of integrated development environments, including Eclipse, IBM Rational Application Developer and ISM Rational Software Architect. It provides rule and application development tools with which one may create and manage the rule vocabulary, business and execution object models and the mappings between them, write, test and deploy business rules and graphical artifacts (decision trees and ruleflows) and debug Java code and business rules, all within the same environment. Rule Studio supports deploying and debugging rulesets to the Rule Execution Server and enables collaboration with business rule authors through its integration with Rule Team Server.

- **The Rule Execution Server** (RES) is a J2SE and J2EE-compliant execution environment for deploying business rule SOA services to web and application servers from IBM, BEA, JBoss, Oracle, and Apache. It includes components for synchronous, asynchronous and web service based invocation of business rules and includes a web administration console. Rule Execution Server is integrated with Rule Studio and Rule Team Server to support business rule deployment intended for both developers and policy managers.

- Lastly, the **Rule Scenario Manager** provides ruleset testing and business simulation capabilities. It provides an integrated environment in which the correctness of rules can be verified and wherein changes in business policy can be simulated. Designed for customization, it can be tailored to enterprise data stores, deployment processes and reporting requirements.

Rule Studio is a single environment for modelling, coding, debugging and deploying rule applications, integrated into Eclipse. Developers and architects familiar with Eclipse will thus benefit from a shortened learning curve. System administrators and operations managers deploy, monitor and manage business rule executions through the JRules administration web console, or via standards-based connectivity to enterprise system management tools such as IBM's Tivoli or HP's OpenView.

The modular architecture of Version 6 of JRules, illustrated in Figure 5.5, supports a business rule management cycle that is independent of application

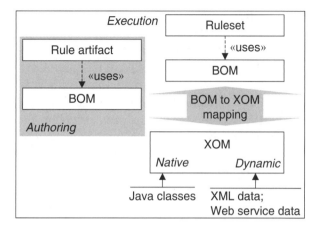

Figure 5-5 JRules architecture.

development cycles, but still allows synchronization between business rule management and application development. Applications can be deployed as stand-alone desktop applications or mid-tier services within a service-oriented architecture (SOA), or as web services. The reliance on Java, while making the technical level of the product higher, allows developers to control the granularity of their components so that architects can design applications or services around the requirements, rather than around the BRMS, as may be useful in some circumstances. JRules is built on a set of Java foundation classes that provide application programming interfaces (APIs), allowing customization of every aspect of a business rule application.

JRules supports development teams of any size through integration with any Eclipse supported source code control (SCC) system. In the execution environment, support for clusters of execution servers provides horizontal scalability.

As with all genuine BRMSs, the rule engine separates business rules from the rest of the source code, executes them (after transformation into executable form) and manages them within the BRMS.

In older versions, the developer approached the product using an authoring and testing environment called Rule Builder. From Version 6.0, this is replaced by a customized version of the Eclipse IDE: Rule Studio for Java. These provide a graphical user interface (GUI) and several editors to write business rules and create a business object model (BOM). The BOM classes map the natural language syntax of the business rules to the underlying application objects, which can be in Java, XML, or exposed as Web services. Rather than a classical repository (to store, organize and manage the rules) JRules generates a series of files that persist in the ILOG projects added to Eclipse. These files can then be checked in to the same source code control (SCC) tool the development team is using for their other code. The SCC tool becomes the repository.

Then an object model must be created, either by defining a business object model (BOM) or a Java object model (or importing an existing one). This is a necessary precursor to writing rules. The repository is accessed using Rule Team Server or may be queried using SQL. RTS has its own DBMS-based repository, which is the repository of record for JRules rule artifacts. New projects are published to RTS from Rule Studio through the RuleSync feature. Then RuleSync keeps the two versions of the project synchronized on demand. This is really quite an impressive innovation: two separate repositories for two separate environments, synchronized on demand.

JRules provides a repository in which to organize and store the rules and a rule engine to execute them. From Version 6 the rule engine is considered a still vital but less visible component of the BRMS. The Rule Execution Server is the focal point for execution. RES provides a managed execution environment, handling pools of engines running multiple heterogeneous rulesets, all remotely monitored and controlled. The managed execution environment is a must-have for some of ILOG's larger customers, who expect the same visibility and control for rule execution in the production environment that they get for other components running on their application servers. Rule projects are persisted in the file system by Rule Studio. This enables full integration with a source code control repository for versioning and collaboration. Rule projects that have been published to Rule Team Server, from Rule Studio, are then persisted in the database layer of Rule Team Server. Applications that have been deployed to Rule Execution Server are persisted in the persistence layer.

A JRules application consists of objects (classes and their instances) and rules. Objects have attributes and methods. Only instances are stored in working memory (because, in Java and C++, classes are not objects). Rules refer to these. Related rules are grouped into rulesets. Rulesets are related to working memory by a JRules 'context', which also holds the current state of the inference process (the 'agenda'). Inference is standard rete forward chaining: execute all applicable rules, remove fired rules from the agenda and then loop until no new applicable rules exist.

Rules are then created, numbered and named. A standard if/then syntax is simplified by making relational operators and connective phrases, such as 'less than or equal to' and '[if] all of the following conditions are true', available from pop-up menus.

There are several rules languages to choose from when writing rules that can then access objects in working memory:

- The BAL (Business Action Language) is a general purpose business rule language with a syntax close to natural language. The BAL is designed to cover most needs when writing business rules.
- Decision tables, which are rules composed of rows and columns and used to lay out in tabular form all possible situations that a business

decision may encounter. The actions to be taken in each of these situations are specified.

- Decision trees, the graphical equivalent of decision tables.

- The ILOG Rule Language (IRL) is the language that can be directly executed by the rule engine. The IRL has a Java-like syntax and is mostly used by developers. Business rule languages, like the BAL or the TRL, can be used by a developer to write rules. These are then translated to IRL.

- The Technical Rule Language (TRL), which is a syntax driven form of the ILOG Rule Language (IRL), and mainly of use to developers. From Version 6.0, TRL is superceded by a version of IRL that operates directly on the BOM. Most users will not be aware that TRL even exists.

JRules provides support for creating a customizable business rule language, using its Business Rule Language Definition Framework (BRLDF). This enables languages to be defined in XML files. The Business Rule Language Definition Framework (BRLDF) can be used to develop a custom business rule language. The BRLDF sits on top of the token model, which can be used for advanced customization. It seems to us that there is a considerable amount of effort involved in creating a custom business rule language.

The relationships among these rule languages are shown in Figure 5.6.

The Business Object Model is translated into the XOM (eXecution Object Model) which can access Java instances and XML data. The rule engine works on this. To write business rules in Rule Studio you must first have a BOM defined. Alternatively, ILOG Rule Language (IRL) can be used by developers. The BOM defines the classes and methods to which the business rules will be

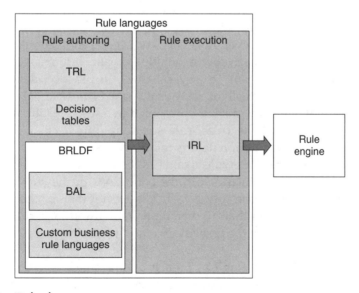

Figure 5-6   JRules languages.

applied and maps the 'natural language' syntax of the business rule language to these classes.

Based upon my experience, the skills needed to use the business rule language are beyond those of a typical knowledge engineer, business analyst or policy manager – unless that person is closely coupled with an IT developer, who must continually be on hand to change the BOM in advance of authoring or updating the rules.

When the business rules have been written and tested they are translated into ILOG Rule Language, which is the language understood by the rule engine. During the translation of business rules into execution rules, the BOM classes are translated into XOM classes. Execution rules are business rules that have been translated into IRL for execution in the rule engine.

The classes available to the rule engine in the XOM and can be dynamic or native in nature. The XOM classes are said to be **native** if they originate from an existing Java object model or **dynamic** if they originate from XML schemas or Web service schemas. To execute a ruleset, it must first be parsed by a rule engine instance. The XOM classes provide the rule engine with the data required to evaluate the business rules.

Data sources to be converted into objects for inclusion in the XOM may be XML, a web service, Java objects, databases, or any combination of them.

There are good debugging facilities, and consistency checking features let the rule author identify broken or redundant rules. Rule templates are supported to aid rapid rule editing. A template can be based on any rule language, such as the BAL or the IRL. A template library contains a set of templates and a BOM that defines the vocabulary of these templates.

The product supports different policy and rule expression formats: if/then, constraints, declarative definitions. Rules can also be entered in the form of row-oriented decision tables, which is sometimes useful if the knowledge is presented in this way. However, not every knowledge engineer likes this form because of its 'verbosity': each row in a table is a rule, but a single rule (with ANDs or ORs) can correspond to several rows. In practice, decision tables get far too large to be practical for realistically sized rulebases. However, this feature is useful if one's raw data are presented in a suitable tabular form.

If you need to extract the rules, rule subsumption checks can be use to tidy them up. Rule subsumption detects relationships between rules and helps debug the rulebase. A business rule is said to subsume another if the conditions of the subsumed rule are included in the conditions of the subsuming rule. Thus, if the antecedent of one rule says 'if X is greater than 20 then do A' and another says 'if X is greater than 10 then do B', then the second rule subsumes the first. We need to correct the first rule to read 'if X is between 10 and 20 then do A'.

Rules can be written in English, French and Japanese and embedded in web services. There are good rule query facilities. Time related conditions and actions can be included in rules, but rule history information is limited. Once written, the rules can be deployed – using the APIs – to either J2EE or JSE environments.

On deployment, instances are inserted into working memory either using keywords within rules or from the application, using this kind of syntax:

```
mycontext.insert(customer);
```

To execute we need to call the following method on IlrContext object:

```
myContext.FireAllRules();
```

The rete algorithm and any custom code now handle the execution.

The repository handles versioning, permissions, change history, persistence and locking. It also provides a query service that allows one to query business rules using any rule property, including user-defined properties such as business rule author, effective/expiration date, and business rule status. You can also query on classes, attributes and methods referenced in the rules. Queries are written using the Business Query Language (BQL). BQL is a language derived from the BAL tailored for querying rules. BQL has SQL-like syntax. Standard management queries can be created.

Ruleflows allow the developer to define the execution order of rulesets. A ruleflow is defined by a diagram (reminiscent of a UML activity diagram) that defines a sequence of tasks (rulesets, other ruleflows or functions) that solve a particular problem or execute a business process. It consists of tasks and transitions between these that define their chaining. A transition can have a guard, which must be true for the transition to be allowed. Rule execution is controlled by task properties, which can be set by the user. These properties determine:

- the rule ordering, using static or dynamic priorities or following a user-defined sequence;
- the rule firing strategy (e.g. fire all eligible rules, or fire one rule and stop); and
- the execution algorithm (rete or sequential bytecode generation for optimal performance).

JRules conforms with current and emerging Object Management Group (OMG), Java Community Process (JCP), and World Wide Web Consortium (W3C) standards.

JRules is a sound product with a rich range of tools and features for developing business rules management systems. On a purely technical level, most business rule applications can be built using this product. However, it failed to pass my tests for usability by non-technical business analysts. Much of the documentation is largely written in terms that can only be fully appreciated by Java programmers. The business analyst is protected from this to some extent but, I feel, not nearly enough. In older versions of JRules the two rule languages and the translation between them was confusing for the analyst new to the product, as is the distinction between the BOM and XOM to this day. In other words, JRules sacrifices simplicity to its powerful architecture. Fortunately, from Version 6, the BAL can be used by both the technical and business teams. The IRL is still there but is unlikely to be used by new adopters.

JRules is most suitable for use within projects where considerable technical skills are on call. Even though business analysts can use elements of Rule Studio, to make this possible will require a significant amount of customization by IT professionals and a deal of tuition. To be fair, Rule Studio is intended for developers; it is RTS that is meant for business analysts and policy managers. Thus my remarks apply to rule creation rather than rule maintenance.

JRules will sit comfortably in developer-centric organizational cultures, especially where Java and J2EE constitutes the prevailing development environment and the flexibility offered by the open Java-based architecture is considered an important benefit. If users are to maintain the rules, the extra effort needed to customize the rule language using the BRLDF should be planned for.

Related ILOG Products

ILOG also supplies constraint logic programming tools. These are more specialist and aimed at a particular kind of artificial intelligence search problem where the knowledge is stored in the form of constraints. Inference then proceeds by backward chaining over the constraints and applying mathematical algorithms to search for feasible solutions. Typical applications include planning and scheduling, resource allocation, transport and logistics, and circuit design and verification. We do not consider constraint programming further in this book.

5.2.4   PegaRULES and Versata

PegaRULES from Pegasystems Inc is a BRMS with good Java integration and full repository management. In the same spirit as Blaze Advisor, it offers HTML-based rule forms to help build and maintain rules. It provides a standardized classification of rule types, including:

- declarative rules, which compute values or enforce constraints as data change;

- decision tree rules, which perform inference on if/then-type statements;

- integration and transformation rules that are intended to streamline interfaces to the legacy; and

- process rules to deal with the receiving, assignment, routing and tracking of work.

The rule engine is proprietary but, so far as I can establish, is similar to the rete-based approached of the other products covered here. One is a little sceptical when the company literature describes forward chaining as 'procedural logic', but the product has a reputation that belies this *faux pas*.

Valid and effective dates for rules may be specified.

PegaRULES comes from a business process modelling tradition, and one of the company's leading products is Process Commander, which is a BPM system built on top of and integrated with the PegaRULES rule engine, although most users use packaged applications rather than the raw Process Commander.

PegaRULES is worth considering, especially when a BPM application is contemplated.

Versata is another BRMS product that appears to meet most of our criteria, although only certain types of rules (decision rules) are subject to rete inferencing. Its focus is on database-oriented applications. In addition to decision rules, Versata defines three other kinds of rule:

- Process Rules describe sequences of activities or workflow. These rules are typically used to coordinate the work of people and systems in conjunction with the other rule types.

- Transaction Rules are mostly static, behavioural features of the underlying components and objects, used to automate business transactions. These rules represent constraints, derivations, validations and actions.

- Data Rules enforce database integrity under update and represent choices in respect of policies about persistence, caching, access, etc. Data rules should help to ensure consistency and optimization.

Like JRules, the development environment is built on top of the Eclipse IDE and provides Java-based development and interoperability with other Eclipse tools. It exploits the Eclipse Modelling Framework for metadata, and is compliant with the XML Metadata Interchange, making it possible to integrate with other corporate metadata. The workbench also contains tools such as Java editors and debuggers and integrates with source code control systems. The repository is centralized, and stores both rules and metadata required for rule development. It uses XML to help tool and model interoperability.

In common with many other BRMS products, Versata supports decision tables, English-like rule expression, and graphical workflow depictions.

Versata emphasize their database focus using a graphic similar to that shown in Figure 5.7, which treats data and transaction rules as distinctly non-inferential – an emphasis with both conceptual and performance implications. The implication is that only Versata covers all these kinds of rule. Of course, other vendors would counter by saying that there is no reason why data and transaction rules should not be treated as inference rules, and that

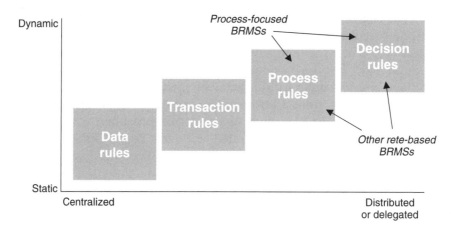

Figure 5-7 Versata rule types.

optimizations can overcome any performance problems. However, if your application is data-intensive (to use Versata's own phrase) there may be some advantage in keeping such rules conceptually separate.

5.3   A Simple Application

In this section we look at a small application designed to test the features typically required of a rule-based application. The sample application scenario is this. A life assurance company employs sales representatives who visit potential customers in their homes. The reps have laptops or PDAs on which they can perform various financial calculations to do with disposable income, requirements for retirement income, death benefit, school fees, marital outlays, etc. The problem is to add to this an application that can recommend the best type of product for a particular client, based on both the numerical data and more 'soft' factors, such as their personal aversion to or preference for taking risks with their money.

Here are the rules for our simplified life assurance advisory system as they might be in an actual business policy or requirements statement.

> *The system needs to recommend a best policy for each client.*
>
> *An annuity is best for clients that are retired and risk averse. An endowment policy is best for clients that are young and not averse to risk. An equity-linked policy is recommended if the client is a mature adult and is risk prone or at least neutral about risk. A bond-linked policy is recommended for a client that is averse to risk unless the client is retired. In any case, we assume that a client is averse to risk if the client has one or more children.*

It would normally be good practice to use a more consistent style and sentence structure. The second paragraph might be clearer if written as follows:

An Annuity is recommended for a client if the client is retired and is risk averse. An Endowment policy is recommended for a client if the client is young and is not averse to risk. An Equity linked policy is recommended for a client if the client is a mature adult and is prone to risk or is neutral about risk. A Bond linked policy is recommended for a client if the client is averse to risk unless the client is retired. A client is averse to risk if the client has children.

The classic approach is to invent some simple pseudocode, readily understandable to most technically savvy knowledge engineers, such as this:

```
Goal = Client.bestProduct
If Client.status is 'retired'
     and Client.preference is 'riskAverse'
     then Client.bestProduct is 'Annuity'
If Client.status is 'young'
     and Client.preference is not 'riskAverse'
     then Client.bestProduct is 'Endowment'
if Client.status is 'matureAdult'
     and Client.preference = 'riskProne' or
client.preference = 'riskNeutral'
        then Client.bestProduct is 'EquityLinked'
If Client.preference is 'riskAverse'
     then Client.bestProduct is 'BondLinked'
If Client.children: > 0
     then Client.preference is 'riskAverse'
```

Note that backward chaining will be required to resolve this ruleset. In a procedural language we would have to put the rule about children first, in order to avoid asking for preference unnecessarily.

Implicit in these rules is the ontology given by the UML type diagram in Figure 5.8. Note that the association is irrelevant to the ruleset, but that it implies a business process wherein, after advice is given, an actual policy may be purchased.

5.3.1 The Application in Blaze Advisor

First, we have to set up the types, as in Figure 5.8, but this is really easy to do. Here is how the rules came out in the Blaze Advisor SRL rule language:

```
if    client.status is retired
      and   client.preference is riskAverse
      then  {client.bestProduct is ''Annuity'', return
```

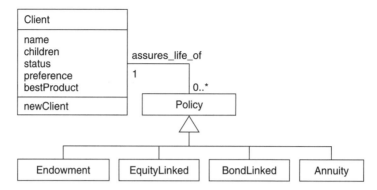

Figure 5-8 Vocabulary for the life assurance adviser ruleset.

```
client.bestProduct}.
if    client.status is young
      and   client.preference <> riskAverse
      then  {client.bestProduct is ''Endowment'', return
client.bestProduct}.
if    client.status is matureAdult
      and   (client.preference = riskProne or
client.preference = riskNeutral)
      then  {client.bestProduct is ''EquityLinked'',
return client.bestProduct}.
if    client.preference is riskAverse
      then  {client.bestProduct is ''BondLinked'', return
client.bestProduct}.
if    client.children > 0
      then  client.preference is riskAverse.
```

Note that the syntax is quite a long way away from our original statement of the rules in English. However, it is only little changed from my crude pseudocode, except for the need to include the return statements. It looks a little more like a programming language than the original; but it is a fairly easy language to learn for a technically competent knowledge engineer or business analyst. Using SRL's alternative syntax would also have allowed me to write in a different style, for example:

```
if    client's status is retired
      and   client's preference is riskAverse
      then  {client's bestProduct is ''Annuity'',
      return client's bestProduct}.
```

There are still five rules. The equivalent of the goal statement is two 'event rules' as follows:

```
event rule getStatus is
```

```
whenever status of a Client is needed do { it.status =
promptEnumerationItem(status, ''What is the client's
status?'')}

event rule getChildrenNumber is
whenever children of a Client is needed do {
it.children = promptInteger( ''How many children has the
client?'')}

event rule getPreference is
whenever preference of a Client is needed do {
it.preference = promptEnumerationItem(preference,''What
is the client's risk preference?'')
```

The 'it' object is the current instance (this in Java; self in Smalltalk). This is looking a bit like programming but it's not that frightening. Of course, we had to create the attributes of a Client class and two enumeration lists. The only other programming was the creation of a main routine to test the rule execution. Here it is:

```
client is a Client.
print (''A few questions about the life to be
assured...'').
      client.bestProduct = apply matchingRules(client).
print (''The best product for this client is ''
client.bestProduct).
```

Here are the results of test executions, showing that backward chaining is working exactly as expected:

```
A few questions about the life to be assured...
Question: What is the client's status?
Answer: retired
Question: What is the client's risk preference?
Answer: riskAverse
The best product for this client is Annuity

A few questions about the life to be assured...
Question: What is the client's status?
Answer: matureAdult
Question: What is the client's risk preference?
Answer: dontKnow
Question: How many children has the client?
Answer: 2.0
The best product for this client is BondLinked

A few questions about the life to be assured...
Question: What is the client's status?
```

```
Answer: matureAdult
Question: What is the client's risk preference?
Answer: riskNeutral
The best product for this client is EquityLinked

A few questions about the life to be assured...
Question: What is the client's status?
Answer: retired
Question: What is the client's risk preference?
Answer: riskProne
Question: How many children has the client?
Answer: 0.0
The best product for this client is unavailable
```

The last result merely shows that the ruleset does not cover the state space and that more rules would be needed in a live application.

However, it should be noted that rules 2 to 3 were given a higher priority than rules 1 and 4. If we relax this and also move rule 4 to the beginning of the list of rules, then rule 4 fires first and we get an erroneous result of BondLinked for a retired and risk averse client. In other words, rule order can have an effect that may not be obvious prior to debugging. Against this, the ability to assign priorities to individual rules is a powerful tool in the hands of analysts who know what they are doing.

5.3.2   The Application in HaleyAuthority

The approach of HaleyAuthority is quite different, in that one can start with writing the rules and work back to the ontology. Also, the rules come out in much plainer English. One is able to write statements as sentences almost identical to the more structured version of the original policy. My first version came out like this:

BestProductRules
Statements:

```
An Annuity is recommended for a client only if the client
      is averse to risk and the client is retired
An Endowment policy is recommended for a client only if the
      client is young and the client is not averse to risk
An Equity linked policy is recommended for a client only if
      the client is a mature adult and the client is prone
      to risk or is neutral about risk
A Bond linked policy is recommended for a client if the
      client is averse to risk unless the client is retired
A client is averse to risk if the client has children
```

As I familiarized myself with the product, I soon discovered a more structured way to write and present the rules, as follows:

BestProductRules
Statements:

```
An Annuity is recommended for a client
     only if : the client is retired
     only if : the client is averse to risk
An Endowment policy is recommended for a client
     only if : the client is young
     only if : the client is not averse to risk
An Equity linked policy is recommended for a~client
     only if : the client is a mature adult
     only if : the client is prone to risk or is neutral
     about risk
A Bond linked policy is recommended for a client
     if : the client is averse to risk
     unless : the client is retired
A client is averse to risk
     if : the client has children
```

We have used the 'applicability condition' rule style here. There are three kinds of applicability condition: 'if' conditions are OR-ed and 'only if' conditions AND-ed. 'Unless' conditions are self-explanatory and help to make rulesets (modules) more concise.

Realizing this I went back to Blaze Advisor and corrected one of my rules to read as follows:

```
if      client.preference is riskAverse
        and client.status is not retired
then    {client.bestProduct is ''BondLinked'', return
        client.bestProduct}.
```

The and/not construction is used here instead of 'unless'.

As explained in Chapter 6, writing rules in HaleyAuthority is guided by Haley's knowledge acquisition method:

1. Identify the decisions to be made;
2. For each decision write the policies or rule logic and indicate any exceptions or qualifications;
3. Define the business vocabulary and phrasings that HaleyAuthority needs to know about in order to understand and interpret the rules that you have defined;
4. Test and simulate your rules incrementally as you go.

This makes the applicability condition style very natural.

Note that the first rule can also be written (as above) as:

```
An annuity is recommended for a client if the client
        is averse to risk and the client is retired
```

In fact, if you type this in, HaleyAuthority suggests the next permissible words as you type.

Rule execution transcripts for a few test cases were put out by the system as follows:

```
Test Case: Clapton
Execute: condition 10: the client is a mature adult.
Execute: condition 11: the client is prone to risk or is
neutral about risk.
Execute: statement 9: An Equity linked policy is recommended for a client.

Test Case: Idle
Execute: condition 4: the client is retired.
Execute: condition 15: the client has children.
Execute: statement 14: A client is averse to risk.
Explanation: [client] 32 is averse to risk
Execute: condition 17: the client is averse to risk.
Execute: condition 20: the client is retired.
Execute: condition 5: the client is averse to risk.
Execute: statement 3: An Annuity is recommended for a client.

Test Case: Jong
Execute: condition 7: the client is young.
Execute: condition 17: the client is averse to risk.
Execute: statement 12: A Bond linked policy is recommended for a client.

Test Case: Leach
Execute: condition 4: the client is retired.
Execute: condition 5: the client is averse to risk.
Execute: condition 17: the client is averse to risk.
Execute: condition 20: the client is retired.
Execute: statement 3: An Annuity is recommended for a client.

Test Case: Redhand
Execute: condition 7: the client is young.
Execute: condition 8: the client is not averse to risk.
Execute: statement 6: An Endowment policy is recommended for a client.
```

All the results are as expected.

In many BRMS products, priorities can be set for rule modules. This enables the analysts to control the order of execution. In Blaze Advisor, for example, priorities can be set at the individual rule level, giving some finer control but at the risk of complexity. To do this in HaleyAuthority, one has to write rules about the priorities in the same natural language style as the main rules. One approach to this, in the above example, is as follows. First, deduce possible or allowable conclusions and then write explicit policies about such preferences. Another approach is to use unless conditions, but still using a representation that is aware of preferences.

The first approach might write policies such as 'An annuity may be (could be) recommended for a client'. Subsequent policies may state:

```
A bond linked policy is recommended for a client
    only if: An annuity may not be recommended for the
client
    only if: A bond linked policy may be recommended to
a client
```

The second approach would generalize to the understanding that certain products are preferred to others, but still distinguishes between what 'may be' and what 'is'. For example:

```
An annuity is preferred to a bond linked policy
    if: An annuity may be recommended for a client
A product is recommended to a client
    only if: the product may be recommended for the client
    only if: no product is preferred to the first product
```

Either of these approaches may be employed to convey the additional desired knowledge that certain products are 'more applicable' or 'preferable' under certain circumstances. The approach is slightly wordy but very clear in meaning and less prone to error.

5.3.3 The Application in JRules

To set up the same application in JRules required a little more effort and some knowledge of programming. JRules requires the creation of an object model as a pre-requisite to creating the rules. You can either import a Java or UML model to create an XOM or create the BOM classes and set their properties using the editor and wizards. This involves naming classes and attributes and providing more English-like alternative names or 'verbalizations'. This 'vocabulary' is automatically generated from the BOM and can then be manually adjusted to optimize the natural language 'look and feel'. Where an RMA might be required in Blaze Advisor, this gives the option of a readily readable and customizable natural-language-like rule syntax. It was quite easy to create the six objects of Figure 5.8 and the attributes of Client. The rules can now be written using a 'guided' editor. This produced errors in relation to the subtypes of Policy, until I went back and declared the four policy types as *members* of Policy and gave the latter a domain of type 'static references'. Then I had to declare each of these members as 'static' and 'final'. Then my rules compiled. Here's how they came out:

```
if the status of the client is "Retired"
    and the preference of the client is "Risk Averse"
    then set the best product of the client to Annuity;
if all of the following conditions are true :
    - the status of the client  is "Young"
    - the preference of the client is not "Risk Averse"
    then
    set the best product of the client to Endowment;
if the status of the client is "Mature Adult"
    and any of the following conditions is true :
    - the preference of the client is "Risk Prone"
    - the preference of the client is "Risk Neutral"
    then
    set the best product of the client to EquityLinked;
if the preference of the client is "Risk Averse"
    then set the best product of the client to BondLinked;
if the children of the client is more than 0
    then set the preference of the client to "Risk Averse";
```

Note the variation in rule style, which I have done to show what is possible rather than to illustrate good style. Note also the terminating semicolons; they are necessary – just like in Java! In Rule Team Server the situation is better; the semicolons are invisible when authoring rule artifacts.

As with Blaze Advisor, testing the rules required writing a main routine; but the syntax of Java was needed to create test instances using the Java 'new' keyword. There is another way to do this, involving use of an 'assert' dialogue to set up attribute values. Individual rules can be tested in Rule Studio without the need to deploy them, but there must be a XOM present to do this. After my tests, all the results came out as expected.

By this point, I had formed a number of impressions about JRules. It was clearly up to doing the job I had in mind. I could see that, with sufficient effort, I could build sophisticated and complex applications. Though not quite natural language, the rules looked a bit friendlier than they did in the Blaze Advisor SRL but the object model looked a bit more complex, which the need to use terms like 'static' and 'final'. And there was no way to avoid building a XOM, which requires some knowledge of Java. This wasn't a tool that you could just give to non-technical people. Even with the advantage of the UML graphical editor (which none of the other products boast), only someone who was comfortable with Java would take to it naturally. For a typical business analyst, set up time would be longer than that with Blaze Advisor or, indeed, HaleyAuthority. On the other hand for a Java developer, the environment is natural and very friendly.

5.4   Usability Issues

Usability is as important for business rules applications as it is for any other kind of application. As always the user experience will be improved by the use of strong metaphors and the illusion of direct manipulation of objects. Metaphors like the desktop or filing cabinets still work. Standard and custom icons can still be used to represent objects. Bear in mind that the user must be able to learn by exploration, and that the interface should be consistent both across this application and with other applications in use.

It is in the area of consistency where BRMS interfaces raise some special issues. We must write rules in a consistent and understandable style. The way the interface works will depend to the product(s) you have selected. In Blaze Advisor you will probably use an RMA to control much user interaction. Therefore, plan to spend some time on the usability design and testing of your RMAs. In Haley Authority you will pay more attention to interacting via the rules themselves. In JRules you may also create Java applications to handle interactions, giving you great freedom to design. ILOG's new verbalization technology, which helps generate a vocabulary of natural-language business terms from the business object model, also allows users of the Rule Team Server to interact directly with the rules.

Products, such as JRules and Versata, that use Eclipse as their IDE benefit from transfer effects when used by developers already familiar with Eclipse. For example, JRules Rule Studio plug-ins for Eclipse adhere strictly to the default style and usage patterns defined by Eclipse.org.

In any case, base error messages on the rules that you have stored. Try to base other interactions on the rules too. Try to use grammatically correct forms of language. Avoid acronyms and abbreviations; they slow the reader. If possible, use (good) punctuation; it too speeds reading and removes ambiguity.

Usability must be tested. Set time and resources aside for this too.

A few of the patterns in Chapter 7 refer to usability issues.

5.5   Summary

Modern BRMS products separate rules from application code and store them in a repository. A separate inference engine can be applied to chain the rules together and deduce new facts. Procedures may also be stored as rules in the repository. Most products allow rules to be phrased in ways different from the standard if . . . then . . . form. Products vary in the degree to which rules can be expressed in a form close to natural language. Some offer alternative ways for users to author rules, often using devices like web forms.

A good BRMS should:

- allow business analysts to create and modify the rules;

- use a fully-featured repository;
- support backward chaining;
- allow the rule engine to be a component or service within larger applications;
- allow applications to be deployed in a service oriented architecture;
- focus on business rules management (as opposed to just workflow) problems;
- provide good report generation facilities;
- provide evidence of successful commercial applications;
- be compatible with a component-based or service-oriented architecture; and
- offer commercial-standard professional support.

Most products offer facilities for rule syntax checking, rule templates, ruleflows and decision tables; some also offer equivalent decision trees. All products support forward chaining inference, most of them utilizing some version of the rete algorithm; most also support backward and mixed chaining. No current major BRMS product offers sophisticated uncertainty management or inference under uncertainty. It is quite hard to design completely general-purpose user-friendly explanation and help facilities, though this can be done with many products.

Of the dozen or so available BRMS offerings, we have looked at only a few in any detail. What emerged was that different products are suitable in different organizational cultures and application development scenarios. Products must be evaluated in the light of this, as explained further in Appendix B.

Usability is as important for business rules applications as it is for any other kind of application .

5.6   Bibliographical Notes

Up to date information on BRMS products may be found on the various companies' websites and in the reports of industry analysts.

Development Methods

You know my methods. Apply them.
Sir Arthur Conan Doyle *(The Sign of Four)*

Adopters of BRMS technology are well advised to follow documented development methods. There are two particularly significant areas where methods are important in this context: methods for knowledge acquisition and analysis; and methods for component, service and system development. In addition, standards are now emerging concerning the style in which rules are to be written.

6.1   Knowledge Acquisition and Analysis

Just as requirements engineering is both difficult and critical for the success of any computer system, one of the hardest and most crucial problems in the development of rule-based systems is knowledge acquisition: the process of discovering the knowledge assets of the organization. These may be found in documentation, but are often locked up in the heads of domain experts and other staff. Business analysts will need to learn a repertoire of knowledge elicitation techniques to implement BRMSs successfully.

There are several informal knowledge acquisition techniques that have been used successfully:

- *Informal, structured and focused interviews*. Informal interviews are the most obviously straightforward type of knowledge elicitation procedures. However, their lack of structure can be wasteful of time, so

143

that advance preparation can pay dividends. This leads to the notion of structured and focused interviews, wherein there is more of a plan. However, experience has shown that in informal interviews, the meeting often seems to be going badly until a critical point is reached. Then a great deal of knowledge pours forth in the last 10% of the available time. This shows that relaxing the interviewee is as important as preparation, and that one must always be prepared for the unexpected.

- *Presentations by experts.*

- *Verbal protocols* are transcripts (written or taped) of sessions wherein the analyst asks a domain expert what she is doing and why. The situation should be a natural one for the expert and consumes minimal expert time. The method is particularly effective when cases have been selected in advance and can reveal considerable detail. However, the questioning can interfere with the task, especially if it is normally performed under pressure; the expert may adopt an uncharacteristically systematic approach. Also, it can take a long time to analyze the protocols. During analysis it is useful if the expert is available to clarify points that are not obvious from the transcripts.

- *Observational studies* can only be undertaken in certain circumstances, but do help the analyst to break free from preconceived ideas and find out what experts actually do, rather than what they say they do. They also provide information on the sequence in which activities or tasks are carried out, the rôles adopted by actors and any time constraints on tasks. On the down side, observational studies are time-consuming and expensive.

- *Questionnaires* are rarely used in knowledge elicitation exercises, but the (pseudo-) science of psychometrics places heavy reliance on the way that questionnaires objectify certain traits; so their use should not be ruled out, especially when expertise is widely distributed geographically. In the latter case, questionnaires may reveal local variations in the applicability of the rules or their BOUNDARY OF COMPETENCE (35). Normally a list of questions will be prepared as part of an interview plan anyway, and it may be useful to give experts advance notice of the questions – to allow preparation. If multiple users are to be consulted a questionnaire will save time, but this will only work if a few face-to-face sessions are carried out as well.

- *Simulation and prototyping.* One form of simulation has the expert pretend to be a machine in conversation with the analyst. In another, the expert sets problems for the team to solve, acting as experts under supervision. Or an artificial test case is fed gradually to an expert whose responses are carefully monitored. One of the aims of simulation is to overcome potential *post facto* rationalizations of knowledge; i.e. dissembling or saying that you did something for reasons that were not present in your mind at the time that you actually did it, but emerged as rational in hindsight. As BRMS products become more friendly and powerful, it becomes possible to knock out quick prototype systems based on elicited rules. These can be shown to experts for comments. This usually reveals errors and omission more quickly and effectively than any amount of formal checking of paper-based models of the knowledge.

- *Introspection* – when the analyst asks 'How would I do that?'–is used as a last resort and has the obvious dangers.

- *Background reading* on the subject will almost always help, if only to familiarize analysts with the terminology of the domain. Sometimes, a great deal of the knowledge is available from written material such as procedure manuals, and these often contain many of the business rules in explicit form. Many analysts jump at the chance to build systems in this way. Of course, if you read (and practise) enough, you are on the way to your own expertise.

- *Becoming an expert yourself* is a viable option if the domain is not too esoteric or skill intensive.

There are also a few more formal techniques:

- *Probes* are open questions based on the question words: what, why, when, where, how and who. There are five types of probe. A **definitional** probe asks 'What is a … ?' A **directive** probe asks 'Why is that?' or uses the word 'how'. An **additive** probe is used when you say something like 'Go on.' A **mode change** probe could be a question like 'How would your colleagues view that?' or 'Can you give a more concrete/abstract example.' Mode change probes are thus all about scope, viewpoints and generalization (inheritance). A **reflective** probe involves saying the equivalent of 'What you're saying is … ' In that case you are far better off when the expert replies 'No, I didn't mean that.' A 'Yes' doesn't give you the chance to ask 'Why?'

- *Teachback* generalizes the reflective probe. The analyst absorbs knowledge from users, an expert or experts and then make a presentation of that knowledge to the people from whom it was elicited or their peers. The hope is that errors of understanding will be uncovered in this way.

- *Kelly grids* emerged from psychoanalytic studies of how people construe their personal situations. The main technique is rarely used and concerns how knowledge is ranked in terms of clarity or importance. However, there are subsidiary techniques that are very useful for eliciting the structure of object knowledge (laddering, triads) and revealing latent concepts in the ontology. (*Cf.* ASK FOR THE OPPOSITE (34).)

- *Data mining* or rule induction was mentioned in Chapter 4. It is very useful for eliciting business rules that are implicit in the history of transactions, especially when these have been recorded in a database. Induction can provide a useful 'first stab' at the rules, but depends on the analyst's ability to structure the problem well; i.e. to decide what the decision categories and significant variables are. The induced rules will usefully benefit from manual refinement and reorganization.

- *Workshops* generalize interviews and are generally to be preferred over them in terms of efficiency and thoroughness, as discussed in RUN A WORKSHOP (27).

Several of the above techniques are distilled into patterns in Chapter 7, notably patterns 25 to 35.

In general, no one technique will be enough on its own. A good analyst will bring a toolbox of techniques to every interview or workshop and be prepared to use the most appropriate ones.

Following knowledge elicitation, the analyst must produce a model of the knowledge, usually in the form of text and diagrams. The model will consist of a type model (the ontology) and rules organized into rulesets around the type model. There may also be decision trees and tables, activity diagrams, use case models and so on. Again, Chapter 7 contains several patterns to help with this organization. Here too prototyping may throw useful light on the model's completeness and correctness.

The whole process of knowledge elicitation and analysis is as much art as it is science. Perhaps in no cognate field of systems analysis will the cunning, creativity and insight of the analyst be tested so thoroughly.

None of the tools considered in Chapter 5 offer specific knowledge acquisition facilities, but the natural language facilities, of the products will help to widen the knowledge acquisition bottleneck. However, in each case, business analysts will still have to mine the object knowledge to create the object model.

Organizations adopting such products will almost certainly need training and – even better – mentoring on knowledge acquisition techniques. Proprietary and published knowledge acquisition methods, such as KADS (Gardner *et al.*, 1998), may be used.

Haley Systems publishes a knowledge acquisition method specific to HaleyAuthority. It includes advice and procedures for breaking the rules up into modules that I think could be better represented as patterns: DO THE ANALYSIS RULES BEFORE THE ACTION RULES, DO THE VALIDATION RULES EARLY ON, DISTINGUISH POSSIBLE FROM FINAL ACTIONS. I will subsume these under more general patterns: DEFINE A RULE-WRITING STYLE (23) and WRITE THE CONSEQUENT FIRST (24). The company recommends the following procedures.

1. Identify output decisions.
2. Create analysis statements that make recommendations in a medium priority module.
3. Create statements that lead to actions in a low priority module.

4. Create a module to handle exceptions in a high priority module.

5. Write applicability conditions for each module, showing the circumstances under which each conclusion is true.

6. Ensure that the conditions match the consequences of other rules where appropriate.

Writing rules in HaleyAuthority is also guided by Haley's knowledge acquisition method:

1. Identify the decisions to be made;

2. For each decision write the policies or rule logic and indicate any exceptions or qualifications;

3. Define the business vocabulary and phrasings that HaleyAuthority needs to know about in order to understand and interpret the rules that you have defined;

4. Test and simulate your rules incrementally as you go.

This makes the applicability condition style very natural. This method leads to a natural order of questioning domain experts. It could be used in conjunction with almost any BRMS.

We have considered knowledge elicitation and knowledge analysis from the viewpoint of extracting and structuring rules around a type model or ontology. Another aspect of knowledge analysis concerns the type of inference (if any) that will be used to chain the rules together.

It is important that the analyst understands how the rules will be used in groups; i.e. what kind of problem is being solved. The use case analysis should reveal tasks of the 'solve problem' type. The way you interrogate experts will vary according to the problem type. The KADS method (Gardner *et al.*, 1998) identifies over twenty different problem types and supplies flowcharts to guide knowledge acquisition for each one of them. The problem types include analysis types and synthesis types. Analysis types involve the manipulation of existing data or concepts, so that new components may be derived of new relationships discovered. Examples of analysis types include:

- classification problems;
- suitability assessment;
- alarm monitoring;
- fault diagnosis; and (closed related to diagnosis)
- repair.

Synthesis types aim to generate new concepts or components from applying the rules. Typical of these are:

- planning (e.g. creating a school timetable or meeting schedule);
- electronic circuit or computer network design;
- configuration; and (arguably)
- forecasting.

The problem type will not only affect the method of knowledge acquisition, but may also give a guide as to the type of chaining that will be the most appropriate inference method. To over-simplify, analysis problem types tend to indicate backward chaining as the primary inference method, while synthesis types point to forward chaining.

Figure 6-1 shows, as an example, the KADS problem solving template for the problem type it calls 'heuristic classification': classification where rules of thumb are used. The bubbles are knowledge acquisition processes and the rectangles are artifacts used or produced by the processes.

Determining the inference method involved in solving a problem implicitly involves choosing the logic to be used. The conventional assumption is that FOPC is the logic, whether the inference method is forward or backward chaining. However, when uncertainty is present in the problem or the rules, this may not be the case. Perhaps a modal, deontic or temporal logic is needed to describe the problem solving strategy adequately. Or perhaps even fuzzy logic would be better. The classic application of fuzzy logic is process control, although it has application to various business decision problems. Not only is the inference method of fuzzy logic quite different from FOPC. The rule of inference (fuzzy *modus ponens*) is different from standard *modus ponens* and forward chaining is a one-shot affair; i.e. all the rules fire in parallel; so that the efficiencies of the rete algorithm are quite irrelevant. Furthermore, the defuzzification step of the inference method used for process control is different to the one used for business decision-making applications.

These questions are addressed by patterns 36 to 38 in the RulePatterns language presented in Chapter 7.

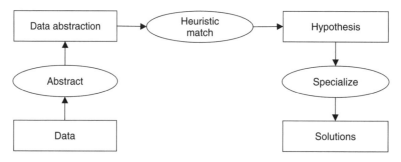

Figure 6-1   A KADS problem solving template.

6.2   System Development

It is not the purpose of this book to regurgitate all the good advice about systems development methods published elsewhere. However, I do want to emphasize that a business rules application needs to apply such methods just as rigorously as any other project.

All the BRMS products we have covered are compatible with published system development methods and we think that, in general, they are more compatible with agile methods. Within such methods, a microprocess for component based development is beneficial and we recommend Catalysis™ for this purpose (D'Souza and Wills, 1999). Any adopted method must also include a knowledge acquisition component.

The earlier patterns in the RulePatterns language distil an agile approach to system development that is compatible with BRMS development. The chiefest relevant patterns are as follows:

- ESTABLISH THE BUSINESS OBJECTIVES (1).
- BUSINESS PROCESS MODEL (2).
- ESTABLISH THE USE CASES (3) [includes Catalysis techniques].
- BUILD A TYPE MODEL (ONTOLOGY) (4) [includes Catalysis techniques].
- DISCOVER BUSINESS RULES (5).
- USER CENTRED SERVICE STRUCTURE (6) [SOA focused projects].
- TIMEBOXES (7).
- GRADUAL STIFFENING (8).
- AUTOMATED TESTING (9) [XP influenced].

Strong involvement by business users militates against developer-centric methods such as RUP or XP. However, taking good ideas and fragments from these methods may well be appropriate. For example, we like the XP-like idea of writing test cases for every ruleset and using the tests to control system evolution. Also, the choice of product will affect the method selected. The method appropriate for a business rules management system like Blaze Advisor or JRules proceeds as follows:

1. Knowledge acquisition
2. Translation of policy into rule format
3. Programming the application
4. Validation
5. Programming the environment (glue code)
6. Production.

HaleyAuthority eliminates some of these steps using automatic .NET or Java code generation from the rules, as follows:

1. Knowledge acquisition

2. Validation

3. Programming the environment (glue code)

4. Production.

Once again, we see the strengths of systems like HaleyAuthority in non-developer-centric cultures. In other cultures, the abbreviated method may throw up problems.

If using Versata, Sapiens or similar, one might well proceed from an initial data modelling exercise and structure the knowledge acquisition around that model, as recommended by Date (2000).

The repository must record the rule authors and maintain permissions. You would not create a database application and then allow any Tom, Dick or Harry to change the data it stores or alter the schema. If the business rules are hidden in the application code then it is normal to put that code under source code control to prevent unauthorized updates. But if the rules are stored separately and in smaller chunks than would be the case for a conventional application, then the rules or rulesets need to have identified owners who are responsible for making or authorizing changes. At a minimum, one must assign a knowledge base administrator and set up review and authorization procedures involving rule authors. See DETERMINE OWNERSHIP AND PERMISSIONS (22) and CHOOSE RULE MAINTENANCE RÉGIME (40) in Chapter 7.

6.3   Halle's Guidelines

Barbara von Halle (2002) is the most notable author to have presented a complete system development method aimed at BRMS projects. Her method consists in a six-phase waterfall that can be 'done incrementally'. Its phases are Scope, Plan, Discover, Analyze, Design and Deliver. Orthogonal to these phases are four 'tracks': Technology (i.e. technical architecture), Process (i.e. use cases, business processes, etc.), Rules and Data. Within the data track things like the ontology are established as well as any underlying databases or mappings to existing systems. Each phase is divided into detailed task-like steps. Most usefully, each step contains one or more pattern-like 'guidelines'. For example, The 'do initial research' step of Scoping contains a guideline that says 'Consider reading the last two years' annual reports'.

The Analyze phase is broken down into subphases for analyzing data, rules and processes. In rule analysis we have steps like 'make each rule atomic' with the guideline 'make sure each rule has only one result'. This, of course, may not be the most natural thing to do when a rule triggers multiple procedures; but it does suggest a good discipline. It is for this reason that I suggest that the guidelines are pattern-like; they may be ignored if the circumstances (the context) justify it. Many of Halle's guidelines for rule analysis overlap the advice on rule style discussed in Section 6.4.

Halle's method differs from other methods in several ways. Of course, rule execution is separated from applications and core process flows, and rules and processes are thus much easier to change. She sees pulling out rule considerations from those concerning data and applications as a benefit, whereas I think there are cons as well as pros, especially in relation to data. While the separate focus on rules (as opposed to applications) *must* be beneficial, developing the ontology separately from the rules may be fraught with dangers: notably the danger of basing the rules on an inadequate component (and therefore service) model – which often is a legacy model. Another difference is an emphasis on wrapping core process flows around rule dependencies; the idea of which is to help refine and vary the sequences of user interactions based on the rule dependencies.

Halle's method is a very valuable contribution, and especially so for its guidelines, but there is a lot of it to read. It lacks, somehow, a notion of *saliency* and may appeal to the sort of management that places more emphasis on having a detailed, fully documented system development method than on instilling good but simple principles into the members of development teams. One motivation for this book is to present the simplest possible guidelines for developing a BRMS. This is not to say that the reader will not benefit from reading Halle's excellent book (I have not reproduced every jot and tittle of its advice herein), but that the pattern format is more readily memorable.

The method contains most valuable advice under the heading of rule management. As an example of how such advice can be 'patternated', CHOOSE RULE MAINTENANCE RÉGIME (40) is an attempt at a condensation of this guidance.

6.4   Rule Style Guidance

There are two well-known published sources offer advice on rule writing style: Morgan (2002) and Ross (2003). Their advice is distilled in pattern 23, in the next chapter.

Ross categorizes rules into rejecters, permissions, producers and projectors. Rejecters address database integrity and disallow any action that violates them in real time. Permissions are merely their flip side. Producers, by contrast, derive new data when an action or event occurs. Ross sees this kind of rule as a function or computation, as opposed to an inference. He calls inferences and triggers 'projectors'. A fourth category, 'suggesters', involves relaxing the hard-and-fast nature of rules; such rules delegate to humans the authority to decide if a rule applies.

Ross's guidelines may be summarized as follows.

- Rules must be unambiguous and refer to the vocabulary (terms and facts). [Lots of his rules are special cases of this one.]
- Rules should be non-procedural and avoid references to how, when and where the rule is enforced or to who enforces it.
- A rule should be clearly written and possible to achieve.
- No redundant words (fluff).
- Remove plural nouns, events as subjects and imperatives.
- Write the consequent first instead of starting with 'if'.
- Avoid ands and ors. [See below.]
- Write computations as separate rules and break down rules with complex logic.

RuleSpeak builds on these principles and Ross's classification by providing a set of rule templates or sentence patterns. These patterns mandate that rules should use a certain restricted vocabulary; so that the word 'must' appears somewhere in every rejecter rule, as does 'may' in every permission rule. Logical connectives (and/or) are avoided in favour of constructions like 'one/all of the following are true'. Recall from Chapter 5, how JRules supports this idea. RuleSpeak nominates specific words to deal with time, such as 'before' and 'by'.

RuleSpeak also includes guidance on when and when not to use decision tables.

Morgan also provides dos and don'ts and rule templates. He divides rules into computations, basic constraints and list constraints. In addition, he gives templates for definitions (classifications and enumerations). Of course, his guidance on rule construction overlaps with Ross's to some extent. It may be summarized as follows.

- Rules must be unambiguous and refer to the vocabulary (terms and facts).
- Write computations as separate rules and break down rules with complex logic.
- Define terms exactly (not too widely or narrowly).
- Make associations explicit, as in 'Every project should *be managed by* a project manager.'
- Avoid vague phrasings such as 'there may be . . .'
- Don't use permissions.
- Avoid padding. [Same as no redundant words.]
- Write the consequent first instead of starting with 'if'.

- Avoid ands and ors.
- Remove plural nouns, events as subjects and imperatives.
- Rules should be non-procedural and avoid references to how, when and where the rule is enforced or to who enforces it.
- A rule should be clearly written and possible to achieve.
- Look out for rules that overlap, duplicate or merely rephrase each other.

Patterns 21, 23 and 24 in Chapter 7 refer to the above guidance more or less obliquely.

In Section 5.3, we saw that there was a range of options for expressing the following rule statement concerning a simplified life assurance advisory system.

The system needs to recommend a best policy for each client.

An Annuity is best for clients that are retired and risk averse. An Endowment policy is best for clients that are young and not averse to risk. An Equity linked policy is recommended if the client is a mature adult and is risk prone or at least neutral about risk. A Bond linked policy is recommended for a client that is averse to risk unless the client is retired. In any case, we assume that a client is averse to risk if the client has one or more children.

First we moved to a more consistent style and sentence structure, as follows.

An Annuity is recommended for a client if the client is retired and is risk averse. An Endowment policy is recommended for a client if the client is young and is not averse to risk. An Equity linked policy is recommended for a client if the client is a mature adult and is prone to risk or is neutral about risk. A Bond linked policy is recommended for a client if the client is averse to risk unless the client is retired. A client is averse to risk if the client has children.

Then we wrote the rules in a vendor neutral style using the 'consequence first' styles recommended *inter alia* by Ross and Morgan:

An Annuity is recommended for a client if the client is retired and is risk averse.

An Endowment policy is recommended for a client if the client is young and is not averse to risk.

An Equity linked policy is recommended for a client if the client is a mature adult and is prone to risk or is neutral about risk.

A Bond linked policy is recommended for a client if the client is averse to risk unless the client is retired.

A client is averse to risk if the client has children.

Note that this is exactly the same as the preceding version with only the addition of line breaks between rules. We also gave the 'if/then' form and noted that there are an infinite number of ways to phrase a ruleset. This is one reason why it is so important for every organization to adopt a standard format. We saw too in Chapter 5 how the rule style could be affected by the technology used, giving the above ruleset as implemented in Blaze Advisor, JRules and HaleyAuthority. What your standard style is may then be influenced by the implementation technology to be used, but must reflect the culture and style of the organization. By default we would recommend the 'consequence first' style, as above.

However, some rulesets may be easier to write and understand in if/then form. For example, here are some rulesets from a different domain, tax benefits assessment. Note the *variations* in style.

Disqualification policies

The taxpayer does not qualify for the EITC if the taxpayer is filing Form 2555

> or the taxpayer is filing Form 2555-EZ

> or the taxpayer's filing status is married filing separately

> or the taxpayer's SSN is not valid

> or the taxpayer's total earned income is $0

> or the investment income is more than $2600

> or the taxpayer's AGI is not less than the applicable income limit for the taxpayer

> or the taxpayer has 0 qualifying children and the taxpayer is at least 25 years old

> or the taxpayer qualifies as a nonresident alien

> or the taxpayer's age is less than 65 years and the taxpayer has 0 qualifying children

> or the taxpayer's total earned income is not less than the applicable income limit for the taxpayer

The taxpayer qualifies as a nonresident alien if

> the taxpayer was not a citizen of the United States for the entire tax year

> or the taxpayer was not a resident alien of the United States for the entire tax year

The taxpayer does not qualify for the EITC if a taxpayer is claimed as a dependent

> or the taxpayer's filing status is married filing jointly and the taxpayer's spouse is claimed as a dependent

> or the taxpayer is a qualifying child

or the taxpayer's filing status is married filing jointly and the taxpayer's spouse is a qualifying child

or the taxpayer did not reside in the United States for more than 6 months

and the taxpayer has 0 qualifying children

Qualifying children

If a person does not pass the age test then the person is not a qualifying child of the taxpayer

If a person does not pass the relationship test for a second person then the first person is not a qualifying child of the second person

If a person resided with a second person for less than 6 months then the first person is not a qualifying child of the second person

If the SSN of a person is not valid then the person is not a qualifying child of a taxpayer

Relationship Test

If a person that is not married is a son or daughter or descendent thereof of a person then the first person passes the relationship test for the second person

If a person can be claimed as an exemption by a second person then the first person passes the relationship test for the second person

If a person that is married is a son or daughter or descendent thereof of a second person and the first person can be claimed as an exemption by the second person then the first person passes the relationship test for the second person

If a person is a sibling or descendent thereof of a second person and the second person cared for the first person as a child then the first person passes the relationship test for the second person

If a person that is not married is a sibling or descendent thereof of a person then the first person passes the relationship test for the second person

If a person that is not married is an eligible foster child of a person then the first person passes the relationship test for the second person

Age Test

A person that was totally disabled permanently passes the age test

A qualifying child that is less than 19 years old passes the age test

If a person was a fulltime student and the person is less than 24 years old then the person passes the age test

Applicable income limit

> The applicable income limit for the taxpayer is the EITC income limit by children for the taxpayer unless the taxpayer is filing jointly

> If the taxpayer has 0 qualifying children then the EITC income limit by children is $11,230

> If the taxpayer has 1 qualifying child then the EITC income limit by children is $29,666

> If the number of qualifying children of the taxpayer is more than 1 then the EITC income limit by children is $33692

> The applicable income limit for the taxpayer is the EITC income limit by children plus $1,000 if the taxpayer is filing jointly

Recommendations

> The taxpayer qualifies for the EITC unless the taxpayer does not qualify for the EITC or an answer to a question is required

Information Requirements (people)

> If a person does not have an SSN then the SSN of the person is required

Information Requirements (taxpayer)

> The filing status of the taxpayer is required A if the taxpayer does not have a filing status

> The marital status of the taxpayer is required if the taxpayer does not have a marital status

> The number of qualifying children of the taxpayer is required if the taxpayer does not have a number of qualifying children

> The SSN of the taxpayer's spouse is required if the taxpayer is filing jointly and the taxpayer's spouse does not have a SSN

> The SSN of the taxpayer is required if the taxpayer does not have a SSN

> The age of the taxpayer is required if the taxpayer does not have an age

Some of these rules look a little stilted because the knowledge engineering process has massaged them into a certain style. For example, a rule that reads

If a person does not have an SSN then the SSN of the person is required was almost certainly converted from

The SSN must be filled in.

or some such phrase. But many of the rules are pretty much what the domain expert would have said or written. So, adopt a standard style but be prepared to vary it to fit in with the product you are using and the style of expression used by your subject matter experts and users.

6.5 Summary

Techniques for knowledge acquisition and analysis must be added to system development methods for BRMS. As well as data analysis and object modelling techniques (to establish the ontology) these may include the following.

- Informal, structured and focused interviews.
- Presentations by experts.
- Verbal protocols.
- Observational studies.
- Questionnaires.
- Simulation and prototyping.
- Introspection.
- Background reading.
- Becoming an expert.
- Probes.
- Teachback.
- Kelly grids.
- Data mining or rule induction.
- Workshops

Different BRMS products require slightly different approaches to knowledge acquisition.

Knowledge acquisition involves determining inference methods – as well as the rules and ontology. Inference methods are closely related to problem types. If uncertainty is involved in the problem type, this too will affect the choice of inference method.

The developers of a BRMS system must pay attention to best practice in system development and the corpus of knowledge about object-orientation, data modelling, component based development and service oriented architecture. Chapter 7 presents several patterns to this effect. Barbara von Halle's method contains much excellent guidance on good system development practice in the specific context of BRMS.

It is a good idea to write the natural language version of rules in a consistent, standard, readable and concise style. Ron Ross and Tony Morgan's guidance is worth paying careful attention to.

6.6 Bibliographical Notes

I am not aware of a really good general text on knowledge elicitation and analysis. I still refer to the excellent short monograph by Margaret Wellbank published privately by BT (1983). Graham (2001) gives extensive guidance on how to organize and conduct workshops. It also contains an appendix describing fuzzy logic and fuzzy inference. Graham and Jones (1988) give even more detail on fuzzy inference.

Halle (2002) presents her system development approach for BRMS projects. Morgan (2002) and Ross (2003) are essential reading on rule style. You will also need to refer to the documentation of your selected BRMS product(s) on these matters.

CHAPTER 7

A Pattern Language for BRMS Development

By different methods different men excel;
But where is he who can do all things well?

Charles Churchill *(Epistle to William Hogarth)*

This chapter presents a distillation of the advice and guidance to be found in earlier chapters of this book, in the works of other authors on the subjects of business rules management systems and software development and upon the practical experience of myself and my colleagues. The idea is not to present a normative method, but to give nuggets of commonly understood wisdom that the developer can use or discard or adapt, according to the concrete circumstances that she faces. In this way the language helps the developer generate a solution to a concrete problem. This distillation is done in the form of a small pattern language broken into two parts: Sections 7.3 and 7.4. To help understand this language and the patterns that comprise it, we must start by reviewing the basic ideas of patterns and pattern languages. Readers already familiar with these ideas may skip directly to Section 7.3.

7.1   What are Patterns?

The idea of a design pattern has been influential in software development since about the mid 1990s. Design patterns are standard solutions to recurring problems, clearly named to help people discuss them easily and to think about design. They have always been around in computing, so that even such old terms as 'linked list' or 'recursive descent' are readily understood by people in the field.

Patterns are abstract solutions to problems that recur in different contexts but encounter the same mutually opposing forces each time. The actual implementation of the solution varies with each application. Patterns are not, therefore, ready-made solutions. They are often represented by commonly recurring arrangements of types and the structural and dynamic connections between them. Perhaps the best known and useful examples of patterns occur in application frameworks associated with graphical user interface building or other well-defined development problems. In fact, some of the motivation for patterns came from the apprehension of already existing frameworks that led people to wonder how general the approach was.

Software developers took the idea of patterns from architects of the built environment. Victorian builders used huge pattern books to design houses with their clients. These books contained pictures of ornamented windows, doors, cornices, fireplaces and other architectural features. They would go through these illustrations selecting the styles and discussing the consistency of their choices. The result is a surprisingly wide-ranging stock of Victorian housing, much of which is pleasant to inhabit to this day. Software patterns are closely related to the idea of software architecture.

Software patterns are most useful because they provide a language for designers to communicate in. Rather than having to explain a complex idea from scratch, the designer can just mention a pattern by name and everyone will know, at least roughly, what is meant. This is how designers in many other disciplines communicate their design ideas. In this sense they are an excellent vehicle for the collection and dissemination of the anecdotal and unquantifiable data that must be collected before we can see real advances in the processes of building systems.

There are two different views of patterns; both of which have value. To examine these we must first look at the roots of the patterns concept that lie outside the domain of software development.

Patterns are associated with the radical architect of the built environment, Christopher Alexander. From the beginning of his career Alexander was driven by the view that the vast majority of the building stock created since the end of World War II (which constitutes the great majority of all construction works created by human beings in the history of the species) has been dehumanizing, of low quality and lacking all sense of beauty and human feeling. In his earliest publication, Alexander (1964) presented a powerful critique of modern design contrasting the failures of the professional *self-conscious* process of design with what he called the *unselfconscious* process by which peasants' farmhouses, Eskimos' igloos and the huts of the Mousgoum tribesmen of the Cameroon, amongst others, create their living spaces. In the latter, 'the pattern of building operation, the pattern of the building's maintenance, the constraints of the surrounding conditions, and also the pattern of daily life, are fused in the form', yet there is no concept of 'design' or 'architecture', let alone separate designers and architects. Each man builds his own house.

Alexander argues that the unselfconscious process has a homeostatic (i.e. self-regulating) structure that produces well-fitting forms even in the face of change; but in the self-conscious process this homeostatic structure has vanished, making poorly-fitting forms almost inevitable. Although, by definition, there are no explicitly articulated rules for building in an unselfconscious process, there are usually a lot of unspoken, unwritten, implicit rules that are sustained by culture and tradition. These traditions provide not only the bedrock of stability but a resistance to all but the most urgent changes – usually when a form 'fails' in some way. When such changes are required, the simplicity of life itself and the immediacy of the feedback (since the builder and homeowner are one and the same) mean that the necessary adaptation can itself be made immediately. Thus the unselfconscious process is characterized by quick reactions to failures combined with resistance to other changes. This allows the design process to make a series of minor, incremental adjustments instead of spasmodic global ones. Changes have local impact only, and over a long period of time; the system adjusts subsystem by subsystem. Since these minor changes happen at a faster rate than does the culture, equilibrium is constantly and dynamically re-established after each disturbance.

In the self-conscious process, tradition is weakened or becomes non-existent. The feedback loop is lengthened by the distance between the 'user' and the builder. Immediate reaction to failure is not possible because materials are not close to hand. Failures for all these reasons accumulate and require far more drastic action because they have to be dealt with in combination. All the factors that drive the construction process to equilibrium have disappeared in the self-conscious process. Equilibrium, if reached at all, is unstable, not least because the rate of cultural change outpaces the rate at which adaptations can be made.

Alexander does not seek a return to primitive forms, but rather a new approach to a modern dilemma: self-conscious designers, and indeed the notion of design itself, have arisen as a result of the increased complexity of requirements and sophistication of materials. They now have control over the process to a degree that the unselfconscious craftsman never had. But the more control they get, the greater the cognitive burden and the greater the effort they spend in trying to deal with it, the more obscure becomes the causal structure of the problem that needs to be expressed for a well-fitting solution to be created. Increasingly, the very individuality of the designer is turning into its opposite: instead of being a solution, it is the main obstacle to a solution to the problem of restoring equilibrium between form and context.

Alexandrian 'theory' is currently expressed in an 11-volume-strong literary project that does not include the 1964 work. Eight of these volumes have been published so far. The ninth volume in the series, *The Nature of Order*, is eagerly awaited as it promises to provide the fullest exposition yet of the underlying theory. A common theme of all the books is the rejection of abstract categories of architectural or design principles as being entirely arbitrary. Also rejected is the idea that it is even possible to design successfully 'very abstract forms at the big level' (Alexander, 1996). For Alexander, architecture attains its highest expression, not at the level of gross structure, but actually in its finest detail: what he calls 'fine structure'. That is to say, the macroscopic clarity of design comes from a consistency; a geometric unity holds true at all levels of scale. It is not possible for a single mind to imagine this recursive structure at all levels in advance of building it. It is in this context that his patterns for the built environment must be understood.

Alexander *et al*. (1977) presented an archetypal pattern language for construction. The language is an interconnected network of 253 patterns which encapsulate design best practice at a variety of levels of scale, from the siting of alcoves to the construction of towns and cities. The language is designed to be used collaboratively by all the stakeholders in a development, not just developers. This is predicated, in part at least, on the assumption that the real experts in buildings are those who live and work in them, rather than those who have studied architecture or structural engineering. The patterns are applied to the construction sequentially; each state change caused by the application of a pattern creates a new context to which the next pattern can be applied. The overall development is an emergent property of the application of the pattern language. The language therefore has a generative character: it generates solutions piecemeal from the successive addressing of each individual problem that each of the patterns addresses separately.

WAIST-HIGH SHELF (pattern number 201 in the language) proposes the building of waist-high shelves around main rooms to hold the traffic of objects that are handled most, so that they are always ready to hand. Clearly the specific form, depth, position and so on of these shelves will differ from house to house and workplace to workplace. One common realization is the hall table that we throw our keys onto when we return from work each day. The implementation of the pattern creates, therefore, a very specific context in which other patterns such as THICKENING THE OUTER WALL (number 211) can be used since Alexander suggests the shelves be built into the very structure of the building where appropriate, and using THINGS FROM YOUR LIFE (number 253) to populate the shelves. It may be interesting to note that patterns can have negative as well as positive effects (which is why they are sometimes referred to as antipatterns). Thieves often steal the keys off waist high shelves using a long hook pushed through the letterbox. Thus armed, they can enter your home or steal your car!

The pattern that, more than any other, is the physical and procedural embodiment of Alexander's approach to design, however, is pattern number 208, GRADUAL STIFFENING, wherein he argues that the fundamental philosophy behind the use of pattern languages is that buildings should be uniquely adapted to individual needs and sites; and that the plans of buildings should be rather loose and fluid, in order to accommodate these subtleties. Recognize that you are not assembling a building from components like an erector set, but that you are instead weaving a structure which starts out globally complete, but flimsy; then gradually making it stiffer but still rather flimsy; and only finally making it completely stiff and strong.

In the description of this pattern Alexander invites the reader to visualize a 50-year-old master carpenter at work. He keeps working, apparently without stopping, until he eventually produces a quality product. The smoothness of his labour comes from the fact that he is making small, sequential, incremental steps such that he can always eliminate a mistake or correct an imperfection with the next step. He compares this with the novice who with a 'panic-stricken attention to detail' tries to work out everything in advance, fearful of making an unrecoverable error. Alexander's point is that most modern architecture has the character of the novice's work, not the master craftsman's. Successful construction processes, producing well-fitting forms, come from the postponement of detail design decisions until the building process itself so that the details are fitted into the overall, evolving structure.

Alexander's ideas seem to have been introduced into the software community first by Kent Beck and Ward Cunningham. In a 1993 article in *Smalltalk Report*, Beck claimed to have been using patterns for six years already, but the software patterns movement seems to have been kicked off by a workshop on the production of a software architect's handbook organized by Bruce Anderson for OOPSLA'91. Here met for the first time Erich Gamma, Richard Helm, Ralph Johnson and John Vlissides – a group destined to gain notoriety as the Gang of Four (GoF). Gamma was already near to completion of his PhD thesis on 'design patterns' in the ET++ framework. He had already been joined by Helm in the production of an independent catalogue. By the time of a follow-up meeting at OOPSLA in 1992, Vlissides and Johnson had joined the effort and, sometime in 1993, the group agreed to write a book that has been a best seller ever since its publication in 1995. In fact, outside the patterns movement itself, many in the software development industry identify software patterns completely and totally with the GoF book.

However, the 1991 OOPSLA workshop was only the first in a series of meetings that culminated first in the formation of the non-profit Hillside Group (apparently so-called because they went off to a hillside one weekend to try out Alexander's building patterns) and then the first Pattern Languages of Programming (PLoP) conference in 1994. PLoP conferences take place in various places around the world annually.

A characteristic of the way in which patterns are developed for publication in the patterns movement is the so-called pattern writers' workshop. This is a form of peer-review that is loosely related to design reviews that are typical in software development processes, but more strongly related to poetry circles.

While the GoF book has won deserved recognition for raising the profile of patterns, for many it has been a double-edged sword. The GoF patterns form a catalogue of standalone patterns all at a similar level of abstraction. Such a catalogue can never have the generative quality that Alexander's pattern language claims for itself and, to be fair, the Gang of Four freely admit that this was not the aim of their work.

The GoF book includes 23 useful design patterns, including the following particularly interesting and useful ones.

- FAÇADE. Useful for implementing object wrappers: combines multiple interfaces into one.

- ADAPTER. Also useful for wrappers: converts interfaces into ones understandable by clients.

- PROXY. Mainly used to support distribution: creates a local surrogate for a remote object to enable access to it.

- OBSERVER. This helps an object to notify registrants that its state has changed and helps with the implementation of blackboard systems.

- VISITOR and State. These two patterns help to implement dynamic classification.

- COMPOSITE. Allows clients to treat parts and wholes uniformly.

- BRIDGE. Helps with decoupling interfaces from their implementations.

Some cynics have claimed that some of the GoF patterns are really only useful for fixing deficiencies in the C++ language. Examples of these might arguably include DECORATOR and ITERATOR. However, this very suggestion raises the issue of language-dependent *versus* language-independent patterns. Buschmann *et al.* (1996) (also known as the Party of Five or PoV) from Siemens in Germany suggest a system of patterns that can be divided into architectural patterns, design patterns and language idioms. They present examples of the first two categories. Architectural patterns include: PIPES AND FILTERS, BLACKBOARD systems, and the MODEL VIEW CONTROLLER (MVC) pattern for user interface development. Typical PoV design patterns are called:

- FORWARDER RECEIVER;
- WHOLE PART; and
- PROXY.

The reader is advised by the PoV to refer to all the GoF patterns as well. The PoV book can therefore be regarded as an expansion of the original catalogue, not merely through the addition of extra patterns, but by addressing different levels of abstraction too. The WHOLE-PART pattern is exactly the implementation of the composition structures that form part of basic object modelling semantics. In that sense, it appears to be a trivial pattern. However, since most languages do not support the construct, it can be useful to see the standard way to implement it. It is a rare example of an analysis pattern that maps directly to an idiom in several languages: a multi-language idiom. The best known source of idiomatic (i.e. language-specific) patterns is Jim Coplien's book on advanced C++, which predates the GoF book by some three years (Coplien, 1992). C++ 'patterns' (the book does not use the term) that Coplien presents include:

- HANDLE CLASS, used to encapsulate classes that bear application intelligence;
- REFERENCE COUNTER, managing a reference count to shared representation;
- ENVELOPE-LETTER permits 'type migration' of classes;
- EXEMPLAR enables the creation of prototypes in the absence of delegation;
- AMBASSADOR provides distribution transparency.

Whilst experienced programmers will feel immediately familiar with many of these patterns, almost everyone will recognize the ideas behind caches and recursive composites. These too can be regarded as design and/or analysis patterns. CACHE should be used when complex computations make it better to store the results rather than recalculate often; or when the cost of bringing data across a network makes it more efficient to store them locally. Clearly this is a pattern having much to do with performance optimization. It is also worth noting that patterns may use each other; this pattern may make use of the OBSERVER pattern when it is necessary to know that the results need to be recalculated or the data refreshed.

The above examples indicate that a standard pattern layout may be beneficial, and many proponents (though not the GoF) adopt a standard loosely based on Alexander's work: the so-called Alexandrian form. This divides pattern descriptions into prose sections with suitable pictorial illustrations as follows – although the actual headings vary from author to author.

- Pattern name and description.
- Context (Problem) – situations where the patterns may be useful and the problem that the pattern solves.
- Forces – the contradictory forces at work that the designer must balance.
- Solution – the principles underlying the pattern and how to apply it (including examples of its realization, consequences and benefits).
- Also Known As/Related patterns – other names for (almost) the same thing and patterns that this one uses or might occur with.
- Known uses.

Actually this deviates quite a lot from Alexander's presentation, as we shall see later.

The overwhelming majority of software patterns produced to date have been design patterns at various levels of abstraction, but Coad *et al.* (1992; 1997) and Fowler (1997) introduced the idea of analysis patterns as opposed to design patterns. Fowler's patterns are reusable fragments of object-oriented specification models made generic enough to be applicable across a number of specific application domains. They therefore have something of the flavour of the GoF pattern catalogue (described in that book's subtitle as 'elements of reusable object-oriented software'), but are even further removed from Alexander's generative concepts. Examples of Fowler's patterns include:

- PARTY: how to store the name and address of someone or something you deal with;
- ORGANIZATION STRUCTURE: how to represent divisional structure;
- POSTING RULES: how to represent basic bookkeeping rules;
- QUOTE: dealing with the different ways in which financial instrument prices are represented.

Apart from systems development, there has also been interest in developing patterns for organizational development (Coplien, 1995; Coplien and Harrison, 2005). These authors apply the idea of patterns to the software development process itself and observe several noteworthy regularities. These observations arose out of a research project sponsored by AT&T investigating the value of QA process standards such as ISO9001. They were able to identify the commonly recurring key characteristics of the most productive organizations and develop a 42-strong pattern language to aid the design of development organizations. Included in the language are patterns such as these:

- CONWAY'S LAW states that architecture always follows organization or *vice versa*;
- ARCHITECT ALSO IMPLEMENTS requires that the architect stands close to the development process;
- DEVELOPER CONTROLS PROCESS requires that the developers own and drive the development process, as opposed to having one imposed on them;
- MERCENARY ANALYST enables the 'off-line' reverse engineering and production of project documentation;
- FIREWALL describes how to insulate developers from the 'white noise' of the software development industry;
- GATEKEEPER describes how to get useful information in a timely manner to software developers.

A typical application of such organizational patterns is the combined use of GATEKEEPER and FIREWALL in, say, a situation where a pilot project is assessing new technology. The software development industry excels at rumour mongering, a situation fuelled by the practice of vendors who make vapourware announcements long in advance of any commercial-strength implementations. Over-attention to the whispers on the industry grapevine, let alone authoritative-looking statements in the trade press, can seriously undermine a pilot project. Developers lose confidence in Java, say, because of its reputation for poor performance or a claimed lack of available tools. Yet, at the same time, some news is important: for example, the publication of Platform 2 for Java. A solution is to build official firewalls and then create a gatekeeper rôle where a nominated individual is responsible for filtering and forwarding the useful and usable information as opposed to unsubstantiated scare stories, junk mail and even the attention of vendors' sales forces.

More interesting than the individual patterns themselves, however, is the underlying approach of Coplien's language, which is much closer to the spirit of Alexander's work than anything to be found in the original GoF or PoV books, for example. First, since its very scope is intercommunication between people, it is human-centred. Second, it is explicitly generative in its aim. Coplien argues that while software developers do not inhabit code in the way that people inhabit houses and offices, as professionals they are expert users of professional processes and organizations. Therefore, just as Alexander's language is designed to involve all the stakeholders of building projects (and, above all, the expertise of the users of the buildings) so process designers have to base themselves on the expertise of the victims of formal processes: the developers themselves. Coplien's attempt to create an avowedly Alexandrian pattern language seems to push the focus of his patterns away from descriptions of fragments of structure (as is typical in the GoF patterns) much more towards descriptions of the work that has to be done. In going beyond mere structure, Coplien's patterns have much more of a feel of genuine architecture about them than do many other pattern types available.

In fact, it is clear that from common roots there are two polarized views of patterns abroad today. One view focuses on patterns as generic structural descriptions. They have been described, in the UML literature especially, as 'parameterized collaborations'. The suggestion is that you can take, say, the structural descriptions of the rôles that different classes can play in a pattern and then, simply by changing the class names and providing detailed algorithmic implementations, plug them into a software development. Patterns thus become reduced to abstract descriptions of potentially pluggable components. A problem with this simplistic view occurs when a single class is required to play many rôles simultaneously in different patterns. The other view regards them simply as design decisions (taken in a particular context, in response to a problem recognized as a recurring one). This view inevitably tends toward the development of patterns as elements in a generative pattern language. This is the approach taken in this book.

7.2 Why a Pattern Language?

The debate about the character of software patterns ('parameterized collaborations' *versus* 'design decisions', pattern catalogues *versus* pattern languages) both reflects and affects debates about software architecture. That relationship was highlighted by Coplien's guest editorship of *IEEE Software* magazine (Autumn 1999), a special issue on software architecture in which Coplien republished Alexander's keynote talk to the 1996 OOPSLA conference. In his editorial, re-evaluating the architectural metaphor, Coplien identified two fundamental approaches to software development: the 'blueprint' or 'master plan' approach *versus* that of 'piecemeal growth'. Coplien suggests that the immature discipline of software architecture is suffering from 'formal envy' and has borrowed inappropriate lessons from the worlds of both engineering and the built environment. Symptoms of the crisis are the separation of the deliverables of architecture from the artifacts delivered to the customer and the reification of architecture as a separate process in a waterfall approach to software development. Following the architects of the built environment, Alexander and Ludwig Miles van der Rohe, Coplien argues strongly that the Devil is in the details, and that clarity at the macro level can only be judged by whether it incorporates the fine details successfully. He further asserts that the object experience highlights what has been important all along: that architecture is not so much about software, but about the people who write the software.'

As Coplien quite rightly points out, the patterns movement has always celebrated the otherwise lowly programmer as the major source of architectural knowledge in software development. Beyond that, he recognizes the deep character of the relationship between the code's structure and the communication pathways between the people developing and maintaining it. In doing so, Coplien argues, patterns have taken software development beyond the naïve practice of the early days of objects, which fell short of its promise because it was still constrained by a purely modular view of programs, inherited from the previous culture. Further advance requires liberation from the weight of 'the historic illusions of formalism and planning'.

Richard Gabriel has suggested that there are two reasons why successful software development is in reality piecemeal growth. First, there is the cognitive complexity of dealing not only with current but possible future causes of change, which make it impossible to visualize completely a constructible software program in advance to the necessary level of detail with any accuracy (Gabriel, 1996). Second, there is the fact that pre-planning alienates all but the planners. Coplien, Gabriel and the entire patterns movement are dedicated to developing practices that combat this social alienation. In doing so they impart a profound social and moral obligation to the notion of software architecture. In the face of these stark realities the only alternative to piecemeal growth is the one once offered by David Parnas: fake the blueprints by reverse engineering them once the code is complete.

Essentially, the difference between a pattern language and a pattern catalogue is that, in the latter, the patterns stand alone as useful pieces of advice. In the former, the patterns are coupled together in such a way that sequences can be built to help practitioners solve concrete problems, each pattern, when it is applied changes the context in which it arose and supplies a context for the application of other, downstream, patterns. Don't forget: the patterns tell you to *consider* a particular solution to a problem and the forces at work when it arises; they do *not* tell you exactly what to do. *You* create the solution.

7.3   The RulePatterns Language – Part I

The language presented here is divided into two major sections, represented by the two navigation charts of Figures 7.1 and 7.2. Figure 7.1 presents some general process patterns (indicated by the grey background) and patterns for requirements, process and architecture, followed by patterns specifically for finding, writing and organizing business rules. Figure 7.2 presents patterns for knowledge elicitation and (again shown against a grey background) patterns for application development and product selection. Within each section the patterns are further classified according to their function.

Pattern numbering is continuous across these sections to emphasize its rather arbitrary nature. The pattern's numbers have no significance except to provide a convenient reference. Each section starts with a map of that section of the language, which provides a high level overview of the section and provides primary navigation. The maps, although not the sections, may overlap slightly. In these maps, the patterns are classified into abstract, concrete and terminal patterns as shown by their colour coding.

Abstract patterns represent the codification of principles and are shown in grey. There is not always a context for such a principle; it's just always a useful one and informs the way downstream patterns are applied and interpreted. **Concrete** (white) patterns are patterns in the usual sense, and we discuss their structure in detail below. Finally, some patterns are **terminal** with this language. Of course, abstract patterns are never terminal.

A pattern being terminal does not mean that design thinking stops with it – merely that the language considers the further design issues as beyond its scope or ambitions. The other cases where the language terminates abruptly usually concern areas of some complexity that, in my opinion, are deserving of a pattern language in their own right, as will be noted. Where such pattern languages exist, this is indicated diagrammatically by an unnumbered rounded rectangle with a dotted background and by a reference in the appropriate pattern text(s).

The simplest way to use the language is to consider pattern number one (ESTABLISH THE BUSINESS OBJECTIVES) first and then follow the links to the other patterns. It is best to have a concrete problem in mind when doing this. Eventually you will reach patterns that are terminal (represented in black on the diagrams). You should also try to construct sequences (or sublanguages) to deal with specific design problems or specific kinds of development.

Rules are made to be broken. The patterns in this chapter may be regarded as rules for successful design, but it is better to think of them as providing suggestions, guidance and checklists of things not to forget to think about. If you do find yourself treating the patterns as rules then pause. Always consider the likely effects of breaking the rules and ensure that you understand the rules that you are going to break and the justification for doing so.

Each pattern is presented using the same layout, semantic structure and typographical conventions. These are very closely based on the structure pioneered by Alexander *et al.* (1977). The pattern number and name are presented first followed, optionally, by a list of alternative names – all in a black header. The alternatives, if present, are labelled aka (also known as) in the same header. Next comes what many people call a **sensitizing image**: a picture or diagram concerning, supporting or illustrating the pattern. In many cases this has been omitted for brevity.

After the sensitizing image we present the **Context** in which one would normally encounter the pattern. This section usually gives the names of patterns that one has already used or considered. This is separated from the body of the pattern by three tildes, thus:

$$\sim\sim\sim$$

Next, the **Problem** is stated in bold text. For the discussion of the **forces** that are at work and the way the pattern deals with them we return to plain text; i.e. text of the sort you are reading in this paragraph. This section may include quite diverse types of commentary and explanations. Where appropriate we highlight known uses of the patterns. Where this is omitted it is because the known uses are so obvious as to not need stating or because they have been intrinsic to the description of the forces and related discussion.

Once the discussion is complete, I state or summarize the recommended solution in bold text. This section is highlighted in the margin with the word **Therefore**. This completes the body of the pattern; so we again delimit it with three tildes.

The next section describes the **Resultant** context and, unless the pattern is terminal, will include the names of the patterns that one may consider applying next. This information is partly represented in Figure 7.1 by the arrows. Interpret these arrows as meaning 'supplies a potential context for'.

Following Alexander again, I have classified the patterns according to my degree of confidence in them. The pattern's 'star rating', shown next to its name,

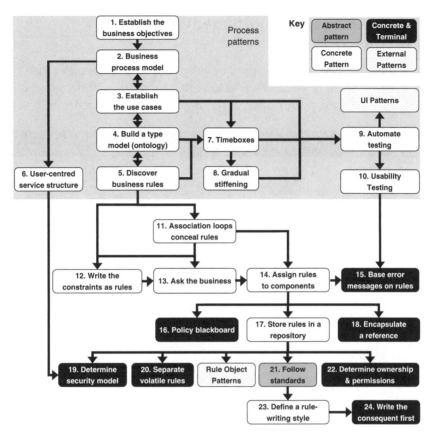

Figure 7-1

indicates this. Three stars means that I am totally convinced of the pattern's efficacy, having used it or seen it used successfully on many projects. Three stars may also indicate that there is some solid theoretical justification of the pattern in the literature and folklore of the subject. If there are no stars it means that I think this is a good idea but would like people to try and see. One and two stars are interpreted on the scale between these extremes in the obvious manner.

The lengths of the patterns vary. Partly, this reflects knowledge and experience of the patterns and therefore confidence in them. However, sometimes a short pattern merely reflects the fact that it is easy to describe and understand. In some cases the pattern is short because either a longer version of the pattern has already been published or an expanded version might be considered useful.

In Figures 7.1 and 7.2, rounded rectangles represent patterns and an arrow from pattern P_1 to pattern P_2 is to be interpreted as meaning 'P_1 possibly generates a context for applying P_2 and indicates that the designer should consider applying P_2 whenever she has applied P_1'. Double headed arrows further suggest that a group of patterns will normally be considered iteratively and in parallel.

7.3.1 Patterns for Requirements, Process and Architecture

Some of the following patterns apply equally well to projects other than BRMS projects; but they are important – and too often ignored – patterns, so I include them in the language, noting any BRMS-specific or SOA-specific points.

Pattern 1	ESTABLISH THE BUSINESS OBJECTIVES ***
Context	You are embarking on a business solution and system development project that may or may not involve business rules. There are very few, if any, that will not.
	~~
Problem	**How can you be sure that the system will be fit for purpose and that project management can be both successful and agile in response to evolving requirements?**
Forces	Many development methods encourage developers to start analysis with use case modelling or, at best, give little concrete advice on how to tie development to business goals. This can lead to dysfunctional results, unused systems or loss of focus during development. Furthermore, as requirements evolve during the project, there can be disputes over which use cases have priority for implementation before the next timeboxed delivery date.
	When you decide to use TIMEBOXES (4) to control iterative development you can only negotiate sensibly on evolving requirements if you have consensus on the things that will *not* change during the project.
	Prioritizing objectives according to some scheme such as 'Must have, Should have, Could have,' often presents difficulties because stakeholders insist that their favourite objective is a 'must' until discrimination is lost completely and the priorities are worthless. An objective numerical ranking can be achieved by pairwise comparison of the objectives, but this can be very time-consuming. It is quicker and just as practically effective to let workshop participants vote, preferably from two points of view.
Example	For example, give each person red and blue stickers to the tune of two-thirds of the number of objectives and

let them place the stickers next to the objectives on a flipchart. Red might represent the view of the organization, while blue represent individual (or departmental) preferences. Next one may add the results (blue and red) together and open a discussion to ensure that there is a consensus on the priorities so computed.

A longer version of this pattern can be found in Graham (2003a). It should also be noted that there are other ways to approach the problem of business objectives, and therefore competing patterns may exist.

Therefore

Run a stakeholder workshop to establish the business objectives. There will typically be between 7 and 30 such objectives. Ensure each objective can be measured numerically and objectively; otherwise reject or reword it. Now assign numerical priorities to the objectives. The quickest way to do this is by voting and consensus-building discussion. Fix the objectives and priorities for the duration of the project.

Involve as many stakeholders as possible. Make sure that potential users are represented. Find a good facilitator. Agree a mission statement to give context to the objectives.

Resultant context

Once the objectives and priorities are fixed you can safely move on to construct a BUSINESS PROCESS MODEL (2). Refer to RUN A WORKSHOP (27).

| Pattern 2 | BUSINESS PROCESS MODEL ** |

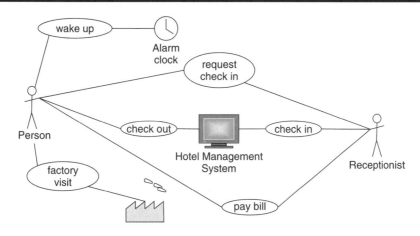

Context

You have ESTABLISHED THE BUSINESS OBJECTIVES (1) and fixed their priorities. You are probably also committed to a service-oriented approach.

~~~

Problem

How can you ensure that the development will take account of current or re-engineered business practices and procedures? The needs of stakeholders that are not direct users of the system must be understood – as well as those of the 'actors' in a conventional use case model. Do the processes, as they mostly will, involve any explicit or latent business rules?

Forces

The philosophy of service-oriented architecture emphasizes that our focus must be on the real user as well as the user who actually interacts with the system; a conventional use case model tends to focus on the latter.

There are two notational styles commonly used to represent business processes. In UML terms, we have activity diagrams or use case diagrams available. Activity diagrams are often useful but they can grow unmanageably large very quickly, often because they attempt to incorporate business rules (as conditionals, etc.) or because they model system activities. Also, they do not show 'who does what' very clearly; in that sense they are 'disembodied'.

Use case diagrams tend to remain manageably concise and are ideal for emphasizing the contract-driven nature of business. Stating contracts for each conversation that occurs in a process can lead directly to statements of business rules. At a minimum, the pre- and post-conditions of the conversations (represented as use cases) always have a rule-like nature.

Known uses

The image above is meant to suggest that actors in use case diagrams should be stereotyped to look like what they represent; if it is a factory, make it look like one. This helps communication in workshop situations and beyond.

This technique has been used successfully on hundreds of projects known to me around the world over thirteen years or so. A longer variant of this pattern can be found in Graham (2003a).

Therefore

Understand first the network of agents and commitments that make up the business. Specify the conversations that take place at an appropriate level of abstraction, so that they are stereotypes for actual stories. Get people to tell these stories. Eliminate conversations that do not correspond to business objectives (or discover the missed objective). Ensure every objective is supported by a conversation.

Emphasizing the contracts that subsist in the business processes will assist in identifying business rules both now and later in the project.

Draw a rich picture of the whole of each business process. Use cases can be used in this picture to represent goal-oriented conversations between actors (including users, non-users, events and artifacts). Ensure that you discuss possible changes to the process, leading to a 'before' and 'after' process model. Use stereotypes in the rich pictures that are meaningful to the business stakeholders present.

~~~

Resultant context

Now ESTABLISH THE USE CASES (3) in the context of the proposed system and the business processes defined. Understanding who the real users are will provide the correct context for building a USER-CENTRED SERVICE STRUCTURE (6).

This pattern is normally applied iteratively, in parallel with all the patterns in the group numbered 2–5.

Pattern 3	ESTABLISH THE USE CASES ***

Context

You have constructed a 'before' and 'after' BUSINESS PROCESS MODEL (2).

~~~

Problem

How can you specify the behaviour of a system and the services it must provide?

Forces

Use case modelling is a very well-known technique. However, current practice tends to produce over-complex use cases with far too much detail. Jacobsen, Fowler and Cockburn all give 'templates' for use cases, which exacerbate this tendency to 'over-document' although, to be fair, I think Cockburn did not intend to encourage their (mis)use.

Theoretically, use cases are completely determined by their pre- and post-conditions. There is really no need to specify them further, apart from the need to state what should happen when the use case encounters an unrecoverable (i.e. fatal) exception. Recoverable exceptions are new, reusable use cases. No steps! No alternative paths!

The second problem with current practice is the use of the semantically ambiguous "extends" association, which tends to over-complicate and enlarge models. It is better to dispense with it and define exception handling by separate use cases, to which error handling messages are delegated. (See Graham (2001) for details.)

Known
Uses

Basically, use case modelling focuses on the functionality of systems as opposed to their data structure. Rule-based methods (e.g. Date, 2002; Halle, 2002) tend to start with the data model. The danger in that approach is that the service structure becomes data-centred rather than user-centred. Much experience says that a method that starts with functionality is both sounder and easier to understand.

Use case modelling is a well-established technique for systems development and is part of most mainstream methods for object-oriented and component based development. A longer version of this pattern can be found in Graham (2003a).

Therefore

Extract the use cases from the conversations in the BUSINESS PROCESS MODEL (2). Write post-conditions for each use case. Compare the vocabulary of the post-conditions to the type model. Write use cases in stimulus–response form. Do not constrain the user's ability to perform steps in any particular sequence.

Use cases are ideal for high level specification but they must be formulated at the right level of abstraction. Very detailed use cases are an impediment to clear understanding. To avoid superfluous detail, define use cases by ONLY their pre- and post-conditions and, if necessary, remarks on what will happen if there is a non-recoverable error during

execution of the task. Write separate use cases to describe how to recover from other types of error.

Write explicit rules based on the pre- and post-conditions (the use case goals).

Ensure the use cases remain cross-referenced to the business objectives and that they inherit the priorities of the latter.

~~~

Resultant context	BUILD A TYPE MODEL (4) by explicating the vocabulary needed to express the pre- and post-conditions. If you have rules, ensure that they are executable and based on the type model. Group the use cases into sets that can be implemented together; base your TIMEBOXES (14) on these prioritized sets. Use the use case model to define tests and AUTOMATE TESTING (9).

This pattern is normally applied iteratively, in parallel with all the patterns in the group numbered 2–5.

Pattern 4	BUILD A TYPE MODEL (ONTOLOGY) ***
Context	You have ESTABLISHED THE USE CASES (3) and written their post-conditions. These statements or rules make no sense without a vocabulary: an ontology that gives the statements meaning.

~~~

Problem	**How can you get a computer to interpret use cases and rules?**
Forces	Getting a machine to understand natural language statements is either impossible or quite beyond any known science. Therefore, we must help the machine by providing an ontology that gives precise meaning to the statements we use in rules or use cases. A UML type model is an ideal way to do this, although semantic networks may also prove valuable.
Known uses	Type modelling is a standard technique for software development, although there are variations in its practice. It is assumed here that a theoretically sound method such as Catalysis (D'Souza and Wills, 1999; Andrews, 2007) or UML components (Cheesman and Daniels, 2000) is the basis for type modelling. It would be inappropriate to reproduce all the details of how to do type modelling here. A few remarks will suffice.

In the context of SOA and CBD it is a good idea to distinguish core (kernel), role and process (association) components – Date (2000), Cheesman and Daniels (2000) and Andrews (2007) all agree on this point. Core objects will be stored in lower architectural layers whereas rôle and process objects tend to be about specific applications. Also Coad's (1999) colour patterns are often very useful in making similar architectural decisions. We discussed them fleetingly in Chapter 2.

Catalysis includes several subpatterns such as MAP TO EXISTING DATABASE (which concerns retrievals from legacy systems). These are worth getting to know.

Most BRMS products provide some level of automated support for this process. Haley Authority walks the user through the construction of the minimal type model needed to interpret the rules. JRules allows developers to import existing Java object models or UML models. At a minimum, all products will fail to compile rules in the absence of an adequate type model.

Therefore

Read all the rules that you have discovered and the post-conditions of all the use cases. Define types that represent the vocabulary of these statements. Some terms may be attributes of the types. Record how types are associated and note any cardinality constraints.

~~~

Resultant context

The type model will contain many business rules, some explicit, some hidden. We need to DISCOVER BUSINESS RULES (6). These two patterns may be applied in any order and their use will be iterative in most cases. That is, you can write the rules before type modelling or *vice versa*.

This pattern is normally applied iteratively, in parallel with all the patterns in the group numbered 2–5.

Pattern 5	DISCOVER BUSINESS RULES

Context

You are building a business rules management system. You have ESTABLISHED THE USE CASES (3). You may have already BUILT A TYPE MODEL (4).

~~~

Problem

How can you discover business rules based on the type model? How can you find rules in other ways?

Forces

The forces at work here depend on how you have arrived at this juncture. Since you have a use case model, the obvious starting point is to rewrite the use case post-conditions as rules. For example, the post-condition of a simple business process such as a sale is 'The vendor has the money and the buyer has the goods'. The corresponding rules might be written as follows.

A sale may be recorded if both of the following are true:

- The Vendor's stock of money has increased by the price of the Good
- The Buyer has the Good.

You can also find rules by examining the type model. Otherwise, you must consider interviews, data mining, workshops and various knowledge elicitation techniques.

Therefore

Rewrite the use case post-conditions as rules.

If there is no type model at the outset, you must use various knowledge elicitation techniques to discover rules. These are covered by the following patterns:

PLAN INTERVIEWS (25)

FILLED-IN FORMS (26)

RUN A WORKSHOP (27)

STRUCTURED INTERVIEW (31)

FOCUSED INTERVIEW (32)

PROBES AND TEACHBACK (33)

ASK FOR THE OPPOSITE (34)

BOUNDARY OF COMPETENCE (35)

If there is a type model then we may also proceed as follows. First realize that ASSOCIATION LOOPS CONCEAL RULES (11). Then rewrite any cardinality constraints as rules WRITE THE CONSTRAINTS AS RULES (12)).

Now BUILD A TYPE MODEL (4) or modify the existing one based on the terms used in the new rules discovered. Next apply:

DETERMINE INFERENCE MODEL (36) if applicable

DETERMINE UNCERTAINTY MODEL (37) if applicable

CLASSIFY YOUR APPLICATIONS (38)

~~~

Resultant context

This is a link pattern that leads to the patterns listed above, in the Solution.

This pattern is normally applied iteratively, in parallel with all the patterns in the group numbered 2–5.

Pattern 6   **USER-CENTRED SERVICE STRUCTURE**

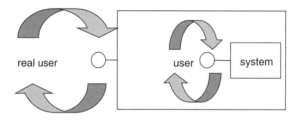

Context

You are building a rule-based application within a service-oriented architecture. You have defined a BUSINESS PROCESS MODEL (2).

~~~

Problem

How can you ensure that the services and components that are provided are pitched at the right level of abstraction?

Forces

All too often, developers focus their attention on implementation concerns, and thus arrive at a design mindset at far too low a level of abstraction compared to the needs of business users. They focus on technical collaborations rather than business processes; the latter often do not – indeed cannot – involve computers. For example, a parcel tracking system needs to understand that a real person has to collect a parcel; the IT systems really can't do that.

The user that actually operates the computer is often not the 'real' user, in the sense of the person who gains the business benefit. Designing the system around use cases (in the conventional sense of actions at the system boundary) will lead to a system that does not serve the real users and whose services are not bundled appropriately for use.

Therefore

Focus on the 'real' user and upon use cases that represent business process that may occur away from the system boundary. Focus on *what* users want to do, rather than *how* they want to do it. Where possible, capture this essence in the form of business rules.

~~~

Resultant context

Since you have a clear idea about who the various kinds of users are, both real and hands-on, you can now begin to DETERMINE THE SECURITY MODEL (18).

Pattern 7	TIMEBOXES ***

Context

You have completed a **BUSINESS PROCESS MODEL** (2), a use case model and begun to extract a type model and some business rules. Now you have to ensure timely delivery of an application that meets current requirements as closely as possible.

~~~

Problem

Time pressure fights against both robustness and the need to respond to changing business requirements during a project. However, timely delivery is nearly always a critical success factor.

Forces

The time-box technique imposes management control over ripple effects and uncontrolled iteration. Control is achieved by setting a rigid elapsed time limit on the iterations and using a small project team. Furthermore, a time-boxed project has a usable (but perhaps incomplete) system as both the end-point of the process and its deliverable. Partial delivery enables benefits (often financial benefits) to be obtained earlier than waiting for an entire system to be delivered. There is no distinction between production, evolution and maintenance as with conventional approaches, which usually ignore maintenance costs during project justification.

Timeboxes should be based on coherent chunks of functionality. These will typically correspond to small group of use cases amongst which there are technical dependencies. Infrastructure use cases may have to be built first, but there should be a strong emphasis on delivering chunks that are of perceived value to the business.

Look for quick wins. For example, when testing your applications there will be instances when a tester hits a problem that surprises the developers but for which the solution is obvious. In a similar category are fixes that require little or no effort or those where a small effort will have a big impact. It is important to give such fixes a high priority and de-scope other features accordingly.

Use the priorities to settle arguments about descoping when new requirements are requested. These are fixed for the duration of a project; the requirements are not fixed.

A longer version of this pattern can be found in Graham (2003a).

Therefore

Divide the use cases into coherent groups, taking into account technical constraints (e.g. client server dependencies, supplier lead times, etc.) and business issues (e.g. unitary business offering). There are three possibilities.

1. **Tackle the easiest area first to boost developers' confidence.**

2. **Tackle the area that solves 80% of the business need first.**

3. **Tackle the area with the greatest technical challenge first.**

The first approach is seldom the right one, because there can be some nasty shocks awaiting the team downstream and because it is not a good way to impress users with the team's skills. A combination of the other two approaches is ideal. The focus too is on the essential requirements early on, rather than those features that the business (or the developers) would like the system to have ideally.

Set definite delivery dates for the software and content that implement each such group of use cases. When deadlines seem endangered, cut functionality instead. But don't expect to get all the requirements right first time. If stakeholders request new or changed functionality, rate its importance against the prioritized business objectives. Negotiate on what must be deferred to the next timebox if the new

features are to be included. Drop use case functionality corresponding to the lowest priority objectives. Never deliver late. Don't compromise on quality unless there is an argument to do so based on the objectives. Don't allow anyone to change the objectives or their priorities:

Resultant context

Now begin to develop the application using **GRADUAL STIFFENING (15)**. Consider **AUTOMATED TESTING (16)** wherever possible. Start **USABILITY TESTING (17)** early on.

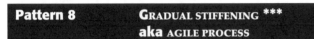

Pattern 8   **GRADUAL STIFFENING** ***
aka AGILE PROCESS

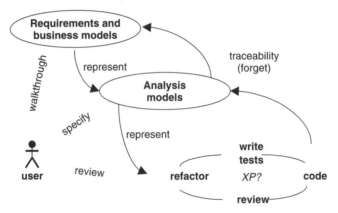

Context

You are managing the project using the discipline of **TIMEBOXES (7)** and you have **ESTABLISHED THE USE CASES (3)** in the context of a **BUSINESS PROCESS MODEL (2)** and a set of fixed, prioritized objectives. However...

~~~

Problem

The requirements use cases and business rules may all evolve during the lifetime of the project. How do you respond to such developments? Should you adhere strictly to the original plan? If not, what is fixed and what should be allowed to vary?

Forces

This is a process pattern of quite general applicability. It is a very minor modification of the one due to Alexander *et al.* They recommend the following procedure for building houses:

The fundamental philosophy behind the use of pattern languages is that buildings should be uniquely adapted to individual needs and sites; and that the plans of buildings should be rather loose and fluid, in order to accommodate these subtleties . . .

Recognize that you are not assembling a building from components like an erector set, but that you are instead weaving a structure which starts out globally complete, but flimsy; then gradually making it stiffer but still rather flimsy; and only finally making it completely stiff and strong.
(Alexander *et al.*, 1977, pp. 963–9.)

In the description of this pattern the reader is invited to visualize a 50-year-old master carpenter at work. He keeps working, apparently without stopping, until he eventually produces a quality product. The smoothness of his labour comes from the fact that he is making small, sequential, incremental steps such that he can always eliminate a mistake or correct an imperfection with the next step. He compares this with the novice who with a 'panic-stricken attention to detail' tries to work out everything in advance, fearful of making an unrecoverable error. Alexander's point is that most modern architecture has the character of the novice's work, not the master craftsman's. Successful construction processes, producing well-fitting forms, come from the postponement of detail design decisions until the building process itself so that the details are fitted into the overall, evolving structure. Another characterization of the process talks about visiting the site *with the client* and, after discussion just placing stakes where the corners of the house will be and heavy stones to mark the entrance and perhaps windows. Detailed decisions, such as where to channel the electrics, will be made much later in the project by the appropriate craftsmen–again in constant consultation with the client.

I think that software design should be like that too. It is also a stance remarkably similar to that taken by the proponents of agile processes.

Beck (2000) introduced the set of ideas called eXtreme Programming (XP): a method that emphasizes frequent delivery of tangible, working results. Beck called the approach extreme because it attempts to take commonplace good ideas and apply them aggressively. For example, as he puts it:

- If code reviews are good, review code all the time (pair programming).
- If short iterations are good, make them really short (hours not months).
- If testing is good, then everyone tests all the time.
- If simplicity is good, then build the simplest thing that could work.

It is an implicit principle of XP that one should listen to the business all the time. However, some particularly extreme advocates of XP take this to mean that there is no need to establish the requirements before coding: 'all that matters is the code!' These people take the view that if you get it wrong you can change the code easily, so why bother. This is wrong for two reasons. First, misunderstood requirements may not bite until the development team has moved on to other projects. Secondly, it is hard believe Beck when he tells us that developers with 'ordinary skills' can make it work – contradicting Alexander's view on the craft nature of good design incidentally. Take the example of a very widely reported success story for XP – at Chrysler. In this case there were very considerably talented people on the team (including Beck himself). Furthermore, the project followed on from an earlier, failed project and many of the team from that project were used. It is inconceivable to me that these very experienced people did not have a good grasp of what the requirements were before the project started. XP is an excellent way of building systems and all its techniques may be useful. However, it must be accompanied (not necessarily preceded) by sound requirements engineering techniques.

Taking the core ideas from XP and the patterns we have already encountered suggests an iterative approach to development. This process starts at the lowest level: that addressed directly by XP, with coding. An agile process will almost certainly benefit from extreme ideas at this level. The good ideas include the process hinted at in the image above: write tests based on use cases, write the minimum code to pass the tests (perhaps working in pairs – but you don't have to!), check the code in and run the automatic test harness (this is essential), run usability tests (this is forgotten by most XP-ers), review with the user(s), refactor and iterate. Agility implies that this is done in very short cycles, perhaps measured in days.

Such an approach implies that the team has mastered good specification and design techniques. It also implies that sound refactoring methods are fully understood. The team will have read and absorbed the techniques in, say, Martin Fowler's book on the subject (Fowler, 2000). However, in a. NET or Java world, refactoring implies a lengthy build cycle. Suppose that the change affects a complex web service offering or, worse still, an application deployed on a mobile device. Users may not be prepared to tolerate the delay or service interruption.

Leaving aside the issues surrounding refactoring, responding to user reviews implies a readiness to embrace any changes requested. How can this be managed without deadlines slipping? Here we get to the stuff that the more ostrich-like XP-ers can't see. DSDM (Stapleton, 1997), in common with most iterative processes, imposes project discipline with time-boxes (and other consequences of its nine principles). This strategy implies that the development team has to negotiate with its customer about which features will be dropped in order to accommodate the requested changes. DSDM recommends that its MoSCoW classification of features is the basis of such negotiations, although many of our clients have faced difficulties in trying to convince users that any requirement isn't an M (must have), as I have already pointed out. We prefer a numerical ranking. But what do you rank: use cases? Clearly not, because the review will often reveal new and changed use cases as businesses evolve.

There must be some fixed points to base the negotiation on. In the first place we can regard the specification as fixed during very rapid cycles of a day of two. But some reviews will imply changes to the spec. The specification should therefore evolve at a slower pace, perhaps in two-week cycles. But still we need fixed points for the duration of an entire project; otherwise the time-box discipline will fail utterly.

Our solution has been to fix absolutely the business objectives and their relative priorities at the outset of projects: changed objectives imply a new project. This suggests a much slower iteration rate of perhaps 6 months or more, because the objectives will typically evolve more slowly than the requirements and may therefore be fixed for the duration of the project to help control runaway change requests. Note that hardly any published method says anything about these business objectives. In RUP (Kruchten, 1999) they are subsumed in a 'visioning' statement and are given no particular structure. The very phrase 'use case driven' suggests that the use cases are the starting point. No! Business objectives are the key fixed point in any project. Of course they are related to the use cases in the sense that a use case may support one or more objectives (if it doesn't you're doing something very wrong!), but they are quite different in kind from use cases.

If you think about the process in the image above, you will see that speed of iteration increases in proportion to the tightness of the representation. A business objectives and use cases model can lead to many specifications. A specification can be designed and coded in many ways, giving what mathematicians call a 'representation'. The transformation from loose to tight representation is characterized as the selection of a representation 'functor'. In mathematics every representation functor has an adjoint 'forgetful' functor, which literally 'forgets' the details of a particular implementation but preserves the invariants of the specification. If you're not a mathematician ignore the jargon; this is just a metaphor. But it does provide a framework for the management of iteration and emphasizes the rôle of traceability in a good process.

A reviewed version of this pattern can be found in Graham (2003b).

Therefore **A project should start with loose design but clear business objectives, defined use cases and types and a sound project plan. Allow the design to stiffen only as the application unfolds and only completely towards the end of the project.**

Taking the core ideas from XP and the patterns we have already encountered suggests the following iterative approach to development:

1. Write tests based on the use cases.
2. Write the minimum code to pass the tests.
3. Release the application and solicit feedback.
4. Modify the tests as necessary.
5. Refactor the code and add new features.
6. Go to step 2.

Remember that the business objectives and priorities must remain absolute fixed points. Stick to the timebox plan already agreed. Ensure that every use case supports at least one business objective, and that every business objective is supported by one or more use cases

~~~

Resultant context

Now ensure AUTOMATED TESTING (9) is enabled and that you do USABILITY TESTING (10).

| **Pattern 9** | **AUTOMATE TESTING** |

Context

You are using TIMEBOXES (4) and GRADUAL STIFFENING (5) to manage the project.

~~~

Problem

This means frequent changes and refactoring of code and design. How do you control the costs of such changes while maintaining quality?

Forces

This is another process pattern that could apply equally well to non-BRMS projects.

It is a principle of XP that if testing is good, then everyone should test all the time. XP is thus said to be test-driven and defines simplicity as 'just enough code to make all the tests work'. Unit tests and key-task tests should be based on known use cases. XP also uses the output from its short cycles to refactor code. Examples of refactoring include creating a superclass to abstract common features, creating new plug-points, splitting classes or methods into two, and renaming components to be more descriptive. Doing all these things frequently relies on the presence of automated testing tools, of course.

Fowler (1999) describes well the techniques necessary for refactoring code. With a BRMS this should be much simpler because the rules are separated from the code and maintained and tested separately. However, the same disciplines should be applied: write tests for the rules and rulesets as you discover them. Retest as new rules are added. Where inference rules are chained there will need to be additional refactoring patterns based on the type of inference being performed and tests based on the comparison of test input data and domain experts' assessments of appropriate results. A library of such tests should be built as application development proceeds.

For code regression testing a number of tools is available. There are now some products that automate stress testing such as SafeTest (www.attenda.com). For Java work many companies currently use Junit for unit testing and Ant for integration tests. Junit and Ant are described well at:

www-106.ibm.com/developerworks/library/j-ant/

Many of the leading BRMS products include facilities for building and storing tests for rule and ruleset execution. Blaze Advisor, for example, goes beyond this and offers interactive inference testing (see Chapter 5).

Therefore   **Refactor continuously; both code and rules. Use automated test tools wherever possible. Retest at every incremental change to the code or the rules.**

~~~

Resultant context   Don't forget USABILITY TESTING (10) after an incremental change. Consider other user interface patterns such as those of Duyne *et al.* (2002), Graham (2003a) or Tidwell (1999).

Pattern 10	USABILITY TESTING

Context   You have ESTABLISHED THE USE CASES (3), BUILT A TYPE MODEL (4) and DISCOVERED BUSINESS RULES (5). You have built a version of the application and completed some AUTOMATED TESTING (9). However . . .

~~~

Problem

You just cannot test things like the understandability of the interface, the consistency of left/right mouse button usage, use of colour or many other aspects of usability automatically. Also, does a business rules approach have an impact on usability?

Forces

The first part of usability testing is based on the use cases. Users must be able to perform all key tasks successfully and without frustration, long delays or using tortuous navigation around the application. The use cases help to define scripts for this kind of test. The tests have a dual aspect: did the user accomplish the task and did they find it easy and pleasurable to do so?

Focus groups may be useful before you begin design. They will help to establish objectives and use cases, but they are no substitute for usability testing. You can start the latter as soon as you have even an outline design in the form of hand-drawn screen mock-ups or storyboards. Usability testing should then continue throughout development. If you do it at the end of the project it will be too late to fix the defects that it uncovers.

Obviously, it is better to test with real users rather than or as well as surrogate ones. Unfortunately, it is not always possible to get hold of real users for the time needed.

Business rules management systems present a special opportunity for enhancing usability insofar as their rules are written in natural language sentences understandable to the business people who use them. The structural simplification and separation of concerns that this implies is bound to make it easier for users to create a mental model of how the system works and what it does. The ability to create a mental model is a key prerequisite for usability.

Some BRMS products, those built on top of expert systems technology, can generate explanations in answer to 'how' and 'why' questions. A system that can generate a well-worded explanation of what it is doing (or refusing to do) is clearly going to have more satisfied users that one that cannot.

A reviewed version of this pattern can be found in Graham (2003b).

Therefore   **Consider hiring a usability consultant from outside the organization to avoid personality or political conflicts.**

Perform usability tests from the first prototype continuously throughout the project. Do not confuse usability tests with output from focus groups. If formal, lab-based tests are not within the budget then test informally with the developers as silent observers. If you can't get real users grab people 'off the street' or from other departments or offices. Video the session if possible. Ask people to think out loud as they use the site. Record their comments. First ask them to browse and react unprompted then give them tasks based on the use cases. Record their successes and failures. Ask them if they're happy after a testing session – and why. Reward them for their trouble and ask if they would help in future.

BRMS usually contain technology that makes it fairly easy to include explanation facilities in applications, and this can vastly improve usability, where the rules are chained together or even when they are stand-alone constraints that may not be obvious to all users. It may be necessary to reword the explanations that are generated to make them understandable to users.

Resist the urge to add features such as help messages and explanations, in response to testers' comments, for their own sake. Instead try to remove features that might have confused or distracted the users.

If the testers were able to get back on track easily after making an error then the cost of fixing it may not be worthwhile. Fix it only if it is easy to do so.

Change-manage requests for new features as you would in any software development project; i.e. make sure there is a justifiable benefit.

Video the test sessions to record both what was on the screen and the user's actions. Record users'

comments and try not to lead. Ask open questions (questions that can't be answered with a yes or a no). Record comments. Let the developers watch – possibly on a screen in a nearby room – but don't let then interfere, criticise, help or explain.

~~~

Resultant context

A business rules approach gives additional opportunities to enhance usability. In particular, you can BASE ERROR MESSAGES ON RULES (15).

7.3.2   Patterns for Finding, Writing and Organizing Business Rules

Pattern 11   **ASSOCIATION LOOPS CONCEAL RULES ***

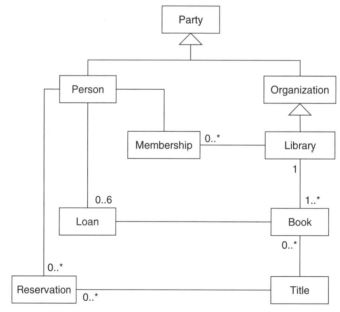

Context

You are trying to DISCOVER BUSINESS RULES (5) and have completed part of BUILDING A TYPE MODEL (4). You know that you must WRITE THE cardinality CONSTRAINTS AS RULES (12).

~~~

Problem

How can you be sure that you have not missed any rules implicit in the type model?

Example	In the image above, start with a person. Do they have a loan? If yes choose one. Every loan is for a unique book that has a unique title. Does the title have an outstanding reservation against it? If yes, go back to the person you started with. Does that person have a reservation? If so, is it for the same title? Perhaps the rule is: 'A member may not reserve a title which they have already borrowed a copy of'.
Therefore	**Look for cycles (loops) in the type diagrams. Start at each type in the loop, choosing a generic instance of that type, and follow the associations to another type. Ask if every route brings you to the same instance. Write down the rule that says it does.**

<div align="center">~~~</div>

Resultant context	The rules you have written down may not be true, so now ASK THE BUSINESS (8) and then ASSIGN THE RULES TO COMPONENTS (9).

Pattern 12	**WRITE THE CONSTRAINTS AS RULES** *
Context	You have started to BUILD A TYPE MODEL (4) and noticed that ASSOCIATION LOOPS CONCEAL RULES (11). You may even have ASKED THE BUSINESS (13) and found that some of these rules are correct. However . . .

<div align="center">~~~</div>

Problem	**Some rules are written as constraints in a style that does not fit into any BRMS. It is unclear at this stage whether there is any interaction (inferencing) among the constraints. How can you clarify the situation?**
Forces	Writing rules in the style of constraints is useful if you want to rewrite them in OCL, as post-conditions in a language like Eiffel, using throw and catch in a language like Java or as database update constraints. On the other hand it may mean that there is a conflict of rule style with other rules elicited by other means (*cf*. Part II of this language). Furthermore, it may be hard to see if there are inferential connections between constraints.
Example	Suppose we have the constraint 'The pilot must be qualified to fly the type of plane assigned to the flight.' Clear enough, but not written as a rule. Why not try this.

```
A pilot may be assigned to a flight if all
of the following are all true:
  A plane has been assigned to the flight;
  The pilot is qualified to fly the plane
  type (of the assigned plane).
```

In this form it is much easier to see that inferences may be possible. Supposing we have other constraints that say, when written as rules:

```
A plane may be assigned to a transatlantic
flight only if it is a Boeing 777.
A pilot may be hired only if she is
qualified to fly Boeing 777s.
```

If we also know the fact 'The flight is a transatlantic flight,' (which may, in turn, be inferred from its origin and destination), then the original constraint may be *inferred* to be true, eliminating the need to check it directly in the database or prompt the user for information.

Therefore   **Rewrite the cardinality and other constraints as rules using a standard style or rule template. Look out for possible inference patterns.**

~~~

Resultant context   Now ASK THE BUSINESS (13) to ensure the rules are (still) correct and whether your discoveries about possible inferences are valid. If you haven't done so already, DEFINE A RULE WRITING STYLE (23) and ensure that you have enforced it when using this pattern.

| **Pattern 13** | **ASK THE BUSINESS **
 aka EXPERT REVIEWER |

Context   You have discovered some rules, perhaps by exploiting the fact that ASSOCIATION LOOPS CONCEAL RULES (7) or by WRITING THE CONSTRAINTS AS RULES (10).

~~~

Problem   **How can you be sure that the candidate rules are indeed veritable rules?**

Forces   Having written a rule after much arduous analysis work, it is tempting to assume that it is true. This need not be the case. The temptation to make assumptions is very strong. For example, if air journeys have an origin and destination then one may jump to the conclusion that these have to be different. Indeed, mostly this is the case. But I remember the days when one could board Concorde at Bradford airport, fly out over the Atlantic for a rewarding sonic boom and then return to – yes, you guessed it – Bradford.

Therefore

A competent user or domain expert must verify every rule. Check also that any inference chains among rules are valid.

~~~

Resultant context

Now that you are confident that the rules are valid, ASSIGN RULES TO COMPONENTS (9).

Pattern 14   ASSIGN RULES TO COMPONENTS *

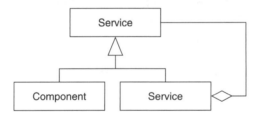

Context

You are developing a rule base. You have DISCOVERED BUSINESS RULES (5), possibly from ASSOCIATION LOOPS (11). You have asked the business (13) to validate the rules. Now you need to store and manage them. Component or service reuse is an important objective.

~~~

Problem

How can you maximize the reuse potential of components and services within a business rules management system?

Forces

Note first that services are built from components and that components, not services, are the units of encapsulation and reuse; components are reused, services are shared. Service sharing is the basis of funding for reuse, but is not the technical means of achieving it. In turn, services may be composed (recursively) of other services. This is an instance of Buschmann *et al.* COMPOSITE pattern, as suggested by the above image.

Some rules obviously belong to component objects, or even to attributes of objects. Attribute constraints might include valid ranges (domains) or there could be rules about attribute default values. Object rules might include simple triggers (relating attributes to methods) or complex rulesets that search for the values of sets of attributes or even the applicable methods dependent on the data presented to the object. If such objects are to be reusable then we need to be able to take them out of one system and drop them in another.

This implies that the objects should contain or encapsulate everything they need to work properly if relocated to a new application. These encapsulating components must include, as well as their own attributes and methods, all references to components and services upon which they depend (i.e. have associations with or send messages to) and *all the rules* that describe how they behave. In other words, if you want reuse, components must encapsulate the rules that apply to them. That way, when you share a service or reuse a component you will get a package of everything needed for that thing to work properly.

On the other hand, the business rules approach recommends that rules should be stored in a central repository for ease of management and update. Also some rules may apply to several objects and be hard to assign to just one. We will need some extra patterns to reconcile these forces. But first . . .

Therefore

Where possible, assign rules and rulesets to the components that they are concerned with or constrain the structure or behaviour of.

~~~

Resultant context

Now consider if a POLICY BLACKBOARD (16) is needed, STORE RULES IN A REPOSITORY (17) and ENCAPSULATE A REFERENCE (18).

Pattern 15	BASE ERROR MESSAGES ON RULES *

Context

You have elicited all or some of the rules and probably have ASSIGNED THE RULES TO COMPONENTS (14).

USABILITY TESTING (10) leads you to think about how friendly the error messages ought to be.

~~~

Problem

How can you ensure that users understand the messages that the system will issue without the need for extensive training or help facilities?

Forces

Rules must be executed by machines but understood by humans, sometimes including business analysts and users. When an error message is generated, this is done on the basis of the statements that the machine understands. The tendency, therefore, is to present error numbers (good to remove ambiguity in debugging) and language that users find hard to interpret. Rewriting the messages involves extra development work. But we have already stored the rules in a form at least close to natural language. Why not exploit that resource?

Therefore

Base as many error and other system generated messages as possible on the natural language versions of corresponding business rules.

Use explanation facilities (that usually work by unwinding the current rule execution stack) to answer as many How? or Why? questions as possible. Again, before presenting the explanations, convert the unwound rules into their natural language equivalents – as stored in the repository. If this is not possible consider handcrafting the natural language versions of explanations or presenting them through purpose-written non-natural-language interfaces.

~~~

Resultant context

This pattern is terminal within this language.

Pattern 16	ENCAPSULATE A REFERENCE *

Context

You want to make your services and components as shareable and reusable as possible but you also need to maintain and manage the rules centrally. You have ASSIGNED RULES TO COMPONENTS (9). Rules that apply to more than one component have been assigned to the POLICY BLACKBOARD (16).

~~~

Problem	**How can you enforce rule encapsulation and not end up with a fragmented, unmaintainable rulebase?**
Forces	Reuse implies encapsulation, although it may be hard to decide where to put the rules. Opposed to this, rule independence implies a separate rule layer. If you encapsulate you lose rule independence; if you centralize you lose the potential benefits of component reuse and service sharing. It seems to be a lose-lose situation. But there is a way out. Decide where the rules *should* go, but instead of storing the rules with the components to which they have been assigned, one can store a reference to these rules in the interfaces of objects that should encapsulate them.
Therefore	**Store the actual rules in the rule repository. When you create or specify any component, ensure that any rules associated with it are both stored in the repository and referenced in the specification and implementation of that component. Perhaps implement these references as methods that invoke the rules on the server. Do this also for the POLICY BLACKBOARD (16).**

$\sim\sim\sim$

Resultant context	This pattern is terminal within this language.

Pattern 17	STORE RULES IN A REPOSITORY ***
Context	You have developed a rule base or discovered some new rules. You have ASSIGNED RULES TO COMPONENTS (14), where possible.

$\sim\sim\sim$

Problem	**How can you make a complex system containing many thousands of business rules manageable?**
Forces	The trouble with encapsulating rules is that it can make them hard to locate. The situation is certainly better than it would be were the rules to be embedded in procedural code; and there are cases where a rule so obviously 'belongs' to a component that it is easy to find it – by finding the component. However, in general, scattered rules will be hard to locate for maintenance.

Furthermore, there are other data that we may wish to store with the rules: author, date created, date retired, containers that realize the rule, etc. Thus, it is natural to consider storing all the rules and ruleset, together with related data and metadata, in a rule database or **repository**. Such a repository will ideally support full version control too.

The repository must include rules that are not implemented in a BRMS as well as those that are.

Just as we ENCAPSULATE A REFERENCE (16) when rules are related to a component, we may even realize the same rules in that component. When this happens the repository must store a reference to the realization.

Morgan (2002) gives a useful list of the sort of things that one might want to store in a repository. Halle (2002) gives step-by-step guidance on how to go about defining a repository, giving examples using the Usoft and Versata products.

Therefore

Store *all* business rules and rulesets in a version-control-enabled repository. Include all data and metadata related to the rules.

~~~

Resultant
context

Now DETERMINE THE SECURITY MODEL (19), DETERMINE OWNERSHIP & PERMISSIONS (22) SEPARATE VOLATILE RULES (20). Ensure that you FOLLOW STANDARDS (21) wherever possible.

Consider the patterns in Arsanjani's (2000) Rule Object pattern language.

Pattern 18	POLICY BLACKBOARD *

Context

You are trying to ASSIGN RULES TO COMPONENTS (14). In some cases this is easy, but in others you face a quandary:

~~~

Problem

If a rule applies to more than one service or component, in which component should it be encapsulated?

Forces

Let's say that there are two candidate components: A and B; and that the rule talks about both of them. If you assign the rule to A then B ceases to be fully reusable because if you reuse it, its rules may be left behind.

Assigning the rule to B causes the same problem for A. How about assigning the rule to both A and B? This would mean you have two points of maintenance for this rule. If you ENCAPSULATE A REFERENCE (16) and STORE RULES IN A REPOSITORY (17) then the maintenance problem goes away; A and B only *refer* to a centrally maintained rule in their interfaces. However, there may still be a conceptual problem.

Some rules may apply to several components and, as well as this, are naturally thought of as 'policy': policy that can change as the business evolves or at the whim of regulators or lawgivers. In such a case, there is an additional complexity in that the new rules may not correspond one-to-one to the old ones. In SBVR terminology, business rules are 'interpretations' of policy to make them 'actionable' or 'practicable'.

A policy blackboard is a central component designed to encapsulate such a policy statement. Rules only encapsulate a reference to these rules *in the blackboard*, which in turn should ENCAPSULATE A REFERENCE (16) and STORE its RULES IN A REPOSITORY (17). In addition to this, each component sets up an OBSERVER to the policy blackboard. There are two variants of this. Either the publisher (the blackboard) broadcasts all changes to rules in which interest has been registered to the subscribed components, allowing them to update their interfaces or stored rules accordingly (if this can be done) or it merely broadcasts an 'I have changed' message, leaving it to the subscribers to decide whether to ask for more information and, indeed, what action to take. To distinguish these alternative architectures we may think of them as subpatterns: PUSH POLICY BLACKBOARD and PULL POLICY BLACKBOARD.

It is sometimes useful, when the rules are grouped into rulesets in a complex way, for example, to segment the policy blackboard into pigeonholes that contain different kinds of knowledge. Subscribing components can register interest in whichever pigeonholes they need to know about.

Such an approach not only makes maintenance changes easier to understand at the business level and implement at the technical level, it also supports a model of complex, cooperative decision making. For example, services implemented as intelligent agents can collaborate in applying the rules to a problem they face, sharing knowledge through the policy blackboard. In that case, the blackboard component may also need methods for handling a problem-solving agenda – which, in turn, may be rule-based.

The alternative to pigeonholes is to divide the rules among several policy blackboards according to the provenance of the rules; e.g. accounting rules, stock control rules, rules of engagement, etc. This approach makes the blackboards themselves more reusable (shareable), but may introduce too much complexity or overhead in agent-based applications.

Example

'Each pilot scheduled for a flight must be qualified to fly the type of plane assigned to the flight,' is a structural constraint. It is almost inconceivable that any policy change would reverse it – except perhaps in Alan Sillitoe's (1971) fictional country, Nihilon. It is not, therefore, an obvious candidate for the policy blackboard, although it could just about conceivably be part of a 'safety rules' blackboard.

'We may not fly more than twenty flights a week out of Bangkok.' 'Our share of transatlantic flights must not exceed 20% of total transatlantic flights.' These rules look more like policy.

This pattern is a specialization of Buschmann *et al.* (1996) BLACKBOARD, which is, in turn, an architectural generalization of PUBLISHER-SUBSCRIBER (the GoF OBSERVER pattern).

Therefore

When rules refer to more than one object, consider encapsulating them (or references to them) in one or more policy blackboard component. This is especially indicated when there is a stated distinction between rules that are 'policy' and those which merely describe the structural relationships between objects.

Remember, too, that it's generally not a good idea to have developers guessing which rules might change and which might not; life is full of surprises.

~~~

| Resultant context | This pattern is formally terminal within this language, although it may be related to SEPARATE VOLATILE RULES (20). |

| **Pattern 19** | **DETERMINE SECURITY MODEL** |

| Context | You STORE RULES IN A REPOSITORY (17). |

~~~

Problem	**How can you prevent unauthorized or malicious access to a business rules application?**
Forces	There is little that is special about BRMS in respect of security, but it needs to be taken just as seriously as for any other business-critical application.
	It is especially the case in the context of SOA that security is an Achilles' heel. Each service is a potential attack point. Until they can properly secure services and applications, companies cannot safely implement B2B relationships with their customers, partners and vendors. And companies increasingly find out (sometimes the hard way) that traditional security protocols, such as SSL, often do not provide adequate security for multiple hop, high value and flexible SOA or web services.
	Several security models for SOA have been proposed. IBM, for example, has proposed a strategy for addressing security within a web services environment. It defines a comprehensive web services security model that supports and integrates several popular security models, mechanisms and technologies (including both symmetric and public key technologies) in a way that enables a variety of systems to interoperate securely in a platform-independent manner. It also describes a set of specifications and scenarios that show how these specifications might be used together. A more general SOA security model is given by Pajevski (2004).
Therefore	**Establish a standard security model for all applications. Ensure that is has been followed for service-oriented and business rules applications.**

~~~

Resultant context	This pattern is terminal within this language but relates closely to DETERMINE OWNERSHIPS AND PERMISSIONS (22), which address the security of the data and the rules themselves.

Pattern 20	**SEPARATE VOLATILE RULES** **aka APPLICABILITY CONDITIONS**
Context	You STORE RULES IN A REPOSITORY (17).

~~~

Problem	**How can you ensure that rules that are volatile (that is, subject to frequent changes) are easy to amend safely?**
Forces	If volatile rules are hidden in big rulesets they may be hard to find when a change is required. On the other hand, they may belong logically in such rulesets. If they cannot be easily and logically separated out, then one may opt to deal with the changes by specifying exception rather than changing the base rule itself. Applicability conditions give one the ability to specify the conditions under which an override or exclusion should apply. Consider the following ruleset:

An Annuity is recommended for a client
> *only if* : the client is retired
> *only if* : the client is averse to risk

An Endowment policy is recommended for a client
> *only if* : the client is young
> *only if* : the client is not averse to risk

An Equity linked policy is recommended for a client
> *only if* : the client is a mature adult
> *only if* : the client is prone to risk or is neutral
about risk

A Bond linked policy is recommended for a client
> *if* : the client is averse to risk
> *unless* : the client is retired

A client is averse to risk
> *if* : the client has children

We have used the 'applicability condition' rule style here. There are three kinds of applicability condition:

'if' conditions are ORed and 'only if' conditions ANDed. 'Unless' conditions are self-explanatory and help to make rulesets (modules) more concise. The other way to do this is to use the and/not construct to represent 'unless'. For example,

```
if   client.preference is riskAverse
        and client.status is not retired
then {client.bestProduct is "BondLinked",
        return client.bestProduct}.
```

The applicability condition style of rule writing is a powerful alternative to the more usual if/then/not style. It can lead to reductions in the number of conditions and overall number of words. Applicability conditions can be shared across rulesets easily by defining these at the module level. It is especially appropriate for rules that are volatile which cannot be easily separated out.

Therefore   **Store volatile rules separately, away from more stable ones. Where this is unnatural, use the applicability rule writing style and handle change by specifying exceptions.**

~~~

Resultant context   This pattern is terminal within this language but related to DEFINE A RULE-WRITING STYLE (23).

Pattern 21	FOLLOW STANDARDS **

Context   You STORE RULES IN A REPOSITORY (17).

~~~

Problem   **How can you maximize and facilitate communication about business rules applications across the organization, and make such applications easy to use and easier to develop?**

Forces   Standards inhibit creativity but they enhance communication within and among teams. It is also true that the essence of all art is repetition with a difference; in other words, adopting a standard may actually increase creativity within its framework. The precondition for this is that the standard must be both sensible and not burdensome.

Of the standards mentioned in Chapter 3, BPMN, BMM, ODM/OWL and SBVR are particularly worthy of note in relation to business rules. But other standards for the general field of system development will be relevant too; perhaps MDA, perhaps CORBA; perhaps ISO 9000; it will depend on your particular environment. You might base your business rules development method on Halle (2002); some organizations have done so. You might, instead, base it on the patterns in this book.

The best thing to do if you want to offer something new is to consider extending a convention rather than replacing it with an entirely new approach. There must be a measurable benefit for you and your users whenever you deviate from a standard.

Standards also help usability due to transfer effects as users move between applications. See Graham (2003a) for further details on this. If your applications have internal conventions, stick to them rigidly on pain of confusing developers and users.

Therefore

Apply *do facto* and *do jure* standards for application development, rule writing, ontology definition, user interface design, repository interoperability/interchange and other relevant areas. If you deviate from a standard, make sure that you can justify doing so. Prefer simple (i.e. short, easily understood and remembered) standards to complex ones. Prefer standards from independent bodies to those pushed by vendors (but beware of the latter's influence on the former).

~~~

Resultant context

Now, as your first standard, DEFINE A RULE WRITING STYLE (23) based as far as possible on proprietary, published or emerging (say OMG) standards.

Pattern 22	DETERMINE OWNERSHIP & PERMISSIONS

Context

You STORE RULES IN A REPOSITORY (17). These rules determine the way you do business. Duff ones could jeopardize the very existence of the organization.

~~~

Problem	**How can you ensure that duff rules don't end up in the rulebase?**
Forces	As pointed out in Chapter 6, you would not create a database application and then allow just anyone to change the data it stores. If the business rules are hidden in the application code then it is normal to put that code under source code control to prevent unauthorized updates. But if the rules are stored separately and in smaller chunks than would be the case for a conventional application, then the rules or rulesets need to have identified owners who are responsible for making or authorizing changes. At a minimum, one must employ a knowledge base administrator and set up review and authorization procedures involving rule authors.
Therefore	**Ensure that every rule has an owner who is a business representative or a domain expert, or both. Assign permissions to entries in the rule repository. Treat the rules as you would treat entries in the database with respect to permissions and ownership. Ideally, get a second user or expert to verify any updates to sensitive rules. The repository should record the rule authors and maintain permissions.**

$\sim\sim\sim$

Resultant context	This pattern is terminal within this language.

Pattern 23	**DEFINE A RULE WRITING STYLE ****
Context	You want to FOLLOW STANDARDS (21) and make your rules as easy to understand and maintain as possible.

$\sim\sim\sim$

Problem	**How can you ensure that rules are readable, understood, easy to maintain and (as far as possible) complete and consistent?**
Forces	The guidelines given by Ross and Morgan, as discussed in Chapter 6, may be combined as follows:
	▪ Rules must be unambiguous and refer to the vocabulary or ontology: the terms and facts.

- Rules should be non-procedural and avoid references to how, when and where the rule is enforced or to who enforces it.
- A rule should be clearly written and possible to achieve.
- No redundant words (fluff, noise, padding).
- Define terms exactly (not too widely or narrowly).
- Make associations explicit, as in 'Every project should *be managed by* a project manager.'
- Remove plural nouns, events as subjects and imperatives.
- Avoid vague phrasings such as 'there may be . . . '
- Avoid permission statements, where possible.
- Write computations as separate rules and break down rules with complex logic.
- Look out for rules that overlap, duplicate or merely rephrase each other.

RuleSpeak builds on these principles by providing a set of rule templates or sentence patterns, as does Morgan. These patterns mandate that rules should use a certain restricted vocabulary; so that the word 'must' appears somewhere in every rejecter rule as does 'may' in every permission rule, if these are allowed. RuleSpeak nominates specific words to deal with time, such as 'before' and 'by'.

It does not really matter whose guidelines and standards you adopt, although the influence of RuleSpeak on emerging standards may be considered significant. What is essential is that you do choose a standard way of writing rules and stick to it – at least within each organization.

Therefore   **Adopt and publish a standard rule-writing style and insist that all rules stored in the repository are checked against the rule styleguide. Ensure that guidelines similar to those above are enforced within the style.**

$\sim\sim\sim$

Resultant context   Ensure your standards take account of the WRITE THE CONSEQUENT FIRST (24) pattern. Embed this pattern when you CHOOSE A RULE MAINTENANCE RÉGIME (40).

Pattern 24	WRITE THE CONSEQUENT FIRST *
Context	You are trying to DEFINE A RULE WRITING STYLE (23).

~~~

Problem

How can you make executable rules easier for users and business analysts to understand?

Forces

The obvious and most general way to write rules is in if . . . then . . . form. This form translates directly into machine understandable languages and is friendly to developers. If also facilitates the observation of inference patterns among the rules.

However, experience has shown that business users find it easier to articulate and read rules written with the outcome preceding the conditions. Inference patterns may still be spotted easily, and there is less likelihood of getting mixed up about ANDs and ORs in antecedent clauses: a common problem in developing rule systems.

Therefore

The 'Consequent if some/all of the following antecedents' style is to be preferred over the 'If Antecedents then Consequent(s)' style.

Avoid ANDs and ORs in rules and use the constructions 'all of the following are true' and 'one of the following is true' respectively.

Avoid the word 'not' in relationship with ANDs or ORs.

This approach also suggests a useful knowledge elicitation method. Ask 'What outcomes are possible?' Then, for each outcome, ask 'Under what conditions does that happen?' This is usually much more effective than asking 'OK then, what are the rules?'

~~~

Resultant context

This pattern is terminal within this language.

7.4 The RulePatterns Language – Part II

The second part of RulePatterns is shown in Figure 7.2. It may be divided into patterns for knowledge elicitation and those for product selection and application development.

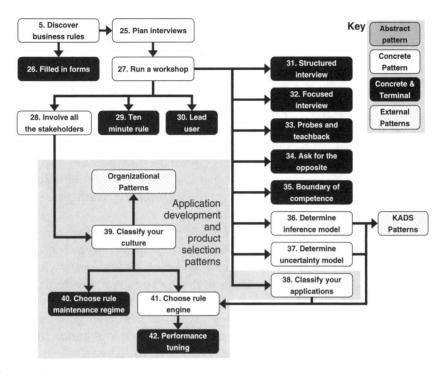

Figure 7-2

7.4.1 Patterns for Knowledge Elicitation

Pattern 25	PLAN INTERVIEWS **
Context	You are trying to DISCOVER BUSINESS RULES (5).

~~~

Problem	**How can you elicit business rules and other knowledge from human beings?**
Forces	People know stuff, lots of stuff. But sometimes they don't know – or can't articulate – what they know. If they do know what they know then all you have to do is ask (assuming no dishonesty or hidden agendas). If there is latent knowledge then you will have to consider more subtle strategies as exemplified by patterns 31 to 37 of this language.
	So why not just interview everyone? The trouble is that that is an expensive, time-consuming procedure. Furthermore, it is common to find that different

people, when interviewed, give different versions of the truth, so you end up having to go round and round the stakeholders, confirming and clarifying points. This suggests that running a workshop is a far better approach. On the other hand, sometimes it is impossible to get people to give up the time to travel to a workshop. In such a case there is no choice but to interview the stakeholders.

Interviews run better if they are planned.

The interview plan can be used to give structure to a workshop, so any effort exerted in creating it is seldom wasted.

Therefore   **Start by outlining plans for stakeholder interviews. The plan should include clear objectives for the outcome of the interview. Select interviewers who have some knowledge of the vocabulary of the domain and who can show humanity and adaptability. It sometimes helps if they have a little knowledge of business rules technology too. Be prepared to abandon the plan during actual interviews or workshops.**

~~~

Resultant
context

Before conducting expensive and time consuming interviews with all the stakeholders, consider RUNNING A WORKSHOP (27). It is usual to conduct STRUCTURED INTERVIEWS (31) before FOCUSED INTERVIEWS (32).

Pattern 26	FILLED-IN FORMS ** aka DATA MINING

Context   You are trying to DISCOVER BUSINESS RULES (5).

~~~

Problem   **How can you exploit the fact that many business rules are already documented or implicit in existing business processes, manuals and other paperwork?**

Forces   Some, though seldom all, business knowledge is nearly always written down somewhere or otherwise recorded. Procedure manuals, legislation, existing databases and applications, forms: all these are potential sources. You may need an interpreter to help you understand the content of these documents.

Obviously, forms are more valuable if they have been filled in with real data.

An existing database is the equivalent of a set of filled-in forms. If one exists then data mining techniques can be used to extract or 'learn' business rules automatically, as we saw in Chapter 4. Data mining uses one of three technologies: multivariate statistics, genetic algorithms or neural networks – or sometimes a mixture of these. We will not examine data mining further within this language. Indeed, data mining may well deserve an entire pattern language of its own.

Where regulatory compliance is an issue, it may be necessary to keep an audit trail showing where the rules have originated. If they have come from paperwork, it might be wise to record this in the repository.

Therefore

Obtain any available procedure manuals, rulebooks, technical documentation and forms. Enlist the assistance of an interpreter of these from within the business. If you are trying to extract rules from forms try to obtain filled-in ones. Use data mining to extract business rules from existing databases. Always check the rules discovered with a human expert or operative (ASK THE BUSINESS (13)).

Consider whether the sources of rules should be included in the repository as metadata.

~~~

Resultant context

This pattern is terminal within this language.

| Pattern 27 | Run a workshop *** |

Context	You are trying to DISCOVER BUSINESS RULES (5) and may have conducted or PLANNED INTERVIEWS (25).

~~~

Problem	**How can you discover requirements efficiently, taking into account all the overlapping and possibly conflicting views of the stakeholders?**
Forces	Interviews are time consuming and can lead to self-contradictory or incomplete information. Workshops, on the other hand, ensure that all participants have heard at first hand the contributions of others, which facilitates compromises where these are necessary. They also generate a sense of shared ownership of the project between and among the developers and users.

On-site workshops may be prone to interruption, but an off-site location is usually more costly, and yet much more focus and relaxation is possible for participants.

The idea is to drive through the core of the requirements gathering process in a very short time, and certainly no more than a week. This implies strong, unbiased facilitation and real-time, technically savvy reporting of the proceedings. The facilitator acts as both guide and interviewer as the event unfolds.

Therefore	**Organize and run a facilitated workshop. Try to hold it off-site. Use a facilitator who has no stake in the project. Appoint a skilled and enthusiastic scribe to record models, rules, decision, and so on.**

~~~

Resultant context	Before running the workshop, make sure you INVOLVE ALL THE STAKEHOLDERS (28). At the beginning of the session announce the TEN-MINUTE RULE (29). Early on in the session identify a LEAD USER (30). Apply patterns 1 to 7 of this language iteratively during the entire session.

During the session consider using all or some of the following knowledge elicitation patterns: STRUCTURED INTERVIEW (31), FOCUSED INTERVIEW (32), PROBES AND TEACHBACK (33), ASK FOR THE OPPOSITE (34), BOUNDARY OF COMPETENCE (35).

Try to DETERMINE INFERENCE MODELS (36) and DETERMINE UNCERTAINTY MODELS (37) where applicable. Try to CLASSIFY YOUR APPLICATIONS (38).

Pattern 28	INVOLVE ALL THE STAKEHOLDERS **		
Workshop participation grid	*Strategic management*	*Tactical management*	*Operational management and clerical staff*
Sales	Sales Director National Sales Manager	Account Managers Regional Managers	Sales Staff Clerical and Telesales Staff
Marketing	Marketing Director	Product Managers	Marketing Assistants
Production	Distribution Director	Production Engineers	Warehouse Supervisors Machinists

Context   You are going to RUN A WORKSHOP (27).

~~~

Problem   **How can you maximize the workshop's coverage of the business area and business rules?**

Forces   Business people are busy, but they are the people who have the knowledge. Not everyone affected by a proposed new business rules system can always be present at requirements capture workshops. A good and oft-quoted example is dealers in financial trading rooms, who are reluctant to leave their investment positions unattended. Furthermore, events involving absolutely everybody could be too large and unwieldy to be managed comfortably. Therefore, some users may act as delegates for their immediate colleagues, managers and subordinates. In the example given, dealer management often stands in for actual dealers. The selection of the right delegates for the task is a key determinant of the success of the event, and the participants must at least include representatives of both the users of the proposed system and the development team.

The presence of key users is both more important and potentially more difficult to organize than one might think. Surely the identity of the correct participants from the user side is obvious and unarguable. Not necessarily! There are several factors to weigh.

Seniority may matter. More senior people may have a better grasp of the wider business issues being addressed in the workshop (or maybe just think they do), but the devil is always in the details, and operational level staff are more likely to be familiar with the detailed intricacies of operations, which will be the things that will break a proposed system if they are not taken into account. So we need people from different levels of seniority – but then we need to be aware that some people will not like to be seen to contradict their boss in public. This is where the facilitator's job of setting ground rules and ensuring fair play becomes important.

Every stakeholder present *must* have authority to commit to the findings of the workshop. Ensuring that this signatory authority is in place is a key job of the sponsor.

The number of people present is hard to get right. The complexity of the interactions will rise exponentially with the number of participants, so life is easier the smaller the number – and the workshop is cheaper to run. But everyone affected by the proposed system should be represented. In the limit, this could mean half the company. What must be avoided is the situation of somebody feeling later that they were improperly overlooked. When the delivered system has a flaw, you do not want to be told that that some stakeholder or user was never consulted in the first place.

Before setting up the workshop, the sponsor, project manager and facilitator should have a prior meeting, generally led by the facilitator, to establish the participant list. They should examine all the options in terms of inclusions and exclusions, probe the emerging list for weaknesses and seek to rectify them and document the reasons for the final invitation list. It can be useful to develop a matrix of candidates, enumerating all the people who could conceivably attend, and then compare possible combinations of candidates from the grid in terms of the impact on the workshop's success. Start with the company's organization chart, and collapse the relevant components into a matrix where the rows are the organizational units, the columns represent approximate seniority levels within the organization, and the cells contain names of logical job descriptions and possible candidates. Note especially that this document is *not* a formal deliverable, because the logical rôles may be the subject of discussion and change during the workshop.

As an example, consider a system to support a new process for product presentation, sales, order taking and manufacturing. This would affect *inter alia* the Sales, Marketing and Production divisions. A possible workshop participation grid is shown in the above image. One should ensure that the grid reflects the actual organizational structure, then fill in the names of the candidates for participation. Considering the options, one representative for each group may make the workshop too large. Beware of the dangers of arguing that a manager can always speak for the troops as well – because he used to be one. This may be true, but it is difficult for people to represent their own needs sincerely as well as those of someone else. The inevitable exceptions that do occur, as with the dealers alluded to above, should be handled with extra care and sensitivity. Otherwise, if any rôle is not to be represented at the workshop, then there is an assumption this rôle will not be affected by the new system – and this should be documented. Some sensitive issues can arise if this is a business process re-engineering project: some rôles may disappear altogether, and asking possible victims of reorganization to contribute enthusiastically to planning the wake may be regarded as unproductive, or in bad taste at the very least. The aim is to produce a participant invitation list along with a supporting document justifying the rôles represented and not represented, and the reasoning behind the choices made.

Users should attend the entire workshop. This is often easier said than done. Freeing people from important work, even for a few days, can have a significant business impact and cost implications. It is also sometimes the case that people will not wish to appear in any way 'dispensable'. Having people attending for a couple of hours, disappearing for a while, then coming back can be very harmful to the progress and ultimate value of a workshop. The sponsor and project manager must work hard with departmental managers to ensure that a block of time is made available to run the event as a block and not as a set of piecemeal sessions with a floating population of participants.

Where at all possible, the complete development team should attend the workshop(s). The challenge is to avoid the development of an 'us and them' attitude: where the user group states its requirements, the developer group goes away and produces something with little contact with or reference to the users. Only later do the users have the opportunity to tell them where they went wrong, when it is often too late to avoid project deadline pressure freezing the mistakes into the end product. The reason for having the whole development team present at the workshops is to help gain *shared* ownership of the system requirements: to understand more fully the content of the formal documents they may be dealing with later in the project.

Importantly, all developers should feel involved in all parts of the project. Of course, someone may be on the team because of specialist skills, because it is known that this will be a key component of the delivered system; but that person should not have the feeling that their contribution is just at the level of their own narrow specialism – they should be regarded as significant contributors to the system as a whole.

Lastly, if the group is very large, it often helps to organize breakout sessions whereby smaller subgroups resolve knotty issues and report back to the main workshop.

Therefore

Involve all the stakeholders: users, IT people, customers, legal experts, workers, managers, regulators, different business areas, whomsoever is affected or knowledgeable. Use the workshop participation grid to check that coverage is complete.

~~~

Resultant context

Now CLASSIFY YOUR CULTURE (39).

Pattern 29	TEN MINUTE RULE ***
	aka TWO MINUTE RULE

Context

You are starting to RUN A WORKSHOP (27). You need to ensure that discussion is focused while not wanting to restrict it so much that information is lost.

~~~

Problem	**How can you shut up vociferous (and possibly senior) bores whilst ensuring that people with valuable information to add are given free rein?**
Forces	Junior or diffident individuals sometimes find it difficult to contribute, and senior or aggressive ones can easily dominate the conversation even though they may have less to contribute. You really don't want long off-topic exegeses in a tightly run workshop. However, so-called 'war stories' sometimes conceal valuable gems of information, and sometimes it needs quite a long presentation to delve into the business rules and processes deeply enough. So exactly how can you, as facilitator, tell the MD to shut the f*** up without causing offence?
Therefore	**At the start of the workshop, announce the ground rules. These may vary, depending on circumstances. They might include a rule that forbids critical remarks (typical of brainstorming workshops). But _always_ announce a ten minute rule: no one may speak on a topic for more than ten minutes. Then, as facilitator, listen to the debate and ignore this rule totally when you feel that useful information is being added by the speaker. Only invoke it when Mr Bigmouth wants to show how clever and interesting he is. Invoke the rule and offer to 'take his issues offline'.**

<div align="center">~~~</div>

Resultant context	This pattern is terminal within this language.

Pattern 30	**LEAD USER** **
Context	You are starting to RUN A WORKSHOP (27). You know that disputes and impasses will inevitably arise.

<div align="center">~~~</div>

Problem	**How can you resolve such disputes quickly in order to move on to the next topic without bureaucratically curtailing the discussion or upsetting anyone?**
Forces	In workshops, when a difficult technical issue arises and there is a significant silence – as people think about it – one often sees eyes turning to one person in the

room. This person may or may not be the most senior individual, but is clearly the focus of respect in the group. He (or she) could be a domain expert or a user or a skilled artisan; there are no rules for this. But he is the guy whose shoulder is cried upon when technical or practical issues need to be resolved. A good facilitator keeps a weather eye open for such people. We call them **lead users** or **lead experts.**

In a workshop, the facilitator may decide to make the identification of the lead expert explicit, saying something like 'Can we agree that Emily is going to resolve issues like this one when we can't agree or just get stuck – at least for this week?' Or it may be more prudent to keep quiet and just make sure that the lead expert is assigned to the teams given open issues to resolve and consulted by the project team regularly throughout the project. This is the right strategy when there is a danger of jealousy arising.

A lead user or lead expert should be appointed as early as possible to resolve disputes. It will be too late to get consensus on who the lead expert is to be after the dispute has arisen. This person will be one respected by other users/experts/colleagues, and need not always be the most heavily involved in the project in terms of time spent. The lead user corresponds somewhat to what DSDM calls an *ambassador* user (Stapleton, 1997). Many users will only be consulted on an *ad hoc* basis, and these then correspond to the *adviser* users of DSDM.

The lead user can help resolve another force: that of confidentiality. The group should be assured that any tapes made will be confidential to the project team, and that they will be destroyed after use or, if required, returned to the lead user for destruction.

Therefore

Identify a lead expert or lead user early in any workshop or in any project. Such a person will resolve disputes and open issues and may also act as the conscience and guardian of the group. It is a matter of discretion (usually the facilitator's) whether the lead user is publicly acknowledged as such. Consult the lead user regularly throughout the project.

~~~

Resultant context	This pattern is terminal within this language.

Pattern 31	**STRUCTURED INTERVIEW ***
Context	You have PLANNED INTERVIEWS (25) or decided to RUN A WORKSHOP (27).

~~~

Problem	**How can you gain a high level overview of a business area, process or problem domain?**
Forces	Structured interviews are high level. They are intended to uncover an overview of a topic or business problem. A structured interview should reveal the key rules, objects and concepts of the domain. Their coverage is 'broad and shallow'. It will result in elicitation of the key objects and concepts of the domain, but not go into detail. In a workshop this corresponds to running a scoping session, where the same techniques can be used.

The plan for a structured interview is always pretty much the same:

- Agree the agenda with interviewee;
- Ask questions, put out PROBES (33);
- Review progress against objectives;
- Move on to the next topic;
- Review and compare with plan: have the objectives been achieved?
- If not, arrange next interview.

Therefore	**Plan to execute structured interviews at the early stages of the project. Use the same techniques in the early parts of a workshop.**

~~~

Resultant context	This pattern is terminal within this language, but structured interviews are often followed by FOCUSED INTERVIEWS (32).

Pattern 32	FOCUSED INTERVIEW *

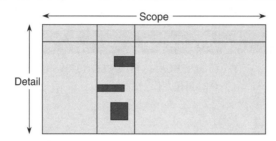

Context

You have PLANNED INTERVIEWS (25) or decided to RUN A WORKSHOP (27).

~~~

Problem

How can you uncover detailed business rules within a business area, process or problem domain?

Forces

Focused interviews are meant to delve into the detail of one area of the problem space covered by structured interviews. Their coverage is 'narrow and deep'.

During the interview process it is essential to search for reusable elements – the grey rectangles in the above image. Analysts should select the area of the domain that gives either 80% of the benefit or 80% of the predicted complexity or reuse/sharing potential as the first area to explore – preferably both. This corresponds, ideally, to about 20% of the scope of the system.

The agenda for a focused interview depends largely on the domain. Focused interviews will be enhanced by applying various knowledge elicitation techniques or patterns such as TEACHBACK (33), repertory grids, ASK FOR THE OPPOSITE (34), task analysis – BUSINESS PROCESS MODEL (2), ESTABLISH THE USE CASES (3) – and BOUNDARY OF COMPETENCE (35).

Therefore

Use a focused interview to uncover details. Use the same techniques in the later parts of a workshop.

~~~

Resultant context

This pattern is terminal within this language.

| **Pattern 33** | **PROBES AND TEACHBACK** ** |

I keep six honest serving men
(They taught me all I knew);
Their names are **What** and **Why** and **When**
And **How** and **Where** and **Who.**

R. Kipling, *Just So Stories* 'The Elephant's Child'

Context

You have PLANNED INTERVIEWS (25) or decided to RUN A WORKSHOP (27).

~~~

Problem

If you are interviewing or running a workshop and you suddenly can't think of the next question to ask, is there a formula to prompt you to think of a suitable question?

Forces

It is essential in interviews of workshops that questions are open rather than closed. Open questions do not permit an answer such as 'Yes' or 'No' that closes further discussion or elaboration. Probes are merely particularly useful types of open question. Probes use all six question words emphasized in the above image.

There are five types of probe. A **definitional** probe asks 'What is a . . . ?' A **directive** probe asks 'Why is that?' or uses the word 'how'. An **additive** probe is used when you say something like 'Go on.' A **mode change** probe could be a question like 'How would your colleagues view that?' or 'Can you give a more concrete/abstract example.' Mode change probes are thus all about scope, viewpoints and generalization (inheritance). A **reflective** probe involves saying the equivalent of 'What you're saying is . . . ' In that case you are far better off when the expert replies 'No, I didn't mean that.' A 'Yes' doesn't give you the chance to ask 'Why?'

Teachback generalizes the idea of reflective probes and involves interviewers, knowledge engineers or business analysts presenting their understanding to the users formally (perhaps with a slideshow) and receiving corrections thereby.

Therefore	**When the obvious question does not come to mind, ask yourself if one of the five probes will help. Consider using teachback when time permits.**

<center>~~~</center>

Resultant context	This pattern is terminal within this language.

Pattern 34   **ASK FOR THE OPPOSITE ****
AKA KELLY GRIDS, LADDERING, CARD SORTS, CONCEPT MINING

	OBJECTS					
CONCEPT	Rolls Royce	Porsche	Jaguar	Mini	Trabant	OPPOSITE CONCEPT
Economical	5	4	4	2	2	Costly
Comfortable	1	4	2	4	5	Basic
Sporty	5	1	3	5	5	Family
Cheap	5	4	4	2	1	Expensive
Fast	3	1	2	4	5	Slow

Context	You have PLANNED INTERVIEWS (25) or decided to RUN A WORKSHOP (27).

<center>~~~</center>

Problem	**Are there any other ways of digging out concepts that are not immediately present in the forefront of a user's or expert's consciousness?**

Forces	One useful knowledge engineering technique for eliciting objects or concepts and their structural relationships is that of Kelly (or repertoire) grids. These grids were introduced originally in the context of clinical psychiatry (Kelly, 1955). They are devices for helping analysts elicit 'personal constructs': concepts which people use in dealing with and constructing their world. Constructs are pairs of opposites, such as slow/fast, and usually correspond to either classes or attribute values in object-oriented analysis. The second dimension of a grid is its 'elements', which correspond to objects. Elements are rated on a scale from 1 to 5, say, according to which pole of the construct they correspond to most closely. These values can then be used to 'focus' the grid: a mathematical procedure which clarifies relationships among elements and constructs. In particular, focusing ranks the elements in order of

the clarity with which they are perceived, and the constructs in order of their importance as classifiers of elements.

To illustrate, first identify some 'elements' in the application. These might be components or concepts, but should be organized into coherent sets. For example, the set {Porsche, Jaguar, Rolls Royce, Mini, Driver} has an obvious odd man out: Driver.

The use of the technique in its full form is not recommended. However, questioning techniques based on Kelly grids are immensely powerful in eliciting new concepts, objects and attributes and extending and refining inheritance structures. There are three principal techniques:

- asking for the opposites of all elements and concepts;
- laddering to extract generalizations;
- elicitation by triads to extract specializations.

Considering the image above, we see that Sporty is a key concept for the user concerned. Asking for the opposite has produced not 'Unsporty' but the concept of 'Family' cars; not the logical opposite but a totally new concept. Thus, asking for the opposite of a concept can reveal a totally new one.

In laddering, users are asked to give names for higher level concepts. 'Can you think of a word that describes all these things: speed, luxury and economy?' This might produce a concept of 'value for money'. It produces more generalizations of concepts.

Elicitation by triads is not a reference to a Chinese method of torture but to a technique whereby, given a coherent set of elements, the user is asked to take any three and specify a concept that applies to two of them but not to the third. For example, with {Porsche, Jaguar, Mini}, top speed might emerge as an important concept. Similarly, the triad {Mini, Jaguar, Trabant} might reveal an attribute such as CountryOfManufacture or the concepts of British and German cars. As a variant of this technique, users may be asked to divide elements into two or more groups and then name the groups. This is known as card sorting, since the elements or concepts are often written on small cards and laid on a table for sorting into groups.

All these techniques are first-rate ways of getting at the conceptual structure of the problem space, if used with care and sensitivity. Exhaustive listing of all triads, for example, can be extremely tedious and easily alienate users.

Therefore

For every concept presented, ask for its opposite and record the new concept if it is not a logical opposite. For every pair of concepts or objects, ask if there is a word that encompasses both; if there is, record the generalization as a new concept. For every triplet of concepts or objects, ask 'Can you think of a feature, attribute, operation or rule that is shared by two of these but not the third?' Alternatively, write the names of all the concepts or objects on cards and ask users or experts to sort them into groups and names the groups. Record the group names as new concepts.

~~~

Resultant context

This pattern is terminal within this language.

Pattern 35	BOUNDARY OF COMPETENCE

Context

You have PLANNED INTERVIEWS (25) or decided to RUN A WORKSHOP (27).

~~~

Problem

How can you be sure that the rules, as stated, always apply?

Forces

Sometimes rules seem to be true because we have limited our perception to the familiar. But there may be unusual circumstances in which the rules cease to be valid. The most common example of this is where a rule is true only between defined applicable dates. A good BRMS will have built-in facilities for handling such time-constrained rules.

In general, one must beware of including rules that may fail when circumstances change. Rules that work fine for a British company may fail when it merges with a German one. These 'boundary conditions' must be made explicit in the way rules are stated.

Example

Suppose the domain is gardening and that we have discovered that 'regular mowing produces good lawns'.

The analyst should not be satisfied with this because it does not show the boundaries of the intended system's competence – we do not want a system that gives confident advice in areas where it is incompetent. We need to go deeper. Thus, the next question asked of the expert might be of the form: 'why?' The answer might be 'Because regular mowing reduces coarse grasses and encourages springy turf'. What we have obtained here are two attributes of the class Turf.

> 'Why does regular mowing lead to springy turf?'
> 'Well, it helps to promote leaf branching.'

Now we are beginning to elicit methods as we approach causal knowledge. To help define the boundaries, ask 'What else?' and 'What about . . . ' questions. In the example we have given, the analyst should ask 'What about drought conditions?' or 'What else gives good lawns?' These questioning techniques are immensely useful.

Therefore

Always ask experts for the boundaries of rule applicability. Consider time, geography, culture, frequency, previous events and so on: anything that may vary. Make the boundary or applicability conditions explicit in the rules statements.

~~~

Resultant context

This pattern is terminal within this language.

Pattern 36	**DETERMINE INFERENCE MODEL** *

Context

You have PLANNED INTERVIEWS (25) or decided to RUN A WORKSHOP (27).

~~~

Problem

How can you ensure that your business rules will be combined in a logical, correct and efficient manner?

Forces

There are basically five inference models to consider for each ruleset:

- *No inference*; each rule is treated as an isolated constraint on database updates or method firing.

- *Procedural execution*; the rules are fired in a fixed order, the results of each firing being passed to the next rule to fire. This is most appropriate for even moderately complex calculations and, more especially, in cases where non-procedural chaining is shown to be too slow.

- *Backward chaining* to determine the value of a given variable, term or fact. This is the method usually most appropriate for analytic problems like classification, matching services to needs, diagnosis and so on.

- *Forward chaining* from given data, where one is hoping to infer the values of one or more currently unknown terms or facts. This is the method usually most appropriate for synthetic problems like planning, scheduling, alarm monitoring (e.g. fraud detection) and so on.

- *Mixed chaining*, where backward chaining is the starting point but, as soon as a value is inferred, then forward chaining proceeds to see if anything else may be deduced. Most problem types can be handled this way, but it can be less efficient than the pure chaining strategies.

A good BRMS will support all the above models.

It is often the case that analysts are so happy to grab hold of a set of rules that they forget to ask the experts about the way they apply the rules. For example, if the domain is fault diagnosis, a skilled mechanic doesn't merely know rules such as 'If the battery is flat then the engine will not start,' they also have a procedure for applying such knowledge. Typically, they might start with the symptom and list a number of rules that could explain it. Then they will conduct tests – usually starting with the cheapest, which might well be the battery. If the battery is not flat and there is fuel in the tank, then the fitter might remove the starter motor to see if it is jammed, and so on. The point is that you need to go through this during knowledge elicitation and leave it until implementation.

It may even turn out that the inference is so complex that it cannot be represented by one of the five models above. In that case a commercial BRMS package is unlikely to be much use to you. As an example, if the problem is to recognize the faces of authorized people entering a secure area, it is unlikely that a conventional rule-based system will be of much use. Less extremely, planning a school timetable is a very hard problem that probably requires purpose built inference code.

The other factor that affects the inference model is uncertainty. Watch out for uncertain inferences being performed by experts.

Therefore **Make sure that you understand the type of inference that is appropriate to the problem. Agree this with your subject matter experts during knowledge acquisition.**

~~~

Resultant context
Determining the inference model prepares you to CHOOSE A RULE ENGINE (41). You should also DETERMINE THE UNCERTAINTY MODEL (37) and CLASSIFY YOUR APPLICATIONS (38) in parallel with this pattern. It is recommended that you consider using the KADS 'patterns' or problem types in relation to determining the inference model.

Pattern 37	DETERMINE UNCERTAINTY MODEL *

Context
You have PLANNED INTERVIEWS (25) or decided to RUN A WORKSHOP (27).

~~~

Problem **How can you be sure that the technology you propose to use can reflect the nature of the problem adequately where it involves some kind of uncertainty?**

Forces
Most BRMS products currently on sale have modest uncertainty management capabilities. But some problems involve uncertainty in an irreducible manner. You need to determine whether this is the case.

It is not reasonable to give here a complete list of all the kinds of uncertainty that might be encountered in the context of business rules. The commonest models that have been used were discussed in Chapter 4.

- Inference under *Bayesian probability*.
- Inference with *certainty factors*.
- *Fuzzy logic*.

- *Verbal labels.* This is the only approach supported by all BRMS products. The inference model is a conventional one as discussed in Pattern 36

- *Special approaches.* Some products offer a proprietary uncertainty management approach. The best known example is Blaze Advisor's scorecards. You will need to determine if your problem can be handled in that way before selecting such a product.

If the problem involves any kind of uncertain inference (other than the last two types) a normal BRMS product will not work – at least not without massive tweaking. You must either buy or build a more specialized product or recast the problem to get rid of the uncertainty management aspect.

In the case of verbal labels you have to determine who will categorize the facts. Should any special facilities be provided in the user interface? For example, if the domain is identifying poisonous mushrooms, there might be a question about colour: 'What shade of yellow is the cup?' To help the user choose, it might help to display pictures and ask something like 'Is is darker or lighter than this one?'

There is a quite different way in which uncertainty might damage your project. It is sometimes said (I think with some justification) that the Sarbanes-Oxley legislation is vague in places and even waffley. Although there have been business rules systems built to support this kind of regulatory compliance, there is not much that you can do with business rules that are not 'clear' – in the legalistic sense of clear. In practice, what you have to do in a case like that is write your own clear rules, interpreting the legislation as you go. Then just pray that the legislation really is vague enough to encompass your concrete version of it.

Therefore

Make sure you understand if your business rules need to use uncertain inference and, if so, what the uncertainty model is. Agree this with your subject matter experts during knowledge acquisition. Consider whether the problem can be recast to eliminate the need for uncertain inferences. Rewrite any unclear rules and check them with experts.

~~~

Resultant context	Determining the uncertainty model may help prepare you to CHOOSE A RULE ENGINE (41). You should also DETERMINE THE INFERENCE MODEL (36) and CLASSIFY YOUR APPLICATIONS (38) in parallel with this pattern.

Pattern 38	**CLASSIFY YOUR APPLICATIONS**
Context	You have PLANNED INTERVIEWS (25) or decided to RUN A WORKSHOP (27).

<div align="center">~~~</div>

Problem	**How can you be sure that the technology you propose to use can reflect the nature of the problem adequately?**
Forces	If you have a hammer, every problem looks like a nail: if you have a BRMS product every problem looks like a business rules application. Well, no! Only some problems can be solved with this technology. To make sure that your problem is one of them, the easiest way is to ask potential vendors for case studies that indicate that they have solved similar problems before. Alternatively, you can try to determine the problem type abstractly, perhaps glancing at the KADS classifications. You might spot that diagnosing a broken customer service process is 'a bit like' diagnosing a malfunctioning car, or that detecting threats to compliance is 'a bit like' spotting hostile incoming aircraft in battle. In such a case it is a fair bet that your problem can be massaged into a form that the technology can handle.
	However, caution is advisable and this analysis needs to be carried out before committing to expensive technology purchases or spending massive effort in design.
Therefore	**Try to classify the application(s) during knowledge acquisition. Is the problem analytic or synthetic? Are there case studies of similar problems that have been implemented successfully using a BRMS or otherwise? Ask the vendors. This is an area where experienced independent consultants may also prove helpful.**

<div align="center">~~~</div>

Resultant context	Classifying your applications prepares you to CHOOSE A RULE ENGINE (41). You should also and DETERMINE THE

INFERENCE MODEL (36) and DETERMINE THE UNCERTAINTY MODEL (37) in parallel with this pattern. It is recommended that you consider using the KADS 'patterns' or problem types in relation to determining the inference model.

7.4.2   Patterns for Product Selection and Application Development

Pattern 39	CLASSIFY YOUR CULTURE **
Context	You INVOLVED ALL THE STAKEHOLDERS (28), so you should be able to understand their *modi operandi*, culture, skills, blind spots and concerns.
	~~
Problem	**How can you ensure that any BRMS product used or business rules application developed will fit in with 'the way we do things round here' and be likely to succeed as a result?**
Forces	BRMS products vary with respect to the skills and backgrounds they assume of their users. The one rooted in the database tradition may assume that your team has good data modelling skills. The ones rooted in the AI tradition may assume that you understand quite a lot about inference strategies. Some expect professional developers to code the rules, others envisage users or non-technical business analysts to do this. Chapter 5 gave several examples of the range of approaches that are current.
	Given a business problem that is to be addressed by a BRMS, you need to enumerate the technical features that characterize the problem and match these against the capabilities of the product, perhaps using the approach set out in Appendix B. However, this is not enough. The product must also be accessed against more cultural criteria. In the spreadsheets of Appendix B this is done by adjusting the weightings of criteria that have a cultural dimension (as well as those of a most technical or financial nature).

This implies that you can decide what kind of cultural environment exists (or is attainable) in your organization.

You need to decide who writes and changes the rules. Are users too busy to do this? Do the users just request rule changes but not implement them? Are the business analysts also skilled programmers? Are developers on hand to talk with users? Will the users enjoy their company or are they regarded as geeks? Is there a 'not invented here' culture? These are the sorts of issues that must be considered. As Appendix B shows, different products fare well or badly when evaluated against different cultural assumptions.

Therefore

Decide who will create the rules. Decide who will maintain them. Establish the skills available to each group. Determine the technical culture. Is it database, Java, mainframe, distributed, COBOL, artificial intelligence, waterfall, agile, etc? Are the users computer literate?

~~~

Resultant context

This pattern prepares you to CHOOSE A RULE MAINTENANCE RÉGIME (40) and CHOOSE A RULE ENGINE (41). You will also be able to apply appropriate published organizational patterns such as those of Coplien and Harrison (2005).

Pattern 40	CHOOSE RULE MAINTENANCE RÉGIME

Context

You have STORED RULES IN A REPOSITORY (17), DETERMINED OWNERSHIP & PERMISSIONS (22) and CLASSIFIED YOUR CULTURE (39) but . . .

~~~

Problem

Who is to maintain the rules? How are they to be managed? How can you ensure that they are consistent across geographical areas, functional units and processes? Can they be easily updated without danger of duplication?

Forces

The rules may exist in several forms: a natural language form and a machine executable form at least. Some products will convert the former into the latter automatically whilst others require a manual (coding) step.

The users can maintain the natural language version of the rules, but only if they are not too busy. If they are, then business analysts must be marshalled to this task.

Business analysts or developers can maintain the machine executable rules (depending on the language used to express them).

Rule ownership implies that owners must give permission before any changes are made.

The repository must record the rule authors and maintain permissions. Assign a knowledge base administrator and set up review and authorization procedures involving authors. Halle recommends doing this during the initial scoping phase. This administration must define what is to be stored in the repository: not just rules but associated data and metadata such the business objective(s) addressed by the rule, who created it, etc. Rôles must be clearly defined too. These should include the administrator, analyst, and, most importantly, a rule steward who has the ultimate say on rule quality, use, consistency, certification and evolution. They may also need to be a steering committee (sometimes called the Rule Council) to resolve conflicts about such issues.

It is impossible to improve rule management if you don't measure results.

Therefore

Define strict procedures for collecting, recording, storing, accessing and changing rules. Ensure that people can challenge rules within this procedure. Create a rule management function with a rule metrics responsibility. Create clearly defined rôles for rule management and maintenance.

~~~

Resultant context

This pattern is terminal within this language.

Pattern 41	**Choose rule engine**

Context

You have CLASSIFIED YOUR CULTURE (39), determined the technical features and CLASSIFIED YOUR

APPLICATIONS (38), and DETERMINED THE INFERENCE AND UNCERTAINTY MODELS (36,37).

~~~

Problem	**What is the best BRMS product?**
Forces	In a few cases there will not be a suitable product, such as when uncertainty is a dominant issue, and you will have to build one or abandon the project. Otherwise this is a classic product selection exercise. Appendix B documents a simple, pragmatic method for choosing between products based on the technical and cultural issues. The material has been placed in an appendix to keep this pattern short and readable. Other, perhaps more rigorous, methods exist, but this one seems to work well enough for the purpose at hand.
Therefore	**Adopt a standard product evaluation method. Ensure it covers cultural as well as technical factors. After applying the method and making a provisional decision, build a prototype of the application to identify any issues that might arise in development. Ensure that adequate product training for staff is provided.**

~~~

Resultant context	This pattern is terminal within this language.

Pattern 42	**PERFORMANCE TUNING**
Context	You have CHOSEN A RULE ENGINE (41) or BRMS product set.

~~~

Problem	**How can you get the technology to execute tens of thousand of rules in times acceptable to the business?**
Forces	All current BRMS products include features that let users tune applications for performance.
Therefore	**When evaluating a BRMS, pay close attention to its tuning facilities. Budget for applying the tuning techniques. Consider executing slow rulesets procedurally. Consider re-writing complex calculations as**

> **conventional programs, but ensure they are linked to the original statement in the repository.**

<div align="center">~~~</div>

Resultant
context

This pattern is terminal within this language.

7.5   Related Patterns and Pattern Languages

The RulePatterns language refers to three external sets of patterns that may contain useful guidance to the specifier or builder of a business rules management system.

7.5.1   Arsanjani's Rule Object Patterns

The only other pattern language concerned specifically with business rules that I have been able to discover was developed by Ali Arsanjani (2000). Rule Object 2001 is a pattern language with 20 or so patterns for the architecture and design of business rules management systems. Some of these patterns overlap (or even contradict) those in RulePatterns, but others follow on neatly from this language at STORE RULES IN A REPOSITORY (17). His patterns are especially applicable when business rules are implemented as methods of objects and are aimed at solving design problems that arise as rules change and evolve.

Here, by way of example, are very brief thumbnail sketches of seven of Arsanjani's patterns, abstracted from his paper:

- RULE OBJECT is based on the assumption that rules change faster than the rest of the object that encapsulates them and recognizes that rules should be stored centrally but still encapsulated locally. Define abstract and concrete rule objects that allow rules to be added dynamically. Rule objects then mediate between separated conditions and actions, applying the rules. This pattern is very loosely related to our patterns 14 and 16.

- CONFIGURABLE WORKFLOW allows developers to modify workflow without disrupting the software architecture. Use a domain-specific language to model the business. Components should read in their workflow description at startup and configure themselves dynamically.

- RULES HAVE STATE insists that state must be maintained between rule checks and application.

- RULES ARE TRACKED. Track the history of changes to condition/action pairs.

- RULE OBJECT REPOSITORY. This is approximately the same as our store rules in a repository (17).

- RULE ACCESS RIGHTS. Managers can create, change and manage rules. This is related to our patterns 22 and 40.

- HASH AND CACHE provides efficient access to subclasses and instances as their numbers increase.

7.5.2 KADS Patterns

The guidance to be found in published knowledge acquisition methods, such as KADS (Gardner *et al.*, 1998), may be useful in conjunction with RulePatterns. In the case of KADS, its 'patterns' are quite different from what normally pass for patterns; they are largely chunks of system building advice presented as process flowcharts. However, KADS does contain a well thought out classification of different inference and problem types, and this may be useful after this language's possibilities have been exhausted. Specifically, you might refer to KADS after or during what you do when you DETERMINE THE INFERENCE MODEL (36) or CLASSIFY YOUR APPLICATIONS (38). KADS was discussed very briefly in Chapter 6.

7.5.3 Organizational Patterns

Coplien and Harrison (2005) present well researched and tested organizational patterns in the form of two languages. These patterns will be as much use to BRMS developers as to those working on any other kind of project. Indeed they quote patterns 1, 2 and 8 from this language. After you CLASSIFY YOUR CULTURE (39), it would be as well to consider if any of Coplien and Harrison's patterns could be usefully applied.

The Business Rules Manifesto*
The Principles of Rule Independence

Article 1. *Primary Requirements, Not Secondary*

1.1. Rules are a first-class citizen of the requirements world.

1.2. Rules are essential for, and a discrete part of, business models and technology models.

Article 2. *Separate From Processes, Not Contained In Them*

2.1. Rules are explicit constraints on behavior and/or provide support to behavior.

2.2. Rules are not process and not procedure. They should not be contained in either of these.

2.3. Rules apply across processes and procedures. There should be one cohesive body of rules, enforced consistently across all relevant areas of business activity.

Article 3. *Deliberate Knowledge, Not A By-Product*

3.1. Rules build on facts, and facts build on concepts as expressed by terms.

3.2. Terms express business concepts; facts make assertions about these concepts; rules constrain and support these facts.

3.3. Rules must be explicit. No rule is ever assumed about any concept or fact.

3.4. Rules are basic to what the business knows about itself – that is, to basic business knowledge.

3.5. Rules need to be nurtured, protected, and managed.

Article 4. *Declarative, Not Procedural*

4.1. Rules should be expressed declaratively in natural-language sentences for the business audience.

4.2. If something cannot be expressed, then it is not a rule.

4.3. A set of statements is declarative only if the set has no implicit sequencing.

4.4. Any statements of rules that require constructs other than terms and facts imply assumptions about a system implementation.

4.5. A rule is distinct from any enforcement defined for it. A rule and its enforcement are separate concerns.

4.6. Rules should be defined independently of responsibility for the who, where, when, or how of their enforcement.

4.7. Exceptions to rules are expressed by other rules.

Article 5. *Well-Formed Expression, Not Ad Hoc*

5.1. Business rules should be expressed in such a way that they can be validated for correctness by business people.

5.2. Business rules should be expressed in such a way that they can be verified against each other for consistency.

5.3. Formal logics, such as predicate logic, are fundamental to well-formed expression of rules in business terms, as well as to the technologies that implement business rules.

Article 6. *Rule-Based Architecture, Not Indirect Implementation*

6.1. A business rules application is intentionally built to accommodate continuous change in business rules. The platform on which the application runs should support such continuous change.

6.2. Executing rules directly – for example in a rules engine – is a better implementation strategy than transcribing the rules into some procedural form.

6.3. A business rule system must always be able to explain the reasoning by which it arrives at conclusions or takes action.

6.4. Rules are based on truth values. How a rule's truth value is determined or maintained is hidden from users.

6.5. The relationship between events and rules is generally many-to-many.

Article 7. *Rule-Guided Processes, Not Exception-Based Programming*

7.1. Rules define the boundary between acceptable and unacceptable business activity.

7.2. Rules often require special or selective handling of detected violations. Such rule violation activity is activity like any other activity.

7.3. To ensure maximum consistency and reusability, the handling of unacceptable business activity should be separable from the handling of acceptable business activity.

Article 8. *For the Sake of the Business, Not Technology*

8.1. Rules are about business practice and guidance; therefore, rules are motivated by business goals and objectives and are shaped by various influences.

8.2. Rules always cost the business something.

8.3. The cost of rule enforcement must be balanced against business risks, and against business opportunities that might otherwise be lost.

8.4. 'More rules' is not better. Usually fewer 'good rules' is better.

8.5. An effective system can be based on a small number of rules. Additional, more discriminating rules can be subsequently added, so that over time the system becomes smarter.

Article 9. *Of, By, and For Business People, Not IT People*

9.1. Rules should arise from knowledgeable business people.

9.2. Business people should have tools available to help them formulate, validate, and manage rules.

9.3. Business people should have tools available to help them verify business rules against each other for consistency.

Article 10. *Managing Business Logic, Not Hardware/Software Platforms*

10.1. Business rules are a vital business asset.

10.2. In the long run, rules are more important to the business than hardware/software platforms.

10.3. Business rules should be organized and stored in such a way that they can be readily redeployed to new hardware/software platforms.

10.4. Rules, and the ability to change them effectively, are fundamental to improving business adaptability.

A Simple Method for Evaluating BRMS Products

This appendix is provided in support of Pattern 41: CHOOSE A RULE ENGINE. It presents a relatively simple pragmatic method for evaluating and comparing BRMS products. More sophisticated and scientifically well-founded approaches are possible, of course, but this one has proved practical in actual studies. We consider three anonymous products in the context of three different scenarios, representing three different sets of cultural and technical imperatives and concerns.

In scenario 1, the customer is an early adopter where the users are keen to be involved in rule creation, with the help of their colleagues in IT. The business analysts are not typically skilled programmers, but do understand the business and their clients well. The IT department is relatively small. The application is a knowledge intensive extension to a larger business system. Imagine, if you will, a sales advisory system, like the one used in the example in Chapter 5, or a system for regulatory compliance or perhaps one for benefit entitlement. In this scenario, therefore, the emphasis is on the ease of rule authoring and maintenance by users or relatively non-technical business analysts.

Scenario 2 maintains the viewpoint of Scenario 1, but lays greater stress on the level of integration with the commercial and technical environment. Furthermore, in this scenario, rule input by users and non-technical business analysts is not required, because the users are too busy. They will maintain rules via custom applications, where appropriate. Scenario 2 envisages a large, more conventional IT department where the users are available for knowledge elicitation but do not have the time or inclination to create the rules and the ontology themselves. There is a strong mainframe culture and the applications must be integrated closely with the legacy. Imagine, in this case, an application like credit card fraud detection or credit scoring where the BRMS will be closely integrated with multiple existing databases. In this scenario the users are busy, and do not want to interact with the rules often. They do, however, require rule-based data validation at the time of data entry.

Development resources are available to create the rules and write predefined rule maintenance applications (RMAs).

Scenario 3 abandons the emphasis on rule creation by end users and assumes a strong commitment to a modern distributed technical architecture, such as J2EE. In this scenario users will have a rule maintenance rôle but will not get involved in the initial set up of the BRMS. Plenty of skilled IT people are available to do this, with assistance from the users. However, the users are keen to interact with the rulebase using a natural language interface rather than an RMA. Imagine, here, an investment bank developing a credit rating system that must integrate with an existing J2EE application suite and architecture.

The product scores in each scenario are, of course, the same but the weightings vary from scenario to scenario, depending on the technical and cultural imperatives given in each situation. You will be able to enter these weightings if you have CLASSIFIED YOUR CULTURE (39).

In every scenario, support for object modelling features such as inheritance and encapsulation is regarded as essential. All three products score well on this. Help and explanation are limited in all three products. In each case they can be coded in applications. Uncertainty management is also limited in all three products.

Product P majors on natural language rule authoring and use by non-technical staff. Product Q adopts a different approach, preferring to let users edit rules using rule maintenance applications. Product R majors on architectural flexibility and allows users to maintain but not create rules using natural language.

The results of our evaluation of features are summarized in the multi-attribute decision making (MADM) analyses shown in tabular form in the following sections. Scores are on a scale from 0 to 5 with 0 meaning 'not worth considering at all' and 5 being 'as good as could be expected'.

The weightings given to each attribute reflect the needs of the particular environment envisaged. Similar weightings would apply to many application types such as loan or credit approval, fraud detection, eligibility screening and so on. However, there is obviously scope for amending the weights in particular contexts. You can easily rerun the analysis with your own weights. The final scores are the sum of the individual scores for each product multiplied by their weightings (SUMPRODUCT($B3:$B82,C3:C82) in Excel). The normalized scores are arrived at by dividing the totals by the sum of the weights (if non-zero) and are thus on a scale from 0 to 1.

Clearly, there is a subjective element involved in arrived at some of the scores, but one should try to minimize the effect of this. In point of fact, some of the factors that lead to product acceptance within an organization are often subjective ones.

Bearing these points in mind, the analysis should be taken as a fairly rough indication of which product is fittest for purpose, rather than as a definitive description. However, with so many attributes, it is actually quite hard to bias the result in practice; so you can usually be quite confident of the conclusions in terms of rank ordering.

B.1   Evaluation in Scenario 1

In this scenario, our evaluation concentrates on the ease with which a business analyst can create a business rules management system. We are also interested in the degree of coverage of the full development lifecycle from knowledge capture to implementation and testing, and the level of integration of the knowledge management tool(s) with the rule engine: the number of steps involved, their relative complexity and the level of automation of each step.

Using Product P, users can use alternative syntactic constructs at will, as long as the semantic aspect (the concept model) remains the same. This provides great flexibility to users. It is also important to note that allowing you the map an external implementation model to a business-level conceptual model helps separate the business rules from the implementation model (in all three products) with all the benefits that this entails. For example, as a .NET or Java application changes, you only need change the mappings and not the statements.

Deployment is to be on a variety of machines, from ageing (Win98 to XP) laptops to Palm pilots and XP desktops (often to be used by the laptop/palm users when in the office), so that the memory footprint is an issue in this scenario. The IT organization is committed to agile development methods.

Usability is at the best of times a subjective matter. All three products passed our tests for basic usability, but Products P and Q come out strongest in this respect.

In evaluating and comparing products we use the many criteria shown in the tables below. These include accessibility and ease of use for untrained users, asking what pre-requisite skills are needed for effective use of the tool by subject matter experts, business analysts and IT staff. A high score is achieved when all these are accommodated well. Is there a clear and consistent separation of business knowledge from implementation details? How expressive is the rule language for business users compared with implementation staff? Relevant to this is the question of who does the translation of business rules into the execution language syntax. Product P offers the highest level of automation in this respect.

Metamodel availability and extensibility refers to the availability of built in concept libraries covering such things as time, units and quantities. Product P, in particular, scores well because it provides a library of concepts that can be readily extended into domain specific areas.

For each product, we compared the completeness of representation of concepts within the knowledge base. Does it include concepts, relationships, vocabulary, phrasings, definitions, policies, constraints, rules, and so on? All products score well, but Product P does particularly well. It provided the best support for documenting, defining and standardizing an organizational vocabulary and in preventing ambiguity in rule definitions.

The results of our evaluation of features are summarized in the MADM analysis shown in Table B.1.

Table B-1 Multi-attribute decision making analysis. Scenario 1

	Attributes	*Weight*	P	Q	R
	General Attributes				
1	Price	*2*	4	2	3
2	Defect free	*3*	4	4	4
3	Ease of installation	*3*	5	4	2
4	Interface/Usability	*5*	4	3	3
5	Repository-based	*5*	5	5	5
6	Technical support	*5*	5	5	3
7	Availability and coverage of professional services – including training	*5*	4	4	4
8	Availability of a defined knowledge engineering method	*3*	5	3	3
9	Coverage of full-lifecycle development from knowledge capture to implementation and testing	*5*	5	5	4
10	Availability of a knowledge capture and management (KM) tool	*5*	5	4	4
11	Plans for forthcoming upgrades	*2*	4	4	4
12	Adherence to IT industry standards	*3*	3	4	4
	Integration of KM tool with the rule engine				
13	Steps involved	*4*	4	3	3
14	Simplicity	*4*	4	5	3
15	Level of automation	*4*	5	5	4
	Knowledge Capture and Management Tool				
16	Accessibility and Ease of use by untrained users – pre-requisite skills for effective use of the tool (perspectives of Subject matter experts, business analysts, IT staff)	*5*	4	3	2
	Clarity, depth and coverage of supplied documentation				
17	User manuals	*4*	5	4	3

Table B-1   *(continued)*

	Attributes	Weight	P	Q	R
18	Examples	3	4	4	3
19	Separation and consistency of business knowledge from implementation details	4	5	3	1
20	Availability and expressiveness of language for business users vs. implementation (in particular ability to support description of rules in natural language)	5	5	3	2
21	Automatic translation of business statements into the execution language/syntax?	4	5	4	3
	Knowledge Management features				
22	Meta model availability and extensibility	4	4	4	2
23	Completeness of representation within the KB (concepts, relationships, vocabulary, phrasings, definitions, policies, constraints, rules)	4	4	4	4
24	Support for documenting, defining and standardizing an organizational vocabulary and using it to prevent ambiguity in rule definitions	4	4	3	3
25	Support for different rule expression formats (if/then, declarative/definitional statements, constraints, general English statements)	4	5	3	4
26	Change management and version control features	5	5	5	5
27	Support for archetypes, templates, overrides/ specialization, and exclusions – Including the ability to specify the conditions under which an override or exclusion should apply (i.e. applicability conditions)	4	4	3	3
28	Reuse of applicability statements in relation to rules and rule sets (drag & drop)	4	4	2	3
29	Table and decision table support	3	2	4	4
30	Decision threshold support	2	3	4	2
31	Automatic, multiple, cross-referencing of rules and concepts (ontology)	5	5	3	4
32	Ability to proactively check for ambiguity in statements	4	5	3	4
33	Support for incremental development (selective deployment)	5	4	4	2
34	Ability to create deployment polices with future effective and expiration dates	3	5	5	4
35	Support for multiple evaluation and control strategies	4	4	4	5

Table B-1   *(continued)*

	Attributes	Weight	P	Q	R
36	Support for inexact reasoning	*4*	2	3	1
37	Support for reasoning with time	*3*	4	2	1
38	Built-in support for importing, mapping to business vocabulary, usage, orchestration, and integration with external data representations, procedures, methods (XML, .NET, Java)	*2*	3	3	3
	Multi-user features				
39	Concurrent KB development. Support for a team repository	*3*	5	5	4
	Built in support for testing and simulation within the KM tool – without the need for an external implementation				
40	Ability to specify test cases	*5*	5	4	4
41	Ability to execute test cases	*5*	4	5	3
42	Code generation capabilities	*5*	5	4	3
43	Ability to define/maintain/organize rule groups/sets	*5*	5	5	5
44	Debug/trace facilities	*5*	4	4	3
45	Report generation capabilities	*4*	3	3	3
46	Support for Web Services	*4*	5	4	4
	The Rule Engine				
47	Support for rete	*5*	5	5	5
48	Support for backward and mixed chaining	*5*	3	4	2
49	Automatic truth maintenance	*4*	5	4	4
50	Support for debugging/audit trail of rule firing	*5*	5	4	4
51	Support for XML input	*4*	5	4	4
52	Automation of integration with Java, .NET, and databases	*5*	4	3	3
53	Ability to handle large no. of rules	*5*	5	4	5
54	Performance and scalability (ability to handle large no. of concurrent requests/transactions, users, and rule executions)	*5*	5	3	4
55	Ease of integration with external applications (e.g. Web Services, embedded)	*4*	3	3	3
56	Does the language have the power to handle procedural or technical functions without requiring a call to an external routine?	*4*	2	3	4

Table B-1   (*continued*)

	Attributes	Weight	P	Q	R
57	Can the language call on external and mathematical routines when desired?	*4*	4	5	5
58	Memory footprint (suitability for embedding in small devices)	*4*	5	4	4
59	Availability across multiple platforms	*4*	4	4	3
60	Availability of alternative interfaces (e.g. C, C++, Java, .NET)	*3*	5	3	4
61	Support for dynamic 'hot' deployment	*4*	4	4	3
62	Runtime rule updates	*2*	4	4	4
63	Support for multiple concurrent KBs	*4*	4	4	3
64	Ability to update KBs with minimal user impact	*5*	5	5	3
65	Ability to handle different deployment dates	*4*	5	5	4
66	Maturity in rule engine market with proven rete-based implementations.	*3*	4	5	5
67	Conflict resolution	*4*	3	4	3
68	Interactive testing	*4*	1	3	1
	Other factors (Technical environment, culture, etc.)				
69	Integration with supplier's product range	*0*	1	5	3
70	Need to leverage technical skills	*0*	1	4	5
71	Suitable for mainframe culture	*0*	3	5	3
72	Integration with J2EE environment	*0*	2	3	5
73	UML object model input	*0*	0	1	3
74	COBOL integration	*0*	1	4	2
75	Custom rule maintenance screens	*0*	0	4	1
76	RUP plug-ins available	*0*	0	3	0
77	Supplier involved with standards bodies	*0*	1	4	4
78	Foreign (i.e. not English) Language support	*1*	0	2	3
79	Java compatible coding style	*0*	2	2	5
80	Effectiveness of performance tuning	*0*	1	3	1
	Total weights and scores	*1375*	1172	1059	935
	Normalized scores		**0.85**	**0.77**	**0.68**

The interpretation of the results for this scenario, therefore, is that Product P scores significantly higher than the other two products based both on the feature-by-feature comparison and subjective evaluation.

B.2   Evaluation in Scenario 2

Scenario 2 is a large conventional IT department. The users are busy and have no desire to engage in rule authoring, although they will need to modify rules and need rule-based data validation. Developers and trained analysts will write and test the rules. Resources are also available to create custom rule maintenance applications. There is an historic COBOL and mainframe culture and applications must be closely integrated with channel-hungry mainframe applications: both legacy and evolving. Nevertheless, there is a commitment to service oriented architecture and rulesets must be presented to applications as services, as in Scenario 1. RUP is used as the main development method for new systems.

We assume that this scenario encounters similar price and performance characteristics to Scenario 1.

In this scenario the natural language input that so strongly characterizes Scenario 1 is regarded as a positive disadvantage.

The results of our evaluation of features are summarized in the MADM analysis shown in Table B.2.

In this situation we find that Product R catches up with Product P and Product Q overtakes it. Adding subjective interpretation and in recognition of the fact that these decision tables are only an approximate guide, the interpretation of the results for this scenario, therefore, is that Product Q scores significantly higher than the other two products based both on the feature-by-feature comparison and the subjective evaluation.

B.3   Evaluation in Scenario 3

This scenario is based on a strong IT culture. Initial application and rule development will be done by skilled Java and J2EE staff, based on user interviews and workshops. Implementation will be on an n-tier, networked platform. Users want to maintain and manage their rules. Product R did better in this scenario, just beating Product Q and pushing Product P into a clear third place.

Table B-2   Multi-attribute decision making analysis. Scenario 2

	Attributes	*Weight*	P	Q	R
	General Attributes				
1	Price	*3*	*4*	*2*	*3*
2	Defect free	*4*	*4*	*4*	*4*
3	Ease of installation	*3*	*5*	*4*	*2*
4	Interface/Usability	*4*	*4*	*3*	*3*
5	Repository-based	*5*	*5*	*5*	*5*
6	Technical support	*5*	*5*	*5*	*3*
7	Availability and coverage of professional services – including training	*5*	*4*	*4*	*4*
8	Availability of a defined knowledge engineering method	*3*	*5*	*3*	*3*
9	Coverage of full-lifecycle development from knowledge capture to implementation and testing	*5*	*5*	*5*	*4*
10	Availability of a knowledge capture and management (KM) tool	*3*	*5*	*4*	*4*
11	Plans for forthcoming upgrades	*2*	*4*	*4*	*4*
12	Adherence to IT industry standards	*4*	*3*	*4*	*4*
	Integration of KM tool with the rule engine				
13	Steps involved	*3*	*4*	*3*	*3*
14	Simplicity	*3*	*4*	*5*	*3*
15	Level of automation	*3*	*5*	*5*	*4*
	Knowledge Capture and Management Tool				
16	Accessibility and Ease of use by untrained users – pre-requisite skills for effective use of the tool (perspectives of Subject matter experts, business analysts, IT staff)	*1*	*4*	*3*	*2*
	Clarity, depth and coverage of supplied documentation				
17	User manuals	*4*	*5*	*4*	*3*
18	Examples	*3*	*4*	*4*	*3*
19	Separation and consistency of business knowledge from implementation details	*2*	*5*	*3*	*1*

Continued overleaf

Table B-2   (*continued*)

	Attributes	Weight	P	Q	R
20	Availability and expressiveness of language for business users vs. implementation (in particular ability to support description of rules in natural language)	*0*	5	3	2
21	Automatic translation of business statements into the execution language/syntax?	*2*	5	4	3
	Knowledge Management features				
22	Meta model availability and extensibility	*3*	4	4	2
23	Completeness of representation within the KB (concepts, relationships, vocabulary, phrasings, definitions, policies, constraints, rules)	*4*	4	4	4
24	Support for documenting, defining and standardizing an organizational vocabulary and using it to prevent ambiguity in rule definitions	*2*	4	3	3
25	Support for different rule expression formats (if/then, declarative/definitional statements, constraints, general English statements)	*4*	5	3	4
26	Change management and version control features	*5*	5	5	5
27	Support for archetypes, templates, overrides/ specialization, and exclusions – Including the ability to specify the conditions under which an override or exclusion should apply (i.e. applicability conditions)	*4*	4	3	3
28	Reuse of applicability statements in relation to rules and rule sets (drag & drop)	*0*	4	2	3
29	Table and decision table support	*4*	2	4	4
30	Decision threshold support	*5*	3	4	2
31	Automatic, multiple, cross-referencing of rules and concepts (ontology)	*3*	5	4	4
32	Ability to proactively check for ambiguity in statements	*3*	5	3	4
33	Support for incremental development (selective deployment)	*5*	4	4	2
34	Ability to create deployment polices with future effective and expiration dates	*3*	5	5	4
35	Support for multiple evaluation and control strategies	*3*	4	4	5
36	Support for inexact reasoning	*4*	2	3	1
37	Support for reasoning with time	*2*	4	2	1

Table B-2   *(continued)*

	Attributes	Weight	P	Q	R
38	Built-in support for importing, mapping to business vocabulary, usage, orchestration, and integration with external data representations, procedures, methods (XML, .NET, Java)	3	3	3	3
	Multi-user features				
39	Concurrent KB development. Support for a team repository	3	5	5	4
	Built in support for testing and simulation within the KM tool – without the need for an external implementation				
40	Ability to specify test cases	5	5	4	4
41	Ability to execute test cases	5	4	5	3
42	Code generation capabilities	4	5	4	3
43	Ability to define/maintain/organize rule groups/sets	5	5	5	5
44	Debug/trace facilities	5	4	4	3
45	Report generation capabilities	4	3	3	3
46	Support for Web Services	3	5	4	4
	The Rule Engine				
47	Support for rete	5	5	5	5
48	Support for backward and mixed chaining	5	3	4	2
49	Automatic truth maintenance	4	5	4	4
50	Support for debugging/audit trail of rule firing	4	5	4	4
51	Support for XML input	2	5	4	4
52	Automation of integration with Java, .NET, and databases	5	4	3	3
53	Ability to handle large no. of rules	5	5	4	5
54	Performance and scalability (ability to handle large no. of concurrent requests/transactions, users, and rule executions)	3	5	3	4
55	Ease of integration with external applications (e.g. Web Services, embedded)	3	3	3	3
56	Does the language have the power to handle procedural or technical functions without requiring a call to an external routine?	4	2	3	4

Continued overleaf

Table B-2   (*continued*)

	Attributes	Weight	P	Q	R
57	Can the language call on external and mathematical routines when desired?	4	4	5	5
58	Memory footprint (suitability for embedding in small devices)	2	5	4	4
59	Availability across multiple platforms	4	4	4	3
60	Availability of alternative interfaces (e.g. C, C++, Java, .NET)	2	5	3	4
61	Support for dynamic 'hot' deployment	4	4	4	3
62	Runtime rule updates	4	4	4	4
63	Support for multiple concurrent KBs	2	4	4	3
64	Ability to update KBs with minimal user impact	5	5	5	3
65	Ability to handle different deployment dates	4	5	5	4
66	Maturity in rule engine market with proven rete-based implementations.	5	4	5	5
67	Conflict resolution	4	3	4	3
68	Interactive testing	5	1	3	1
	Other factors (Technical environment, culture, etc.)				
69	Integration with supplier's product range	5	1	5	3
70	Need to leverage technical skills	4	1	4	5
71	Suitable for mainframe culture	5	3	5	3
72	Integration with J2EE environment	0	2	3	5
73	UML object model input	2	0	1	3
74	COBOL integration	5	1	4	2
75	Custom rule maintenance screens	5	0	4	1
76	RUP plug-ins available	4	0	3	0
77	Supplier involved with standards bodies	3	1	4	4
78	Foreign (i.e. not English) Language support	1	0	2	3
79	Java compatible coding style	0	2	2	5
80	Effectiveness of performance tuning	3	1	3	1
	Total weights and scores	1400	1049	1111	931
	Normalized scores		**0.75**	**0.79**	**0.67**

B.4   Analysis of Results

Along with service oriented architectures and component-based development, business rules management systems are an essential component of modern agile businesses. They vastly reduce the problems associated with the evolution of complex and volatile business strategies and policies.

This appendix compared three imaginary products with features based on those to be found in actual enterprise-class BRMS products, and which can be used within a component-based development organization. All three products are capable of delivering effective solutions. However, there are factors that discriminate among them.

Our weighted multi-attribute analysis gave the following results.

In Scenario 1, Product P had the highest score: 85% of the maximum possible score. Product Q came second with 77%. Product R scored 68%; all very respectable scores, indicating that these are all good products.

Product P seems to be ideal for situations where users and non-technical business analysts need to create and maintain the rules and where development resources are at a premium. If you really want to engage users, as well as business analysts, in the development process, and thus reduce the time to market of new versions of an application, as policy evolves, then this is the indicated choice. Its natural language syntax capability and automatic inferencing and code generation facilities make it the clear winner in Scenario 1. It should help reduce knowledge base development and maintenance costs significantly, compared to its competitors. Product P is the right product when you have good access to users and domain experts and need them to help maintain and (especially) create the rulebase.

In Scenario 2, Product Q has the highest score: 79% of the maximum possible score. Product P came second with 75%. Product R scored 67%; all respectable scores again.

Product Q seems to be most suitable for environments where multiple deployment types may be required and business users require customized rule maintenance. It appears to be a more productive environment than Product R, and puts the business more in control of application development than the latter. From the point of view of the rule language, it stands midway between Products P and R, but its rule maintenance application features make it the most suitable in this scenario. Adopting Product Q will reduce development and deployment times. However, the rule syntax is still rather opaque to business users so that RMAs are essential. Product Q is a mature product that technically savvy business analysts can use to create rule-based applications providing they take the time to learn the product.

In Scenario 3, Product R has the highest score: 74% of the maximum possible score only just beating Product Q came second with 75%. Product P scored 70%; all respectable scores yet again.

If your culture is more developer-centric – i.e. the developers create applications largely in isolation from the users after an initial period of knowledge gathering and during acceptance testing – then Product R is a viable option. This is reflected in Scenario 3. Developers will code the knowledge base, but users may read and understand the rules, providing that enough developer effort has been put into the rule language customization that the product makes possible.

All three products have the features needed to support enterprise projects: multiple views of the same rules, rapid code deployment for various installations, easily maintainable code, version control, structured user access, excellent debugging tools, and English-like rule-building languages that makes maintaining rules easy for developers if not for business analysts and users. Product P's natural language approach is superior to that of either of its competitors for pure rule writing, whereas for custom rule maintenance by business users, Product Q's approach may be preferable. Product R excels where the culture is Java and users prefer to interact with their rules in a natural language.

All three products can be used to implement Morgan's or Ross's recommendations on rule syntax and style, but it is a lot easier to do this using Products P and R. The use of a rule maintenance application in Product Q, however, might make these recommendations less relevant.

All three products have weaknesses as well as strengths. No BRMS product should be adopted without training.

B.5   The Method

The method exemplified by the above analysis may be applied to the evaluation of any BRMS product. Decide on the weightings according to your priorities and organizational culture, bearing in mind also the nature of likely applications and deployment considerations. It may be necessary to change, reword or add attributes. Rather than remove attributes, it is better to suppress them by awarding a weighting of zero; then they can be used for future studies and you will be able to see (and justify) what has been explicitly left out of the evaluation. Score each candidate product against each attribute with a non-zero weighting. Then apply professional judgment before coming to a final conclusion.

Your evaluation and scores may well be based on a toy application, like the one used in this book. Where the scores are close, ask the top-scoring suppliers if they can help you build a prototype of part of your actual application.

Table B-3 Multi-attribute decision making analysis. Scenario 3

	Attributes	*Weight*	P	Q	R
	General Attributes				
1	Price	*3*	4	2	3
2	Defect free	*3*	4	4	4
3	Ease of installation	*0*	5	4	2
4	Interface/Usability	*3*	4	3	3
5	Repository-based	*5*	5	5	5
6	Technical support	*1*	5	5	3
7	Availability and coverage of professional services – including training	*5*	4	4	4
8	Availability of a defined knowledge engineering method	*0*	5	3	3
9	Coverage of full-lifecycle development from knowledge capture to implementation and testing	*0*	5	5	4
10	Availability of a knowledge capture and management (KM) tool	*3*	5	4	4
11	Plans for forthcoming upgrades	*4*	4	4	4
12	Adherence to IT industry standards	*5*	3	4	4
	Integration of KM tool with the rule engine				
13	Steps involved	*1*	4	3	3
14	Simplicity	*1*	4	5	3
15	Level of automation	*1*	5	5	4
	Knowledge Capture and Management Tool				
16	Accessibility and Ease of use by untrained users – pre-requisite skills for effective use of the tool (perspectives of Subject matter experts, business analysts, IT staff)	*0*	4	3	2
	Clarity, depth and coverage of supplied documentation				
17	User manuals	*2*	5	4	3
18	Examples	*1*	4	4	3
19	Separation and consistency of business knowledge from implementation details	*2*	5	3	1
20	Availability and expressiveness of language for business users vs. implementation (in particular ability to support description of rules in natural language)	*0*	5	3	2
21	Automatic translation of business statements into the execution language/syntax?	*0*	5	4	3

Table B-3 (*continued*)

	Attributes	Weight	P	Q	R
	Knowledge Management features				
22	Meta model availability and extensibility	1	4	4	2
23	Completeness of representation within the KB (concepts, relationships, vocabulary, phrasings, definitions, policies, constraints, rules)	4	4	4	4
24	Support for documenting, defining and standardizing an organizational vocabulary and using it to prevent ambiguity in rule definitions	1	4	3	3
25	Support for different rule expression formats (if/then, declarative/definitional statements, constraints, general English statements)	1	5	3	4
26	Change management and version control features	5	5	5	5
27	Support for archetypes, templates, overrides/ specialization, and exclusions – Including the ability to specify the conditions under which an override or exclusion should apply (i.e. applicability conditions)	2	4	3	3
28	Reuse of applicability statements in relation to rules and rule sets (drag & drop)	0	4	2	3
29	Table and decision table support	5	2	4	4
30	Decision threshold support	0	3	4	2
31	Automatic, multiple, cross-referencing of rules and concepts (ontology)	1	5	4	4
32	Ability to proactively check for ambiguity in statements	1	5	3	4
33	Support for incremental development (selective deployment)	1	4	4	2
34	Ability to create deployment polices with future effective and expiration dates	1	5	5	4
35	Support for multiple evaluation and control strategies	5	4	4	5
36	Support for inexact reasoning	0	2	3	1
37	Support for reasoning with time	0	4	2	1
38	Built-in support for importing, mapping to business vocabulary, usage, orchestration, and integration with external data representations, procedures, methods (XML, .NET, Java)	2	3	3	3

Continued overleaf

Table B-3   *(continued)*

	Attributes	*Weight*	P	Q	R
	Multi-user features				
39	Concurrent KB development. Support for a team repository	*3*	5	5	4
	Built in support for testing and simulation within the KM tool – without the need for an external implementation				
40	Ability to specify test cases	*3*	5	4	4
41	Ability to execute test cases	*3*	4	5	3
42	Code generation capabilities	*0*	5	4	3
43	Ability to define/maintain/organize rule groups/sets	*5*	5	5	5
44	Debug/trace facilities	*5*	4	4	3
45	Report generation capabilities	*5*	3	3	3
46	Support for Web Services	*3*	5	4	4
	The Rule Engine				
47	Support for rete	*5*	5	5	5
48	Support for backward and mixed chaining	*2*	3	4	2
49	Automatic truth maintenance	*2*	5	4	4
50	Support for debugging/audit trail of rule firing	*2*	5	4	4
51	Support for XML input	*2*	5	4	4
52	Automation of integration with Java, .NET, and databases	*5*	4	3	3
53	Ability to handle large no. of rules	*5*	5	4	5
54	Performance and scalability (ability to handle large no. of concurrent requests/transactions, users, and rule executions)	*5*	5	3	4
55	Ease of integration with external applications (e.g. Web Services, embedded)	*3*	3	3	3
56	Does the language have the power to handle procedural or technical functions without requiring a call to an external routine?	*4*	2	3	4
57	Can the language call on external and mathematical routines when desired?	*5*	4	5	5
58	Memory footprint (suitability for embedding in small devices)	*2*	5	4	4
59	Availability across multiple platforms	*4*	4	4	3

Table B-3   *(continued)*

	Attributes	*Weight*	P	Q	R
60	Availability of alternative interfaces (e.g. C, C++, Java, .NET)	*0*	5	3	4
61	Support for dynamic 'hot' deployment	*4*	4	4	3
62	Runtime rule updates	*2*	4	4	4
63	Support for multiple concurrent KBs	*2*	4	4	3
64	Ability to update KBs with minimal user impact	*5*	5	5	3
65	Ability to handle different deployment dates	*3*	5	5	4
66	Maturity in rule engine market with proven rete-based implementations.	*5*	4	5	5
67	Conflict resolution	*4*	3	4	3
68	Interactive testing	*2*	1	3	1
	Other factors (Technical environment, culture, etc.)				
69	Integration with supplier's product range	*0*	1	5	3
70	Need to leverage technical skills	*5*	1	4	5
71	Suitable for mainframe culture	*2*	3	5	3
72	Integration with J2EE environment	*5*	2	3	5
73	UML object model input	*5*	0	1	3
74	COBOL integration	*1*	1	4	2
75	Custom rule maintenance screens	*0*	0	4	1
76	RUP plug-ins available	*0*	0	3	0
77	Supplier involved with standards bodies	*5*	1	4	4
78	Foreign (i.e. not English) Language support	*5*	0	2	3
79	Java compatible coding style	*5*	2	2	5
80	Effectiveness of performance tuning	*2*	1	3	1
	Total weights and scores	*1050*	732	774	781
	Normalized scores		**0.70**	**0.74**	**0.74**

References and Bibliography

Alexander, C. (1964) *Notes on the Synthesis of Form*, Harvard: Harvard University Press

Alexander, C. (1979) *The Timeless Way of Building*, Oxford: Oxford University Press

Alexander, C. (1996) *A Foreshadowing of 21st Century Art*, New York: Oxford University Press

Alexander, C. (1999) The Origins of Pattern Theory: The Future of the Theory and the Generation of a Living World, *IEEE Software* September/October, 71–82

Alexander, C., Ishikawa, S. and Silverstein, M. (1977) *A Pattern Language*, Oxford: Oxford University Press

Anderson, J.R. (1976) *Language, Memory and Thought*, Laurence Erlbaum

Andrews, D. (2007) *Catalysis II*, in preparation.

Appleton, D.S. (1984) Business Rules: The Missing Link, *Datamation* Oct 15th, 145–50

Arsanjani, A. (2000) Rule Object: A Pattern Language for Pluggable and Adaptive Business Rule Construction; in *Proceedings of PLoP2000*. Technical Report #wucs-00–29, Dept. of Computer Science, Washington University Department of Computer Science, October

Ashby, W.R. (1956) An Introduction to Cybernetics, London: Chapman & Hall

Beck, K. (2000) *Extreme Programming Explained: Embrace change*, Reading MA: Addison-Wesley

Bobrow, D.G. and Winograd, T. (1977) An overview of KRL, a knowledge representation language, *Cognitive Science* 1, 3–46

Brown, T. (1992) Simplicity and Complexity in the Zachman Framework, *Database Newsletter* May/June, 3–11

Bruce, T.A. (1992) Simplicity and Complexity in the Zachman Framework, *Database Newsletter* 20(3), 3–11

Buschmann, F., Meunier, R., Rohnert, H., Sommerlad, P. and Stal, M. (1996) *Pattern-oriented Software Architecture: A System of Patterns*, Chichester, England: Wiley

Charniak, E. and McDermott, D. (1985) *Introduction to Artificial Intelligence*, Reading MA: Addison-Wesley

Cheesman, J. and Daniels, J. (2001) *UML Components*, Harlow, England: Addison-Wesley

Chomsky, N. (1980) *Rules and Representations*, Oxford: Basil Blackwell

Coad, P. (1992) Object-Oriented Patterns, *Comms. ACM* **35**(9), 152–158

Coad, P., LeFebvre, E. and DeLuca, J. (1999) *Java Modeling in Color with UML*, Upper Saddle River NJ:Prentice Hall

Coad, P., North, D. and Mayfield, M. (1997) *Object Models: Strategies, Patterns and Applications*, Upper Saddle River NJ:Prentice Hall

Cockburn, A. (2000) *Writing Effective Use Cases*, Reading MA: Addison-Wesley

Collins, H.M. (1990) *Artificial Experts: Social knowledge and intelligent machines*, Cambridge MA, MIT Press

Cooper, A. (1999) *The Inmates are Running the Asylum*, New York: SAMS

Coplien, J. O. (1999) Reevaluating the Architectural Metaphor: Toward Piecemeal Growth, *IEEE Software* September/October, 40–44

Coplien, J.O. (1992) *Advanced C++: Programming Styles and Idioms*, Reading MA: Addison-Wesley

Coplien, J.O. (1995) A Generative Development-Process Pattern Language. In Coplien and Schmidt (1995)

Coplien, J.O. and Harrison (2005) *Organizational Patterns of Agile Software Development*, Upper Saddle River NJ: Prentice Hall

Coplien, J.O. and Schmidt, D. (Eds) (1995) *Pattern Languages of Program Design*, Reading NJ:Addison-Wesley

D'Souza, D.F. and Wills, A.C. (1999) *Objects, Components and Frameworks with UML: The Catalysis Approach*, Reading MA: Addison-Wesley

Date, C.J. (1983) *An Introduction to Database Systems*, Volume II, Reading MA: Addison-Wesley

Date, C.J. (2000) *What Not How: The Business Rules Approach to Application Development*, Reading MA: Addison-Wesley

Duyne, D.K. van, Landay, J. and Hong, J.I. (2002) *The Design of Sites*, Reading MA: Addison-Wesley

Farhoodi, F. (1994) CADDIE: an advanced tool for organizational design and process modelling. In *Software Assistance for Business Re-Engineering*, Chichester: Wiley

Ferber, J. (1995) *Les Systèms Multi-Agents: Vers une intelligence collective*, Paris: InterEditions

Flores, F. (1997) The leaders of the future. In Denning, P.J. and Metcalfe, R.M. (Eds.) *Beyond Calculation: The next 50 years of computing*, New York: Copernicus

Forgy, C.L. (1982) RETE: A fast algorithm for the many pattern/many object pattern match problem, *Artificial Intelligence* **19** 17–37

Fowler, M. (1996) *Analysis Patterns*, Harlow, England: Addison-Wesley

Fowler, M. (1997) *UML Distilled*, 2nd Edition, Harlow, England: Addison-Wesley

Fowler, M. (2000) *Refactoring*, Reading MA: Addison-Wesley

Gabriel, R.P (1996) *Patterns of Software*, Oxford: University Press

Gamma, E., Helm, R., Johnson, R. and Vlissedes, J. (1995) *Design Patterns: Elements of Reusable Object-Oriented Software*, Reading MA: Addison-Wesley

Gardner, K., Rush, A., Crist, M., Konitzer, R. and Teegarden, B. (1998) *Cognitive Patterns*, Cambridge: Cambridge University Press

Graham, I. (1994) On the Impossibility of Artificial Intelligence, *BCS Specialist Group in Expert Systems Newsletter*, Summer 1994

Graham, I. (1995) *Migrating to Object Technology*, Wokingham: Addison-Wesley

Graham, I. (2001) *Object-Oriented Methods: Principles & Practice – Third Edition*, Harlow, England: Addison-Wesley

Graham, I. (2003a) *A Pattern Language for Web Usability*, Harlow, England: Addison-Wesley

Graham, I. (2003b) Four web usability patterns from the *wu* language, in O'Callaghan, A., Eckstein, J. and Schwanninger, C. (Eds) *Proc. EuroPLoP '02*, UVK Universitätsverlag Konstanz, 159–177

Graham, I. and Jones, P.L.K. (1988) *Expert Systems: Knowledge, Uncertainty and Decision*, London: Chapman & Hall

Guilfoyle, C. and Warner, E. (1994) *Intelligent Agents: The New Revolution in Software*, Ovum Ltd

Halle, B. von (2002) *Business Rules Applied*, New York: Wiley

Hay, D.C. and Healy, K.A. (1997) *GUIDE Business Rules Project*, http://www.softerra.com/files/apbrules.pdf

Hayes-Roth, F., Waterman, D.A. and Lenat, D.B. (Eds) (1983) *Building Expert Systems*, Reading MA: Addison-Wesley

Jackson, M.A. (1995*) Software Requirements & Specifications*, Wokingham, England: Addison-Wesley

Jackson, M.A. (1998) A Discipline of Description, *Requirements Engineering* **3**(2), 73–78

Jackson, M.A. (2001) *Problem Frames*, Harlow, England: Addison-Wesley

Jackson, P. (1986) *Introduction to Expert Systems*, Wokingham, England: Addison-Wesley

Jacobson, I., Ericsson, M. and Jacobson, A. (1995) *The Object Advantage: Business Process Re-engineering with Object Technology*, Wokingham, England: Addison-Wesley

Kelly, G.A (1955) *The Psychology of Personal Constructs*, New York: W.W. Norton

Kendall, E.A., Malkoun, M.T. and Chong, J. (1997) The application of object-orientated analysis to agent-based systems, *J. of Object Oriented Programming* **9**(9), 56–65

Kruchten, P. (1999) *The Rational Unified Process*, Reading MA: Addison-Wesley

Luck, M. and McBurney, P. (2005) Agent-based computing for next generation apps, *ITNOW*, September, 24–25

Melle, W. van, Shortliffe, E. and Buchanan, B. (1981) EMYCIN: A domain-independent system that aids in constructing knowledge based consultation programs, Infotech State of the Art Report **9**, no. 3.

Miller, G.A. (1956) The magical number seven, plus or minus two: some limits on our capacity for processing information, *Psychological Review* **63**, 81–97

Minsky, M.L. and Papert, S. (1969) Perceptions, MIT Press

Morgan, A. (2002) *Business Rules and Information Systems: Aligning IT with Business Goals*, Boston MA: Addison-Wesley

Newell, A. and Simon, H.A (1963) GPS: A program that stimulates human thought. Ln Feigenbaum, E.A. and Feldman, J.A. (Eds.) *Computers and Thought*, McGraw Hill

O'Callaghan, A. (1997a) Object-oriented reverse engineering, *Application Development Adviser* **1**(1), 35–39

O'Callaghan, A. (1997b) Realizing the reality, *Application Development Adviser* **1**(2), 30–33

O'Callaghan, A. (1998) A plethora of patterns, *Application Development Adviser* **1**(3), 32–33

O'Callaghan, A.J. (2000) Patterns for an Architectural Praxis, *Proc. European Pattern Languages of Program Design*, Irsee, Germany

Pajevski, M.J. (2004) www.oasis-open.org/committees/download.php/17573/06-04-00008.000.pdf

Pawson, R. and Matthews, R. (2002) *Naked Objects*, Harlow, England: Addison-Wesley

Riecken, D. (1994) Special issue on intelligent agents, *Comms ACM*, July.

Rising, L. (Ed.) (1998) *The Patterns Handbook*, New York: Cambridge University Press

Ross. R.G. (1987) *Entity Modeling: Techniques and Applications*, Boston MA: Database Research Group

Ross. R.G. (1994) *The Business Rule Book*, Boston MA: Database Research Group

Ross. R.G. (2003) *Principles of the Business Rules Approach*, Boston MA: Addison-Wesley

Ross. R.G. (2005) *Business Rule Concepts, Getting to the Point of Knowledge (2nd edition)*, Boston MA: Business Rule Solutions, LLC

Russell, S. and Norvig, P. (1995) *Artificial Intelligence: A Modern Approach*, Englewood Cliffs NJ: Prentice Hall

Shortliffe, E.H. (1976) *Computer Based Medical Consultations: MYCIN*, American Elsevier

Sillitoe, A. (1971) *Travels in Nihilon*, London: W.H. Allen & Co.

Sims, O. (1994) Business Objects: Delivering Cooperative Objects for Client Server, London: McGraw-Hill

Standish (1995) *CHAOS*, The Standish Group International Inc.

Standish (2004) *CHAOS*, The Standish Group International Inc.

Stapleton, J. (1997) Dynamic Systems Development Method: The Method in Practise, Harlow: Addison-Wesley

Szperski, C. (1998)Component Software: Beyond Object-Orientated Programming, Harlow: Addison-Wesley

Taylor, D.A. (1995) *Business Engineering with Object Technology*, New York: John Wiley & sons

Tidwell, J. (1999) *Common Ground: A Pattern Language for Human-Computer Interface Design*, www.mit.edu/~jtidwell/common_ground.html

Wellbank, M. (1983) *A Review of Knowledge Acquisition Techniques for Expert Systems*, Martlesham: BT Research Labs

Weiner, N. (1948) Cybernetics, Cambridge MA: MIT Press

Winograd, T. and Flores, F. (1986) Understanding Computers and Cognition, Reading MA: Addison-Wesley

Zachman, J.A. (1987) A framework for information systems architecture, *IBM Systems Journal* **26**(3), 276–292

Index

Page references in **bold** indicate tables and those in *italics* indicate figures.